COMPLETE REAL ESTATE OFFICE DESK BOOK

Also by the Author

The Successful Creative Secretary

COMPLETE REAL ESTATE OFFICE DESK BOOK

Carolyn Kristt

Prentice-Hall, Inc. **Englewood Cliffs, N.J.**

Prentice-Hall International, Inc., *London*
Prentice-Hall of Australia, Pty. Ltd., *Sydney*
Prentice-Hall of Canada, Ltd., *Toronto*
Prentice-Hall of India Private Ltd., *New Delhi*
Prentice-Hall of Japan, Inc., *Tokyo*
Prentice-Hall of Southeast Asia Pte., Ltd., *Singapore*
Whitehall Books, Ltd., *Wellington, New Zealand*

Library of Congress Cataloging in Publication Data

Kristt, Carolyn
Complete real estate office desk book.

Bibliography: p.
Includes index.
1. Real estate business. I. Title.
HD1375.K66 333.33'068 80-21088
ISBN 0-13-162370-2

Printed in the United States of America

With Thanks

Introduction

THIS BOOK PROVIDES UNUSUAL PRACTICAL VALUE FOR THE BROKER, THE SALESPERSON, AND THE SECRETARY BECAUSE...

You are given a complete, specialized collection of essential facts, usable data, efficiency ideas and problem-solving procedures—many from actual businesses—all arranged and organized for easiest understanding and fastest reference—and focused squarely on the needs of the busy real estate office.

Real estate involves public contact, so tips are included on how to get the most from a conversation, ways to create and maintain a positive atmosphere, ways to better listen to what is being said, ideas to eliminate tension, tips to be certain you are communicating—all of which are basic and necessary to successful real estate operations.

This is a "how-to" book for real estate documents and forms, and it includes all you need to know for typing from scratch (margins, spacing, tab stops, amounts of money, and more). You are given guidelines to all the steps in a real estate transaction so you can easily coordinate the flow of work. You are shown the key factors in land descriptions and how to type real property descriptions so you can complete the necessary documents properly and quickly. You are also given tips and tricks for putting together an appraisal report—what should go into each kind, a sample of a short form letter report, and an actual outline for a narrative report.

Property management involves money, apartments, tenants, documents, building property and personnel, so the chapter devoted to it illustrates time-saving forms, applications, bills, and even a master filing system.

Newspaper advertising is a major part of real estate and

you must often control the ad from the concept stage through to the actual printing. A form on which you type the advertising copy and all the pertinent information for the newspaper makes checking ads and following up leads easy from your office carbon copy. From major U.S. newspapers comes basic information on the proper way to set up ads, as well as copy and headline ideas. A form helps the salespeople put together information for a newspaper story, and an illustration of a completed press release shows how to properly type it.

Real estate revolves around sales—and it is essential to keep the listings in order. Ideas from a secretary include an office table with directories, telephone books, maps, current Multiple Listings, and a folder with probate sales. Another time saver is to print a property information form directly on the front of the file folder. Television, transparencies, and home inspector's reports are a few of the other innovative ideas discussed.

Another way to advertise the company's "merchandise"—its listed property—is through brochures and mailers. Because you must work with the coordination of the text, art work, and photos, you must have an understanding of the mechanics of preparation. Here are design tricks, space savers, problem solvers, and all you need to know about copier reproduction, putting together camera ready copy, and how to work with stencils. If you know how these things are done, you can initiate ideas and create new projects.

To show you how to apply all of this knowledge, Chapter 13 reproduces three entirely different projects—one uses a rearrangement of letterhead and small photos, one is a booklet with text only and a mailer, and the third uses text and pictures and a mailer. The elements of design are made simple with comments on each page detailing the use of white space, balance, optical tricks, and original color. There are also forms for the preparation of the brochures.

Drawings, charts, lists, and tables provide you with instant information. Here you have 17 illustrations of different architectural styles and accompanying descriptions to help you explain property to a client. There are also drawings of roof types and 113 details of a building's construction—with this knowledge you can understand what the builder refers to, without the dictionary. A temperature conversion chart is also helpful because real estate is closely associated with climate and conservation ideas in today's energy-conscious environment.

For the educational sales meeting, for a community project, for new salespeople, for your office library, and for general information a chapter is included on reference sources for real estate books, magazines, catalogs, booklets, audio visuals (slides and cassettes), courses, seminars, and workshops. Names, addresses, and phone numbers for purchase information are supplied.

For the real estate office staff, the glossary provides definitions which fall into the context of real estate, law, and business.

You can easily apply the treasury of knowledge in this real estate encyclopedia to your own situation for fast, dependable, on-the-job answers and effortless efficiency. It is indeed the *"Complete" Real Estate Office Desk Book.*

Carolyn Kristt

Contents

COMPLETE
REAL ESTATE OFFICE
DESK BOOK

1

How the Real Estate Office Staff Accomplishes More with the Public

In the real estate office you deal with people in everything you do—from public contact on the telephone (with prospects, advertising salespeople, other real estate offices, banks, insurance companies, and the myriad of people who are part of the day-to-day workings of business), to personal interaction with the salespeople and clients in your own office.

It would be impossible to set hard and fast rules for reacting to specific situations, because every personality and every situation is different, but there are *some good basic premises from which to operate.*

To get the most from a conversation, see it as the art of talking together, a verbal exchange of ideas, opinions, and/or facts. To participate fully, follow these guidelines:

DO	DON'T
1. Explain instead of tell.	1. React emotionally.
2. Talk *with* instead of *to*.	2. Demean.
3. Listen intelligently.	3. Antagonize.
4. Question courteously.	4. Wound.
5. Reply candidly.	5. Battle.

HOW TO CREATE AND MAINTAIN A POSITIVE ATMOSPHERE

If three people walk in at once, acknowledge them *each*, and say that you will be with them each in turn. The same applies to the phone. People don't mind being put on hold if they know you are helping someone else. They do mind being forgotten, however.

Try a supply of coloring books or children's reading books and lollipops for customers with children. A current and full magazine rack will also help.

Listen to what is being said. If the customer complains, offer thanks for pointing out something you did not see. If someone is not happy with a certain procedure, find out why. Ask for ideas for improvement, or create a suggestion box (anonymous) and encourage its use.

If there is tension, find out the cause and solve it as soon as possible. Negative attitudes not only drain energy, but they also block thoughts and repel potential clients who may walk into the office.

HOW TO BE CERTAIN YOU ARE COMMUNICATING

If someone uses a word you do not know, stop then and there and find out the meaning, or you might lose the whole point of the discussion and perhaps lose a sale. There is no such thing as a stupid question. Conversely, if you see from an expression or tone of voice that the person to whom you are speaking does not understand, immediately stop and find out where you lost the thought. Then clarify and continue.

As you go through this book you will learn about the functionings of real estate, as well as many projects in use today by real estate offices throughout the country. Let these be ideas for applications in your own office.

Vincent Friia, San Francisco real estate salesman, makes the following suggestions to the real estate secretary from the sales point of view.

Q. If the client calls and you can't be reached because you are out showing property, how do you want the receptionist to handle the telephone?

A. Give *assurance* to the client; tell the client I am out showing property; I may be in my car. She should tell the client she will try to reach me on my mobile phone. See that the client is immediately assured that something is being done to reach me. Take the client's name and number and assure him that you will call back or that I will call him shortly.

Q. What of the caller who says it is an emergency?

A. These people want assurance—they want to be talking to me—speak with them immediately. Otherwise they are antagonized and the situation is out of proportion. Her function in that situation, no matter how antagonized she is by the call, is to still be calming and reassuring, and to show no antagonism within the interaction of the staff. She should not get involved to that degree.

Q. What is important for a healthy working atmosphere among the employees? There should be no antagonism within the interaction of the staff. The secretary is in a situation where she must work with everybody—many different personalities. She is the voice of the office to the client at the other end of the phone, the title companies, and to the people in the office. Could you give her any pointers in doing her job extremely well? What would you want from her? You must work with her. You must interact with her. She has to do your work. She has to do work for others. How do you want to be treated by her?

A. The receptionist, or the office secretary, can only function in a very limited manner. I expect the secretary to organize herself *and* organize me. She should see that my calendar is up to date and that all proper notations appear. She should *assist* but she is always working under my guidance—she can help prepare my letters by suggesting possible changes in sentence structure, but final wording of the letter is my responsibility.

Q. How do you want the telephone handled?

A. She should always take a written message *with date and time and with properly spelled name and correct phone*

> *number. Repeat if necessary.* She should tell the caller that I always call in and that I will be calling shortly and she is sure I will return the call.

A San Francisco real estate secretary offers the following pointers for handling difficulties graciously.

Each office is its own world and it is very important that you always focus on the point that your boss is your boss. Whenever you are in doubt, ask him. Never be afraid to say, "I don't know." Be sure you find the right moment, though. Don't interrupt. Don't play games. You will never get sidetracked if you work with the truth. *Never.*

Develop a discipline. Where you have favorites, be careful. (You won't be able to help it—everyone is human.) Everybody touches your life—everybody in the office. You are a contact point. Do a lot of listening. Remember that you are dealing with independent contractors and that you can become the center of a fire you did not light.

Real estate is a high-tension business and everyone works at a high level of energy. You are going to be in the middle of a lot of highs and lows. You are going to hear a lot of complaints. You are going to see a lot of deals made and a lot of deals fall through. At some point somebody is going to come to you and complain. *Do a lot of listening.* Try not to offer too many opinions because they may backfire on you. These are daily things; the fight that is going on over a deal could be settled inside of an hour and the people involved could go out arm in arm and leave you in the middle. You have to be very careful. Do the best you can; you have to key your temperament to what is going on around you. Ride with the tension and not against it. *Don't take sides.*

You will be hearing a lot of confidential information. Simply say that it is none of your business. Tell the asking party that just because the information went past your eyes and through your head when you typed it, doesn't mean that it is information to be given out. Interaction should be on a one-to-one basis with concerned parties. Don't discuss anybody's business, but only the particular situation with the particular person involved. Put off the question lightly or you will create friction.

To help you work with the public you don't see, Figure 1-1 gives some tips for better coordination with your answering service. And, if you use an answering machine, Figure 1-2 shows you how to do it best.

Figure 1-1a

Figure 1-1b

HOW TO WORK EFFECTIVELY WITH AN ANSWERING SERVICE — MANUAL OR COMPUTER VOICE BANK

Among the types of service an answering service can offer are message taking, paging, radio dispatch, wiring messages to you out of town, placing calls for you, taking orders, quoting prices, making appointments, wake-up calls, second phone lines as message phones only, elevator phone service.

Cross-connecting (answering the phone, locating a salesperson at another number, connecting the caller) is very important to real estate salespeople who must be reachable when an important prospect calls and there is no one in the office. Instruct the answering service, "If Joan Smith calls, tell her to call (meet) salesperson's full name at (name or address).

Once you decide on the type of service, work closely with the operators. Tell the answering service exactly how you want your phone answered, what you want to know from everyone calling, and what to do in an emergency situation. Change your instructions as your situation changes.

Check in often enough—phone in for messages at regular intervals.

Be ready with paper and pencil when you call for messages.

Be patient if your call is interrupted when messages are being given. Remember that the operator may be answering your phone and will get back to you as soon as possible.

If there is a problem, call the supervisor. Her job is to see that things run smoothly. Also call if the service has been "above and beyond the call of duty."

Courtesy of Artson Voice Bank Answering Service,
San Francisco, California.

Figure 1-1

TELEPHONE ANSWERING MACHINES

These machines are recording devices which plug into standard telephone wall jacks and which are available in both department and specialty stores. When the telephone rings, a pre-recorded cassette is activated and the caller hears instructions such as, "Hello, this is Mr. Smith. I am out of my office now and if you will leave a message, I'll return the call. Begin speaking at the sound of the tone."

Different machines have different features, such as:

1. Setting so that the machine will answer on a specific ring.
2. Silent monitor—you can hear the caller's voice as the call comes in and answer if you choose.
3. Announce only—gives only your message to the caller, then hangs up.
4. Dictation capability.
5. Two-cassette system—one for incoming messages, one for instructional messages.
6. Erasing capability.
7. Tape rewind and tape forward.
8. Fixed caller message time or unlimited caller message time.
9. Remote control device which activates the recorder to play messages back and/or allow recording of new instructional messages when you call from an outside telephone.
10. Conversion to a regular cassette recorder when not being used as an answering machine.

Figure 1-2

So that you will be able to make potential customers feel welcome in your office or on the phone, Figure 1-3 gives you 61 English words translated into French, Italian, Spanish, German, Swedish, Portuguese, Dutch, Chinese, and Japanese.

WORD TRANSLATIONS

ENGLISH	FRENCH	ITALIAN	SPANISH	GERMAN
1. Do you speak English?	1. Parlez-vous anglais?	1. Parla inglese?	1. ¿Habia usted ingles?	1. Sprechen Sie englisch?
2. I do not understand	2. Je ne comprends pas	2. Non capisco	2. No entiendo	2. Ich verstehe nicht
3. Yes/No	3. Qui/Non	3. Si/No	3. Si/No	3. Ja/Nein
4. Your name?	4. Votre nom?	4. Il Suo nome?	4. ¿Su nombre?	4. Ihr Name?
5. I, you, he, she	5. Je, vous, il, elle	5. Io, Lei, egli, ella	5. Yo, usted, el, ella	5. Ich, Sie, er, sie
6. Good morning	6. Bonjour	6. Buon giorno	6. Buenos dias	6. Guten Morgen
7. Good evening	7. Bonsoir	7. Buona sera	7. Buenas noches	7. Guten Abend
8. Good night	8. Bonne nuit	8. Bonna notte	8. Buenas noches	8. Gute Nacht
9. Good-bye	9. Au revoir	9. ArrivederLa	9. Adios	9. Auf Wiedersehen
10. How are you?	10. Comment allez-vous?	10. Come sta?	10. ¿Cómo está usted?	10. Wie ghet es Ihnen?
11. How far?	11. A quelle distance?	11. Quant e lontano?	11. ¿Hasta dónde?	11. Wie weit?
12. How much is it?	12. Combien est-ce?	12. Quanto costa?	12. ¿Cuánto vale?	12. Wieviel kostet es?
13. Too much	13. Trop cher	13. Troppo caro	13. Demasiado	13. Zu teuer
14. Very Well	14. Tres bien	14. Benissimo	14. Muy bien	14. Sehr gut
15. Thank you	15. Merci	15. Grazie	15. Gracias	15. Danke
16. You are welcome	16. Je vous en prie	16. Prego	16. De nada	16. Nichts zu danken
17. Excuse me	17. Exusez-moi	17. Scusi	17. Dispénseme	17. Entschuldigen Sie
18. I am sorry	18. Je regrette	18. Mi spiace	18. Lo siento mucho	18. Es tut mir leid
19. Please	19. S'il vous plaît	19. Per piacere	19. Por favor	19. Bitte
20. I want	20. Je veux	20. Vorrei	20. Yo quiero	20. Ich mochte
21. Airport	21. Aeroport	21. Aeroporto	21. Aeropuerto	21. Flugplatz/Flughafen
22. Automobile/car	22. Auto/voiture	22. Automobile/macchina	22. Automóvil/coche	22. Auto/Wagen
23. Bank	23. Banque	23. Banca	23. Banco	23. Bank
24. Barber	24. Coiffeur	24. Barbiere	24. Barbero	24. Friseur
25. Beauty salon/parlor	25. Salon de beaute	25. Salone di bellezza	25. Salón de belleza	25. Frisiersalon
26. Breakfast	26. Petit dejeuner	26. Prima colazione	26. Desayuno	26. Fruhstuck
27. Bus	27. Autobus	27. Autobus	27. Autobus	27. Bus
28. Change (money)	28. Change	28. Cambio	28. Cambio	28. Geldwechsel
29. Check (bill)	29. Addition	29. Conto	29. Cuenta	29. Rechnung
30. Church	30. Eglise	30. Chiesa	30. Iglesia	30. Kirche
31. Dentist	31. Dentiste	31. Dentista	31. Dentista	31. Zahnarzt
32. Dinner	32. Diner	32. Cena	32. Cena	32. Abendessen
33. Doctor	33. Docteur	33. Dottore	33. Médico	33. Arzt
34. Flat tire	34. Pneu a plat	34. Pneumatico forato	34. Neumatico reventado	34. Reifenpanne
35. Gasoline/petrol	35. Essence	35. Benzina	35. Gasolina	35. Benzin
36. Hospital	36. Hopital	36. Ospedale	36. Hospital	36. Krankenhaus
37. Information	37. Renseignements	37. Informazione	37. Información	37. Auskunft
38. Lavatory (toilet)	38. Toilettes (WC)	38. Gabinetto	38. Retrete/excusado	38. Toilette (W.C.)
39. Lunch	39. Dejeuner	39. Colazione/pranzo	39. Almuerzo	39. Mittagessen
40. Men (gentlemen)	40. Messieurs	40. Signori/uomini	40. Señores/caballeros	40. Manner/Herren
41. Occupied (sign)	41. Occupe	41. Occupato	41. Ocupado	41. Besetzt
42. Pharmacy	42. Pharmacie	42. Farmacia	42. Farmacia	42. Apotheke
43. Post Office	43. Bureau de Poste	43. Ufficio postale	43. Oficina de correos	43. Postamt
44. Registered (letter)	44. Recommande	44. Raccomandata	44. Certificado	44. Einschrieben
45. Room (hotel)	45. Chambre	45. Camera	45. Habitación	45. Zimmer
46. Shop (store)	46. Boutique	46. Negozio	46. Tienda	46. Geschaft
47. Sick	47. Malade	47. Ammalato	47. Enfermo	47. Krank
48. Soap	48. Savon	48. Sapone	48. Jabón	48. Seife
49. Stamp (postage)	49. Timbre-poste	49. Francobollo	49. Sello/estampilla	49. Briefmarke
50. Station (railroad)	50. Gare	50. Stazione	50. Estación	50. Bahnhof
51. Suitcase	51. Valise	51. Valigia	51. Maleta	51. Koffer
52. Telephone	52. Telephone	52. Telefono	52. Teléfono	52. Telefon
53. Ticket (travel)	53. Billet	53. Biglietto	53. Billete	53. Fahrkarte
54. Time (of day)	54. Heure	54. Ora	54. Hora	54. Uhrzeit
55. Today	55. Aujourd'hui	55. Oggi	55. Hoy	55. Heute
56. Tomorrow	56. Demain	56. Domani	56. Mañana	56. Morgen
57. Towel	57. Serviette	57. Asciugamano	57. Toalla	57. Handtuch
58. Train	58. Train	58. Treno	58. Tren	58. Zug
59. Waiter	59. Garcon	59. Cameriere	59. Camerero	59. Kellner
60. Water (drinking)	60. Eau potable	60. Acqua potabile	60. Aqua potable	60. Trinkwasser
61. Women/ladies	61. Dames	61. Signore/donne	61. Señoras/damas	61. Frauen/Damen

Courtesy Pacific Telephone Company San Francisco, CA.

Figure 1-3

SWEDISH	PORTUGUESE	DUTCH	CHINESE	JAPANESE
1. Talar Ni engelska?	1. Você fala inglês?	1. Spreekt U Engels?	1. Na Sic Gong Yin Mon	1. Eigo Hanashimasu Ka?
2. Jag forstar inte	2. Não compreendo	2. Ik begrijp U niet	2. Or But May Bach	2. Wakarimasen
3. Ja/Nej	3. Sim/Não	3. Ja/Nee	3. Si But See	3. Hai/Tie
4. Ert namn?	4. Seu nome?	4. Hoe heet U?	4. Na Men	4. Onamae Wa?
5. Jag, Ni, han, hon	5. Eu, você, êle, ela	5. Ik, jiji, hij, zij	5. Knou; Nea; Ha; Coy	5. Watakushi, Anata (proper names)
6. God morgon	6. Bom dia	6. Goeden Morgen	6. Jo Sun	6. Ohayoo Gozaimasu
7. God afton	7. Boa tarde	7. Goeden avond	7. Mon-On	7. Konban Wa
8. God natt	8. Boa noite	8. Goeden acht	8. Mon On	8. Sayonara
9. Adjo	9. Adeus	9. Goeden dag	9. Joy-Gen	9. Sayoonara
10. Hur star det till?	10. Como vai você?	10. Hoe gaat het met U?	10. Na Ho Ma	10. Ogenki Desu Ka?
11. Hur langt?	11. A que distância?	11. Hoe ver is het?	11. Ga Yeun	11. Dono Kurai Arimasu Ka?
12. Hur mycket?	12. Quanto custa?	12. Hoeveel kost het?	12. Ga Dor Chan	12. Ikura Desu Ka?
13. For dyrt	13. Demasiado	13. Dat is teveel (Dat is te duur)	13. Ho Dor	13. Takai Desu
14. Mycket bra	14. Muito bem	14. Heel goed	14. Oh Ho	14. Hai, Shoochi Shimashita
15. Tack	15. Obrigado	15. Dank U wel	15. Dor Jea	15. Doomo Arigatoo Gozaimasu
16. Ingen orsak	16. De nada	16. Tot Uw dienst	16. Min Say Hawk-Hay	16. Doo Itashimashite
17. Ursakta	17. Desculpe	17. Pardon	17. Ger-Ger	17. Gomen Kudasai
18. Jag beklagar	18. Perdão	18. Het spijt mij zeer	18. Yu Leung	18. Doomo Sumimasen
19. Var god	19. Por favor	19. Alst U blief	19. Ching (Um Goy)	19. Doozo
20. Jag skulle vilja ha	20. Eu quero	20. Ik wil	20. Know Surn	20. Itadakimasen Ka?
21. Flygplats	21. Aeroporto	21. Vliegveld	21. Fay Ga Chon	21. Hikoojo
22. Automobil/bil	22. Automóvel/carro	22. Auto	22. Chea	22. Jidoosha
23. Bank	23. Banco	23. Bank	23. Ong Hong	23. Ginkoo
24. Barberare	24. Barbeiro	24. Herenkapper	24. La Fax See	24. Rihatsuten
25. Damfrisering	25. Salão de beleza	25. Dameskapper	25. Dean Fax Deem	25. Byooin
26. Frukoot	26. Café da manhã	26. Ontbijt	26. Jo Chon	26. Asagohan
27. Buss	27. Ônibus	27. Bus	27. Guy-Che	27. Basu
28. Vaxel	28. Trôco	28. Kleingeld	28. San Ong	28. Komakai Mono
29. Rakning	29. Conta	29. Rekening	29. Don	29. Okanjo
30. Kyrka	30. Igreja	30. Kerk	30. Li By Tong	30. Kyookai
31. Tandlakare	31. Dentista	31. Tandarts	31. Knaw-Yee	31. Haisha
32. Middag	32. Jantar	32. Avondeten (Diner)	32. Man-Chon	32. Gohan
33. Lakare	33. Doutor	33. Dokter (Arts)	33. Ye San	33. Isha
34. Punktering	34. Pneu furado	34. Lekke band	34. Che Leung Mo Hay	34. Taiya Ga Panku Shimashita
35. Bensin	35. Gasolina	35. Benzine	35. Hay Yo	35. Gasorin
36. Sjukhus	36. Hospital	36. Ziekonhuis (hospitaal)	36. Yu Yuen	36. Byoin
37. Upplysningar/information	37. Informação	37. Informatie	37. Su Sic	37. Uketsuke
38. Toalett	38. Banheiro	38. Toilet (W.C.)	38. Se Sar	38. Oterai
39. Lunch	39. Almôço	39. Middageten (Lunch)	39. Ang-Jo	39. Obentoo
40. Herrar/man	40. Homens	40. Mannen/Heren	40. Nam Yun	40. Otoko, in speech proper name
41. Upptaget	41. Ocupado	41. Bezet	41. Yo Yung Jo Chu	41. Kore Wa Shiyochu
42. Apotek	42. Farmácia	42. Apotheek	42. Yuk Fon	42. Yakkyoku
43. Postkontor	43. Correio	43. Postkantoor	43. Yo-Jin Gu	43. Yuubinkyoku
44. Rekommenderat	44. Registrado (carta)	44. Aangetekend	44. Dom Bo	44. Kakitome
45. Rum	45. Quarto	45. Kamer	45. Fon	45. Heya
46. Affar	46. Loja	46. Winkel	46. Po Tow	46. Omise
47. Sjuk	47. Doente	47. Ziek	47. Been	47. Byooki
48. Tval	48. Sabão/sabonete	48. Zeep	48. Fon Gon	48. Sekken
49. Frimarke	49. Sêlo	49. Postzegel	49. Yo Peel	49. Ishi
50. Station	50. Estação	50. Station	50. Jarm	50. Eki
51. Kappsack/resvaska	51. Valise/mala	51. Koffer	51. Pay doy (pa Kep)	51. Kaban
52. Telefon	52. Telefone	52. Telefoon	52. Din Wah (Hom Sin)	52. Denwa
53. Biljett	53. Bilhete	53. Kaartje	53. Peel	53. Kippu
54. Tid	54. Tempo	54. Tijd	54. Sea Gan	54. Jikan
55. Idag	55. Hoje	55. Vandaag	55. Gum Yet	55. Kyoo
56. I morgon	56. Amanhã	56. Morgen	56. Ting Yet	56. Ashita
57. Handduk	57. Toalha	57. Handdoek	57. Mo Gun	57. Tenugui
58. Tag	58. Trem	58. Trein	58. For Che	58. Kisha
59. Kyparen	59. Garçom	59. Kelner	59. Kay Toy	59. Kyuuji
60. Dricksvatten	60. Água	60. Water	60. Sher (Shir)	60. Omizu
61. Damar	61. Mulheres/senhoras	61. Vrouwen/dames	61. Nu Yeung	61. Gofujin/Onna

This is only *one* of many dialects.

Translation, courtesy
Mayumi Yamamoto
San Francisco, California.

Courtesy Pacific Telephone Company San Francisco, CA.

Figure 1-3 (cont'd)

All of real estate deals with people. The change of location of buyers and sellers is one of the reasons why property is sold. The information on the Rand McNally United States Mileage and Driving Time Map, which is reproduced in Figure 1-4, could save the office staff, as well as the potential client, research time.

The SONY Corporation Time Zone chart (Figure 1-5) is necessary so that you can be instantly familiar with business hours in foreign countries.

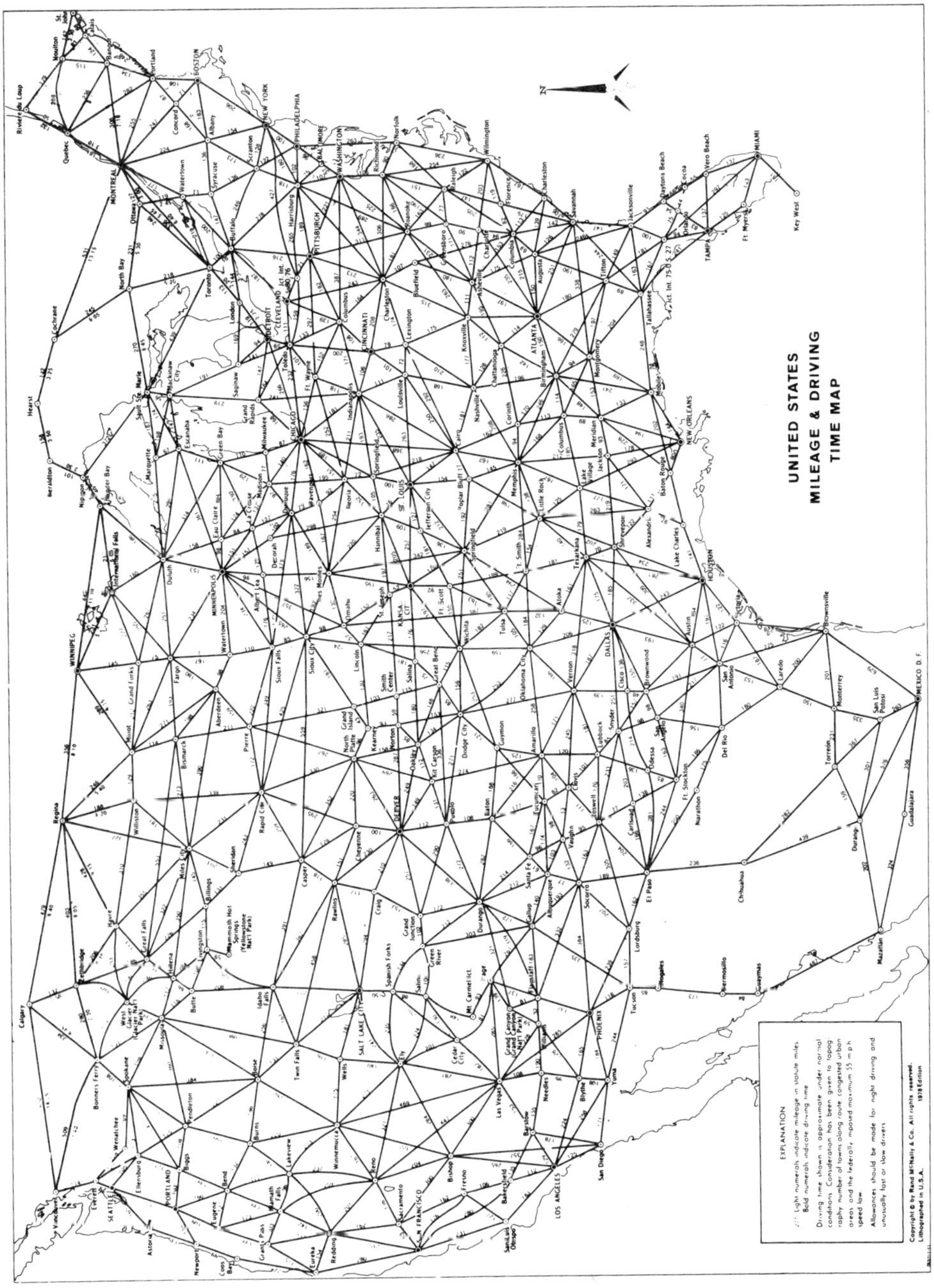

Figure 1-4

©Rand McNally & Company, R.L. 80-4-97.

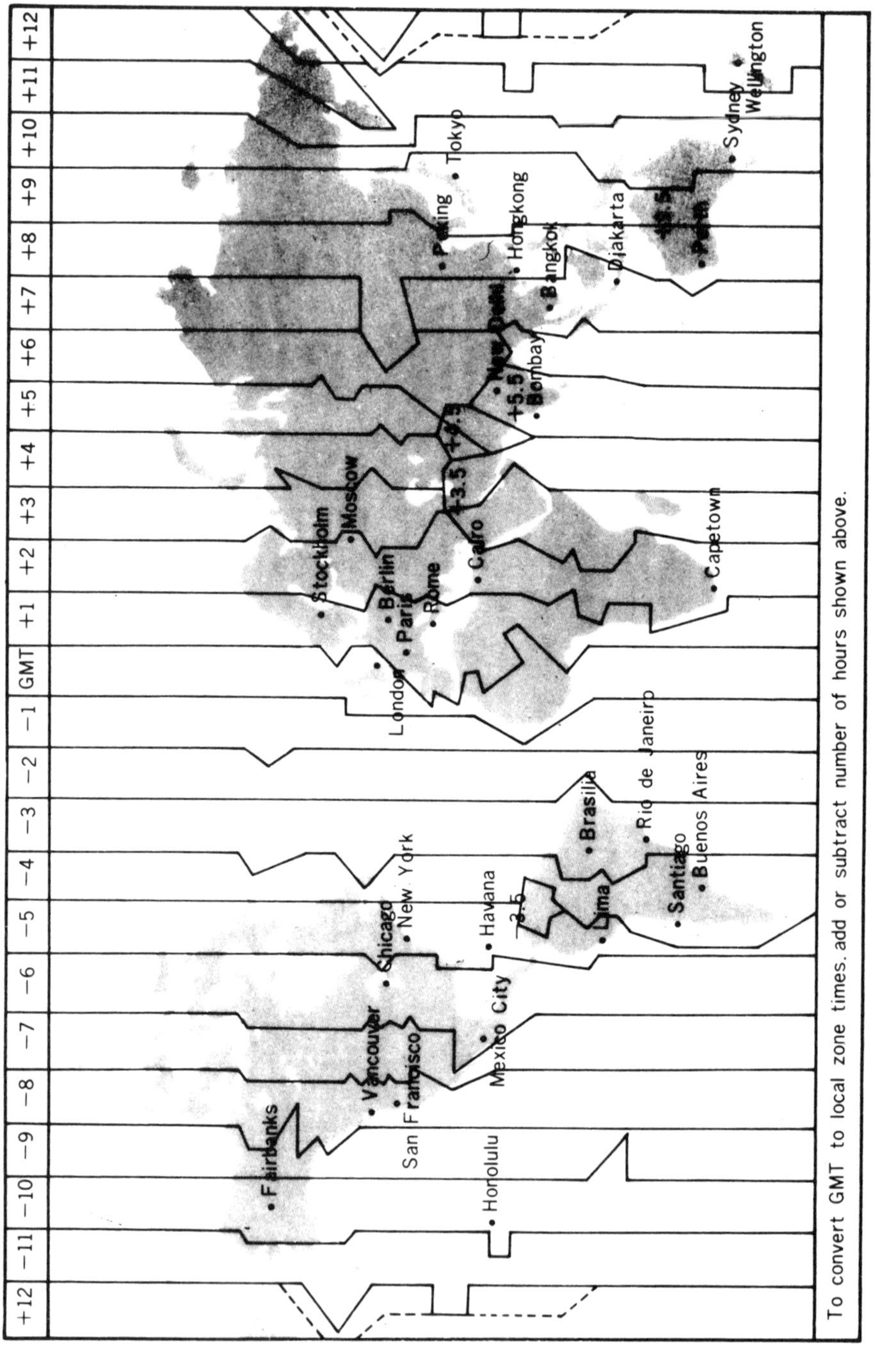

SONY CORPORATION

Figure 1-5

Printed in Japan ©
Courtesy Sony Corporation
Airport P.O. Box 10
Tokyo 149, Japan.

3-993-063-13 (2)

2

Guidelines to the Key Steps in a Real Estate Transaction

In the real estate office you see each transaction not only from beginning to end, but through each phase. You process papers, secure documents, and have them typed.

Part of the job is public relations, explaining to the customer what documents are needed for the closing, dealing with banks for mortgage information, coordinating escrow closings, obtaining pest control reports, insurance policies, tax documents, power meter readings, deeds, and much more—sometimes under deadline pressure.

This chapter contains extensive checklists and actual examples of financial transactions. You have here at your finger tips:

- Checklist of facts and preparations to be made before executing the sales contract
- Checklist of documents to be furnished by seller upon the closing of title
- Checklist for purchaser for the closing of the sale
- Definitions of legal and financial closing

- General escrow rules—procedures—termination
- Checklist of escrow charges for which the seller is responsible
- Checklist of escrow charges for which the purchaser is responsible
- Form for audit
- Forms of closing statement to seller and statement to buyer
- Explanations of items on closing statements

In effect, a real estate transaction begins at the point when a broker secures an agency contract in the form of a listing from the prospective seller. Assume, for simplicity's sake, that this contract remains unchanged until a buyer is secured before the expiration of the listing. We say that the deal is ready to close. There are three meanings of the term *closing*:

1. *Closing the sale.* The buyer and seller agree, and both have signed the agreement or deposit receipt form, which is used when accepting "earnest money" (deposit) to bind an offer for property by a prospective buyer. This is the result of sales effort and negotiation.

After securing a written listing on a piece of property and having a client ready, willing, and able to purchase the property, there are certain facts to ascertain and certain preparations to be made before executing the sales contract. Some of these are included in the following checklist.

CHECKLIST OF FACTS AND PREPARATIONS TO BE MADE BEFORE EXECUTING THE SALES CONTRACT

1. The date of the contract
2. The name and address of the seller
3. Whether the seller is of full age and competence
4. The name of the seller's spouse
5. The name and residence of the purchaser
6. A full description of the property
7. The purchase price, including the amount to be paid on signing the contract, the amount to be paid on delivery

of the deed, existing trust deed(s), and the provisions thereof

8. The kind of deed that is to be delivered (separate, community, joint tenancy, or tenancy in common)
9. What agreement has been made with reference to any specific personal property to be conveyed, such as gas ranges, heaters, machinery, fixtures, window shades, carpets, rugs, hangings, TV antennas, etc.
10. Whether purchaser is to assume the mortgage or trust deed, or take the property subject to it
11. Whether mortgages or trust deeds contain acceleration or restrictive provisions (alienation clause)
12. If there are to be any exceptions or reservations in the deed
13. If there are any special specifications or conditions to be inserted in the contract
14. Stipulations and agreements with reference to tenancies and rights of persons in possession
15. Stipulations and agreements with reference to any facts the survey would show, such as party wall, easements, etc.
16. The items to be adjusted on the closing of the title
17. The name of the broker who brought about the sale, the broker's address, and the amount of commission to be paid
18. Agreements as to any liens, easements, assessments, or taxes, covenants, restrictions, etc., affecting the title, and who is to draw the purchase money mortgage or trust deed and pay the expense thereof
19. The place and date on which the title is to be closed
20. Whether time is to be the essence of the contract
21. Any alterations to be made on the premises between the date of the contract and the date of the closing
22. Name and address of the escrow holder
23. Who pays title, escrow, and recording charges
24. Whether structural pest control report is to be furnished, and who shall pay the cost of recommended work, whether corrective or preventive

25. The date of possession and adjustments of taxes, interest, etc.

2. *Legal closing* means that all instruments necessary to transfer title have been executed and recorded. Title insurance or title evidence has been furnished and the money necessary to pay the seller for his equity, less expense, is in the hands of the broker acting as trustee, or in the hands of an escrow holder. (Transfer of title and transfer of money are thought of as simultaneous acts.)

CHECKLIST OF DOCUMENTS TO BE FURNISHED BY SELLER UPON THE CLOSING OF TITLE

1. The seller's copy of the contract
2. The latest tax, water, and receipted assessment bills
3. The latest possible water meter readings
4. Receipt for the last payment of interest on mortgages or trust deeds, if any
5. The fire, liability, and other insurance policies
6. A certificate or offset statement from the holder of any mortgage or trust deed on the property, showing the amount due and the date to which interest is paid
7. Any subordination agreements which may be called for in the contract
8. Certificates showing satisfaction of mechanic's liens, security agreements (chattel mortgages), judgments, or mortgages which are to be paid at or prior to the closing of the title
9. A list of the names of the tenants, amounts that are paid and unpaid, the dates when rents are due, and an assignment of unpaid rent
10. An assignment of all leases affecting the property
11. Letters to tenants to pay all subsequent rent to the purchaser and reaffirm conditions of tenancy
12. Authority to execute the deed of the seller if acting through an agent

13. Bill of sale of the personal property covered by the contract
14. The seller's last deed
15. Any unrecorded instruments affecting the title, including extension agreements
16. Deed and other instruments which the seller is to deliver or prepare

CHECKLIST FOR PURCHASER FOR THE CLOSING OF THE SALE

1. The purchaser's copy of the contract
2. Examination of the deed to see if it conforms to the contract
3. Comparison of the description to see if it coincides with the description of the deed and a true description of the lot or property to be conveyed
4. Examination of the deed to see if it is properly executed
5. Sufficient cash to make payments required in accordance with the provisions of the contract
6. Disposition of all liens which must be removed
7. Names and details with reference to tenants and rent
8. Assignment of unpaid rent and assignment of leases
9. Certificate with reference to mortgages, showing the principal due and the date of the last payment
10. Letters to tenants from seller reaffirming conditions of tenancy
11. Examination of authority if the seller acts through an agent
12. Bill of sale of personal property covered by the contract
13. Examination of the survey if applicable
14. Examination to see if the policy or certificate of title shows any covenants, restrictions, or other matters affecting the title or the use of the property
15. Bills for any unpaid tax, water, or assessments, and interest computed up to the date of the closing

16. Adjustments completed if called for in the contract
17. Examination of purchase money mortgages
18. Any unrecorded instruments affecting the title, including extension agreements

3. *Financial closing* is closely related to the legal closing but there is more emphasis upon the mechanics, the actual disbursements of funds by checks and an accounting on paper to all parties concerned. In a complicated deal involving refinancing, there may be not only buyer and seller, but an old and new lender to be taken into consideration. The holder or agent will prepare settlement sheets for the interested parties to show that instructions of the escrow have been fully carried out.

Because the consummation of a real estate transaction may take a few hours, or several weeks, and includes the assembling of various documents and moneys, it has been customary for the buyer, the seller, the broker, and the lender to deliver all instruments (money, documents, etc.) to an independent third party, who is the stakeholder or escrow agent. When all conditions necessary to complete the transaction are met, the escrow agent is authorized to close the sale, record the instruments, and make proper disposition of money and documents as directed, to complete transfer of ownership. The cash requirement, the proceeds, the expense or charge allotments, and the prorations in the transactions must be shown in written form to the buyer and seller.

It is customary practice for the broker or salesman to explain the usual division of charges in a settlement to each party in the course of the initial negotiations.

GENERAL ESCROW RULES

When the instructions have been signed by the parties to the escrow, neither party may change the escrow instructions to the detriment of the other. However, by mutual agreement between both parties to the escrow, the instructions may be changed at any time and one party may waive the performance of certain conditions, if in doing so the waiver does not act as a detriment to the other parties to the transaction.

Procedures

The basic steps in an escrow procedure usually include the following:

1. Mutual escrow instructions and initial deposit, which, in the case of escrow holders employing unilateral instructions, may not be prepared until steps 2 through 7 have been completed
2. Title search
3. Demand for payoff, or in the case of an assumption, a beneficiary statement
4. Deposit of termite report, if any
5. Deposit of new loan documents, if buyer is obtaining new financing
6. Deposit of required fire insurance policies
7. Balancing of accounting details, including adjustments and prorations
8. Deposit of balance of moneys required to close
9. Title run to date
10. Recordation
11. Disbursement of funds
12. Escrow statement
13. Title policy

Termination

Escrows are voluntarily terminated either by full performance and closing or by mutual consent and cancellation. It has been held that all the performances required by escrow instructions must be performed within the time limit set forth in the escrow agreement, and the escrow agent has no authority to enforce or accept the performance after the time limit provided in the instructions. When the time limit provided in the escrow has expired, and neither party to the escrow has performed in accordance with the terms, the parties are entitled to the return of their respective papers and documents from the escrow agent.

CHECKLIST OF ESCROW CHARGES FOR WHICH THE SELLER IS RESPONSIBLE

Legal closing

1. Owner's title policy (where applicable)
2. Escrow services
3. Drawing deed
4. Drawing reconveyance
5. Notary fees
6. Recording reconveyance
7. Documentary transfer tax (providing county has adopted this tax)
8. Other agreed charges

Financial closing

1. Mortgage discounts (points)
2. Appraisal charge for advance commitment
3. Termite report or structural repair (if any needed)
4. Interest on existing loan from last monthly payment to closing date
5. Beneficiary statement (balance of existing loan)
6. Loan payoff (1st trust deed and/or 2nd trust deed)
7. Prepayment penalty
8. Other agreed charges
9. Escrow fees in VA transaction

Adjustment between seller and buyer

1. Pay any tax arrears in full
2. Pay any improvement assessment arrears (assessment may have to be paid in full)

3. Pay any other liens or judgments necessary to pass clear title
4. Pay broker's commission
5. Reimburse buyer for prepaid rents and deposits
6. Occupancy adjustments

CHECKLIST OF ESCROW CHARGES FOR WHICH THE PURCHASER IS RESPONSIBLE

Legal closing

1. Standard or owner's policy (if applicable)
2. ALTA policy and inspection fee (if ordered)
3. Escrow services
4. Drawing second mortgage (if used)
5. Notary fee
6. Recording deed
7. Other agreed charges

Financial closing

1. Loan origination fee
2. Appraisal fee
3. Credit report
4. Drawing up note(s) and trust deed(s)
5. Notary fees
6. Recording trust deed
7. Tax agency fee
8. Termite inspection fee (if agreed upon)
9. Interest on new loan (from date of closing until first monthly payment due)
10. Assumption fee
11. Other agreed charges
12. New fire insurance premium, one year prepaid, if applicable

Adjustments between buyer and seller (depends on closing date)

1. Reimburse seller for prepaid taxes
2. Reimburse seller for prepaid insurance
3. Reimburse seller for prepaid improvement assessment
4. Reimburse seller for prepaid impounds (in case buyer is assuming an existing loan)
5. Other
6. Other occupancy adjustments

Reserve (impounds)

1. Reserve to lender to meet next tax payment
2. Reserve to lender to meet next insurance payment (one year)
3. Reserve to lender to meet FHA insurance premium

Variations

1. Any variation from custom in closing a deal should be agreed upon in advance. Sometimes, through sheer bargaining power, one party can demand to be relieved of all or some of the customary charges and offsets generally assigned against him.
2. Accruals: Unless agreed upon in advance, interest bearing debts are accrued up to date of settlement, and constitute a charge against the seller.

AUDIT

The escrow agent or broker may want to check his work before final closing in order to be sure he is not paying out more than he has received. This is accomplished by a cash reconciliation statement, as follows:

Cash Reconciliation Statement

(for Broker's Use Only)

Cash received:		Cash paid:	
Down payment	$2,500.00	Taxes	$1,112.40
Buyer's final check	6,061.55	Documentary transfer tax	11.55
	$8,561.55	Draw deed	5.00
		Recording deeds	6.00
Less check paid seller	4,586.60	Title insurance policy	229.00
	$3,974.95	Escrow service	96.00
		Broker's fee	2,505.00
		Quitclaim deed	10.00
			$3,974.95

Thus, the two totals are in balance and cash in and out is accounted for.

TYPICAL CLOSING

An understanding of closing or "escrowing" a transaction and the preparation of the final settlement sheet (or sheets) may be best understood by following a typical, hypothetical deal from beginning to end. In the following example there will be presented (1) the facts and agreements surrounding a negotiated home sale, (2) computations and explanations, and (3) distribution of the items on the settlement sheets.

Example—Smythe-Porter sale

R. N. Canfield, a real estate broker, has a listing from Martin B. and Donna G. Smythe on the latter's house at a sales price of $41,750. The listing contract provides authority to consummate the sale on the basis of customary charges and prorations of taxes, insurance, rents, etc. The terms are based on cash, and buyer to assume existing trust deed.

1. Canfield locates buyers in the persons of Arnold D. and Joan K. Porter, who sign a written purchase agreement at the price and terms set forth above.
2. Closing date, March 10, 19__.
3. There is an existing trust deed of $34,000, with a net balance of $31,432, as of January 1, 19__. Interest is at 8 percent with payments of principal and interest to be made quarterly. Next payment date, March 30, 19__.
4. The house is presently rented to a tenant who pays rent in advance on the first of the month at $360. Rent has been paid to May 1, 19__, when tenant agrees to vacate.
5. Fire and comprehensive insurance for one year, dated from July 1 of the preceding year, is in force. One-year premium is $162. Policy is to be assigned in favor of buyer.
6. There is a street assessment bond against the property of $1050. Buyer insists in negotiation that this be deducted as an offsetting item.
7. Current taxes are $1080, divided into two installments of $540. Neither has been paid and there is a delinquency on the first of $32.40. Buyer insists that all taxes be paid but agrees to bear his share.
8. Charges to consider: 6 percent broker's fee; documentary transfer tax; preparing papers for seller, $5; recording deed, $3; title insurance policy and escrow service, $325 and $96 respectively, securing quitclaim deed to remove title cloud, $10; recording of quitclaim deed, $3.
9. Buyer paid $2,500 at time of purchase and pays balance at time of closing.

Statement to Seller, Martin B. and Donna G. Smythe
Closing Date, March 10, 19__

	(Debit)	(Credit)
a. Sales price		$41,750.00
b. Insurance prorate in favor of seller for 3⅔ months unexpired, premium one year, $162		49.50

c. Tax prorate in favor of seller		330.00
d. Rent prorate in favor of buyer for rent prepaid to May 1, at $360 per month	600.00	
Liens assumed by buyer		
e. Trust deed $34,000, with present balance of	31,432.00	
Accrued interest on above, 8 percent from January 1, 19__...............	488.95	
Street assessment bond	1,050.00	
Cash charges		
f. Pay current taxes and penalty	1,112.40	
g. Pay documentary transfer tax	11.55	
Pay drawing deed	5.00	
Pay quitclaim deed.................	10.00	
h. Pay recording quitclaim	3.00	
Pay title insurance policy and escrow service	325.00	
Pay broker 6 percent of sales price..	2,505.00	
i. Proceeds check to seller	4,586.60	
	$42,129.50	$42,129.50

Statement to Buyer, Arnold D. and Joan K. Porter
Closing Date, March 10, 19__

	(Debit)	(Credit)
j. Purchase price	41,750.00	
Insurance prorate in favor of seller for 3⅔ months unexpired, premium one year, $162	49.50	
Tax prorate in favor of seller	330.00	
Rent prorate in favor of buyer for rent prepaid to May 1, at $360 per month		$600.00
Liens assumed by buyer		
Trust deed $34,000, with present balance of		31,432.00
Accrued interest on above, 8 percent from January 1, 19__...............		488.95

k. Street assessment bond		1,050.00
Cash items		
l. Pay for recording deed	3.00	
Cash received as down payment		2,500.00
m. Cash received, March 10, 19__, to close		6,061.55
	$42,132.50	$42,132.50

Explanations

a. Sales of real estate and personal property including prepaid items are set up as credits on the seller's statement because the broker or escrow is thought of as "owing" the seller for these items.

b. The seller is being paid for the time that the policy is to remain in force. Of a 12 months' policy with a premium of $162, in the period from July 1, 19__, of the preceding year, to March 10, 19__, 8⅓ months have been used or 3⅔ months remain:

Computation: $\frac{162}{12} = \$13.50$ per month.

$\$13.50 \times 3\frac{2}{3} = \$49.50$

c. This item will be explained in connection with (f), below.

d. Seller has collected rent at the rate of $360 per month beyond closing date:

$360 for April
<u>$240</u> for March 10 to April 1
$600

e. The interest on the trust deed balance of $41,432 must be accrued at 8 percent from January 1, 19__, to March 10, 19__ (70 days).

Computation: $41{,}432 \times 8 \text{ percent} \times \frac{70}{360} = \$488.95$

(It is common to count 30 days per month and use 360 instead of 365 for the denominator.)

f. The escrow holder is required by the agreement to pay all taxes. It is easier to pay this in a single check, showing it as a charge against the seller, and then to give him a "prorate credit," as shown in (c) above, for the amount he pays beyond the settlement date. The tax year is from July 1 of one year to June 30 of the next. The seller has thus paid 3⅔ months beyond his required share. He pays, of course, the first installment and penalty.

Computation: $\frac{\$1{,}080}{12} = \$90.00$ per month.

$90 \times 3\frac{2}{3} = \$330.$

g. Documentary transfer tax on sale of real property is at the rate of $1.10 per thousand, or $0.55 for $500, or any lesser amount. Only the equity sold is taxable, which is the difference between the sale price, $41,750, and the trust deed balance of $31,432, or $10,318.

Computation: 10 x ($1.10 + $0.55) = $11.55

h. Seller pays for all charges to clear up title.

i. The amount is the difference between the sum of the preceding debits and the total of the credit column.

j. It will be noted that the items (a) and (b) on the seller's statement are the same as the items (j) and (k) on the buyer's, except for reversal of account position. These are now debits because the buyer is thought of as "owing" the escrow for these items.

k. A credit to the buyer. Under the purchase terms, the amount of the outstanding street assessment bonds was to be deducted from the purchase price.

l. An example of buyer's responsibility for recording instruments in his favor.

m. This item represents the difference between the sum of the preceding credits and the total debits. Of course it bears no relation to the proceeds check given to the seller because of the down payment and varying charges.

3

How to Complete Real Estate Documents and Forms

The proper typing of legal forms and documents becomes easy if you remember that there is a source to answer any question. Check for *identical* transactions and documents in your own office, call the municipal (city, county, state, or federal) office involved, or the public or law library. For future handy reference, make a card file of sources and include names, addresses, and phone numbers. Keep a copy of each document you type, and set up your own "forms file" in a three-ring binder. Divide the notebook into pertinent sections, tab it, and include a table of contents in the front. Cross-reference the notebook to your card file of sources.

Most real estate offices and/or real estate associations use standard forms. If you use new forms, or prepare any legal document, it is advisable to have the wording and/or the form cleared by an attorney before putting the form into use.

The basic elements for legal documents are presented here, so that you will have a "master reference" book.

Real estate contracts generally include:

1. Contracts for the sale of real property or an interest therein

2. Agreements for leasing of realty for a period longer than one year
3. Agreements authorizing or employing an agent or broker to sell real estate for compensation or a commission

These contracts *must* be in writing and *must* be signed by the party to be charged in order for them to be valid.

In the usual real estate sales transaction, the prospective buyer states the terms and conditions under which he is willing to purchase the property, and these terms and conditions constitute his offer. If the owner agrees to all of the terms and conditions of the offer, it is an acceptance which results in the creation of a contract. All that is then required legally to complete the contract for the sale of real property is to state the terms and conditions in writing and have the parties sign the contract.

Forms such as listing agreements (authorizations to sell), deposit receipts, exchange agreements, and other real estate contracts for the sale or exchange of real estate, should contain:

1. The date of the agreement
2. The names and addresses of the parties to the contract
3. A description of the property
4. The consideration
5. Reference to creation of new mortgages (or trust deeds) if any, and the terms thereof; and the terms and conditions of existing mortgages, if any
6. Any other provisions which may be required or requested by either party
7. The date and place of the closing of the contract
8. A description of the property so that it may be referred to for absolute certainty

A contract of sale normally calls for the preparation of a deed to convey the property. When the deed of the property is signed and delivered to the purchaser of the contract, the contract is executed.

Sales contract (land contract) does not require conveyance of title within one year. Buyer takes possession, paying little or nothing down. He has possession and use of the property for as long as he continues to make regular payments on the sales contract. The title to the property remains with the seller, and does not pass to the buyer until he has paid an agreed amount. These sales contracts may or may not be recorded, and they operate for varying periods of time.

Types of deeds

A deed is presumed to be delivered as of its date. If no date exists, its date is presumed to be the date of delivery. Possession or the rights thereto *must* be given when the deed is delivered.

A *grant deed* carries implied warranties (the law makes them effective whether or not they are expressed), which are that it has not already been conveyed to any other person, and that it is free from encumbrances. It includes rights of way and building restrictions.

A *grant deed* is one in which the grantor makes a gift of the property to the grantee. It is invalid if made to defraud creditors.

In a *quitclaim deed*, the grantor relinquishes any right or claim he has in the property. It is used generally to clear up some cloud on the title. There are no implied warranties.

A *warranty deed* contains express covenants of title.

A *reconveyance deed* conveys title to property from a trustee to the trustor upon termination of the trust.

A *sheriff's deed* is given to a party on foreclosure of property; it is levied under a judgment for mortgage foreclosure or a money judgment against property owner.

HOW TO RECORD A DOCUMENT

The *recording* of a real estate instrument is a device for safeguarding the ownership of land and was designed to protect against secret conveyances and liens.

The process consists of giving the instrument to be recorded to an official, designated by the state statute, who copies it into a book. The information is then indexed in this municipal office in alphabetical order according to the names of the grantors and grantees or mortgagors or mortgagees, the name or nature of the document, the date of recording, and the recording reference.

Instrument means a paper signed and delivered by one party to another:

- Transferring title to, or giving a lien on property
- Giving the right to a debt or duty
- Judgments affecting title or possession of real property
- Notices of locations of mining claims
- Certificates of amounts of taxes, interest, and penalties due, and extensions or releases thereof by certain government agencies
- Leases for the development and extraction of minerals, oil, and gas in which the United States is the lessor
- Copies of interdepartmental letters and decisions of the Department of the Interior

Instruments affecting real property must be recorded in the county where the property is situated and, if it is in more than one county, must be recorded in each. In most states it is recorded with the County Recorder, but you should double-check. The recording fee also varies.

An instrument may be recorded in person or mailed with a covering letter identifying the document, enclosing a check and a stamped, return envelope, requesting recordation and return. It can be sent by registered mail, with return receipt requested.

A document is considered recorded when it has been marked "Filed for Record," given a number, and imprinted with the year, month, day, hour, and minute of (as well as the party requesting) recordation by the County Recorder's office. See Chapter 15 for information on how to research public records.

HOW TO TYPE A DOCUMENT*

Never complete a paragraph at the end of a page. Carry over at least one or two lines.

Marginal and tabular stops. On a typewriter with pica type (pica type is most frequently used in legal instruments), set your marginal and tabular stops as follows:

Paper guide ... 0

Left marginal stop ... 15

Right marginal stop ... 75

---

*This section from the book, *The Real Estate Office Secretary's Handbook*, by Lillian Doris. © 1953, 1966, by Prentice-Hall, Inc. Published by Prentice-Hall, Inc., Englewood Cliffs, New Jersey 07632.

First tabular stop ... 25

Second tabular stop ... 30

Third tabular stop ... 35

With the stops set at these points, practically no adjustment of the typewriter will be necessary for margins, paragraph indentations, proper placement of quotations, and the like.

Numbering pages. Number pages on legal cap one-half inch from the bottom of the page, in the center of the line. The number should be preceded and followed by a hyphen, thus: -4-. If the first page is not numbered, the numbering begins with -2-. Be exact in placing the number so that when the pages are collated the numbers will overlie one another.

Space for fill-ins. When a date is to be filled in later, leave a space instead of typing a line for the fill-in.

June , 1968 (3 spaces)

This day of June, 1968 (6 spaces)

Do not leave the blank for a subsequent fill-in at the end of a line, because it will not be noticeable.

How to write numbers. In legal instruments, write numbers in words and repeat them in numerals in parentheses, as follows:

One thousand three hundred eighty-two (1,382)

Twenty-five and sixty-three one hundredths (25.63) *or* (25 63/100).

Note that when the number is spelled out, *and* is used only for a decimal or fraction.

How to write amounts of money. To insure accuracy, spell out amounts of money and repeat them in parentheses, as follows:

Thirty-eight dollars ($38)

Eight hundred fifty dollars and eighty cents ($850.80)

Note that (1) the figures in parentheses follow the entire amount as spelled out; (2) an amount of dollars without cents is written $1,340, not $1,340.00; (3) *and* is not used unless the amount includes cents.

Dates. Dates may be expressed in figures or spelled out. Even if the day of the month is spelled out, the year may be written in figures. Thus: the twenty-first day of August, 1968.

Ditto marks. Ditto marks are not permissible in a legal instrument. They are used in exhibits and schedules, but not in the instrument to which the exhibits and schedules are annexed.

Erasures and interlineations. If an error is made involving more than a few letters of a word, retype the page. The signer of the document must initial interlineations. Do not insert pages, but retype as many pages of the document as are necessary to work in the additional material.

Many words and phrases commonly used in legal documents, particularly in introductory and closing paragraphs, are customarily written in full capitals. They may be followed by a comma, a colon, or no punctuation, depending upon the sense and preference:

- KNOW ALL MEN BY THESE PRESENTS, That ...
- MEMORANDUM OF AGREEMENT made ...
- THIS AGREEMENT, made October ...
- NOW, THEREFORE, IT IS HEREBY MUTUALLY AGREED, AS FOLLOWS: ...
- IN WITNESS WHEREOF, the parties ...

Filling in plurals, "his" or "her," etc. Where the blank form leaves space for completing a word, insert the necessary letter or letters immediately after the printed word to which it is added.

Filling in surplus space. Some of the blank spaces on printed legal forms are just large enough for insertion of the material, possibly a single word; other spaces are quite large to allow for short or long insertions.

A large space following a land description should be filled in after you have taken the sheet out of the typewriter, a Z with ink, from under the last line of typing to what should be the bottom margin.

This same practice may be followed to close up any other large space and thus prevent anyone from inserting something in the document after the instrument has been signed. In some cases, such as after the insertion of the name of a party, it is advisable to finish the line with dashes to the right-hand margin, just as you would do on a check after you had inserted the name of the person to whom the check is payable.

"Riders" when space is insufficient. Sometimes the space allotted for filling in conditional clauses or other provisions is not large enough for the typewritten material you have to insert. In that case, be careful to leave sufficient space after your last

line of type to permit a "rider" with the rest of the typewritten matter to be pasted to the document. For the rider, use legal cap paper, preferably the same width as the printed legal form, and cut off any part of the sheet that is not used. The piece pasted to the document should be only as large as is necessary to carry the runover plus the initials or signatures of the parties who sign the document. Paste the rider securely to the document (after the document and the rider have been examined and found to be correct), using a glue that will stick permanently. *Do not use rubber cement* for this purpose.

In some instances, riders attached as additions or amendments to documents have a heading to show that they are part of the document to which they are attached.

All separate sheets of paper attached to a document should be signed or initialed by the parties who sign the document.

Matching the printed copies. Printed forms bear a printer's mark showing the number of copies printed and the date of the printing. When filling in more than one copy, use forms that were printed at the same time because a change might have been made in the form.

Before attempting to fill in more than one blank form at one time by using carbons, make sure that the printing on all copies registers exactly. To do this, place the edges of the forms together and hold to the light. You can then see whether the printed matter in one copy lies exactly over corresponding material in the other copy.

Fill-ins on both sides of sheet. When making carbon copies of a printed form that has fill-ins on both sides of the sheet, be sure to have the original front with the original back. Be particularly careful of double sheet forms.

How to copy-type legal documents. The following instructions relate to the copy-typing of a signed document:

1. Copy exactly, even obvious errors, because the copy purports to be a "True and Exact" copy.
2. Indicate obvious errors copied from the original as follows: (a) Underline an incorrect letter or figure. (b) Put "sic" in parentheses or brackets after apparently or obviously incorrect words or phrases. (c) Show an omission by a caret.

agreement entered into the 31th day of April ...
upon reciept ...
as part payment on the principle [sic] of a certain note and mortgage ...
and regulations of the United States, State and ^ in which said premises are situate, ...

3. Copy page for page and line for line as far as practicable.
4. If you do not have a paper holder fitted with an adjustable line spacer, place a ruler or the edge of a "see through" (soft yellow or soft green) engineering triangle directly under the line you are copy-typing, and move it down line by line.
5. When the document is completed, proofread it with another person who reads aloud from the original copy while the typist checks the typewritten material. The reader should indicate paragraphs, punctuation, underlining, full capitals, hyphens, and so on.

SETTING UP THE SECTION FOR EXECUTION OF THE INSTRUMENT*

Meaning of "execution" of an instrument. Technically, execution of an instrument includes signing and delivery. In office parlance, execution frequently refers merely to the signing of an instrument by the party or parties described in it.

You will understand how to set up the section for execution of the instrument from the following explanation of (1) the testimonium clause, (2) attestation, (3) signatures, (4) sealing, and (5) acknowledgment.

Testimonium clause. The testimonium clause is the clause with which the instrument closes. It immediately precedes the signatures and usually begins, "IN WITNESS WHEREOF, ...," typed in solid caps. It is a declaration by the parties to the instrument that their signatures are attached in testimony of the preceding part of the instrument. The testimonium clause is

*This section from the book, *The Real Estate Office Secretary's Handbook*, by Lillian Doris. ©1953, 1966, by Prentice-Hall, Inc. Published by Prentice-Hall, Inc., Englewood Cliffs, New Jersey 07632.

not to be confused with the "witness" or "attestation clause" (see below). The testimonium clause relates to the parties themselves, whereas the witness or attestation clause relates to those who sign the paper as witnesses, not as parties to the instrument.

Quite often, the testimonium clause will guide you in setting up the signature lines. It will indicate (1) what parties are to sign the instrument; (2) what officer of a corporation is to sign; (3) whether the instrument is to be sealed; and (4) whether a corporate seal is to be attached. For example, from the following clause, which is a form commonly used, you know that the president of the corporation is to sign, that the seal is to be affixed, and that the secretary of the corporation is to attest the seal:

> IN WITNESS WHEREOF, Alvin Corporation has caused its corporate seal to be hereto affixed, and attested by its secretary, and these presents to be signed by its president, this 26th day of October, 19__.

On the other hand, from the following clause, also commonly used, you know that the instrument is not to be sealed:

> IN WITNESS WHEREOF, the parties hereto have hereunto set their hands the day and year first above written.

The introductory words to the testimonium clause, *in witness whereof, in testimony whereof,* and the like, are usually typed in solid caps. The following word begins with lower case unless it is a proper name.

Attestation clause. Frequently the signatures to an instrument must be witnessed in order to make the instrument legal. The act of witnessing the signature to a written instrument at the request of the party signing the instrument is attestation. The witness is called a subscribing witness, because he signs his name as a witness. A legend or clause that recites the circumstances surrounding the signing of the instrument often precedes the signature of the attesting witnesses and is called the *attestation clause.* The wording of the attestation clause may be simply "In the presence of."

The legend and the lines on which witnesses sign are written opposite the lines for the signatures of persons who will execute the instrument.

Signatures. The parties signing an instrument vary with the instrument. Thus, all parties to a contract sign, but usually only the grantor signs a deed and only the mortgagor signs a mortgage. As a general practice, lines are typed for signatures. Type the first signature line below the body of the instrument, beginning it slightly to the right of the center of the page. Type a line for the signature of each person who must sign the instrument. There are no special requirements for the spacing of signature lines, except that sufficient space should be allowed for average handwriting and the lines should be evenly spaced. Three or four spaces between lines are sufficient.

When a corporation is a party to an instrument, the instrument is signed in the name of the corporation by the officer or officers authorized to execute it. Type the name of the corporation in solid caps, leave sufficient space beneath it for a signature, and type "By" and a line for signature. Under the signature line, type the title of the corporate officer who is going to sign the instrument, as shown below. The testimonium clause usually recites the title of the officer who is supposed to sign the instrument.

BLANK CORPORATION

By__________________________

(Title)

When a partnership is a party to an instrument, type the name in solid caps, leave sufficient space beneath it for a signature, and type "By" and a line for signature. Since partnerships do not have officers, there will be no title under the signature line.

How to fit the signatures on the page. Arrange the body, or text, of the instrument so that at least two lines appear on the page with the signatures. The signatures must all be on the same page unless there are so many that they require more than a full page. To comply with these requirements you must gauge carefully the length of the material to be typed. This is not difficult if you are copying from a draft; otherwise, you might have to make a test copy and adjust your spacing accordingly. Here are methods by which you may lengthen or shorten the available typing space in order to fit the signatures on the page:

1. Leave wider or narrower top and bottom margins.
2. If you are using paper without ruled margins, leave wider or narrower left and right margins.
3. If the last line of a paragraph is full-length, adjust the right margin of that paragraph so that at least one word carries over to another line, thereby taking up an extra line of space. Or, if a paragraph ends with one word on a line, adjust the margin so that it is not necessary to carry over the one word, thereby saving a line of space.
4. Triple space between paragraphs.
5. Leave less space between the text of the instrument and the signatures.
6. Leave less space between the signatures.

Sealing an instrument. If an instrument is to be sealed, the testimonium clause will so indicate.

An individual's seal. At the end of the signature lines on an instrument that must be sealed, type (SEAL) or (L.S.) in solid caps. Thus:

________________________*(L.S.)*

L.S. stands for *locus sigilli*, which means place of the seal.

A corporation's seal. Almost all corporations adopt a formal seal. It is engraved on a metal plate and impressed by this means upon the paper. An officer of the corporation impresses the seal on the instrument when it is signed. In many cases the corporate secretary must bear witness, or "attest," to the fact that the imprint on the paper is the seal of the corporation. Whenever the testimonium clause recites that the seal is to be attested, type the following on the left side of the page, opposite the signature line:

ATTEST

____

Secretary

The seal will ordinarily be placed in the margin immediately above or below the "attest" line.

Acknowledgment. This is a formal declaration before a duly authorized officer by a person who has executed an instrument that such execution is his act and deed. An acknowledgment is for the purpose of entitling an instrument to be recorded and thus to give constructive notice of its contents. It is an attestation by an official witness. Acknowledgment of certain documents for recordation is not applicable in every state.

How and where to type the acknowledgment. Acknowledgments are usually double spaced. They follow the signatures. Although there is no rule of law governing the placement of an acknowledgment on the page, it is desirable that the entire acknowledgment be placed on the signature page of the instrument, even if single-spacing is necessary to accomplish this. If the entire acknowledgment cannot be placed on the signature page it is preferable to type it all on another page. In the case of some instruments—for example, a power of attorney that authorizes the conveyance of any interest in real estate—it is practically mandatory to type the acknowledgment on the same page as the signatures.

Forms of acknowledgments to be signed by a notary public. The acknowledgments illustrated in the forms below are for the purpose of showing you how acknowledgments are set up when typed and to give you a general idea of the wording of the acknowledgment. They are not supposed to be copied word for word:

(Individual)
STATE OF....................
COUNTY OF..................
ss.:

On the .... day of ...., 19..., before me came ...., to me known to be the individual described in and who executed the foregoing instrument and acknowledged that he executed the same.

....
Notary Public
(Affix stamp and seal)

(Corporate)
STATE OF_______________
COUNTY OF_______________
ss.:

On the .... day of ...., 19..., before me personally came ...., to me known, who, being by me duly sworn, did depose and say that he resides at

........................; that he is .... *(title)* of .... Company, the corporation described in and which executed the foregoing instrument; that he knows the seal of said corporation; that the seal affixed to said instrument is such corporate seal; that it was so affixed by order of the .... of said corporation, and that he signed his name thereto by like order.

....
Notary Public
(Affix stamp and seal)

(Partnership)
STATE OF ....
COUNTY OF ....
SS.:

On this .... day of ...., 19..., before me personally came ...., to me known and known to me to be a member of ...., and the person described in and who executed the foregoing instrument in the firm name of ...., and he duly acknowledged to me that he executed the same as and for the act and deed of said firm of ....

....
Notary Public
(Affix stamp and seal)

TIPS FOR TYPING DOCUMENTS*

Paper. A legal instrument is typewritten generally on "legal cap" or on a legal form. This part of the chapter relates to legal cap, which is white paper 8″ or 8½″ by 13″, with a wide ruled margin at the left and a narrow ruled margin at the right.

Margins. Documents typed on legal size paper are bound at the top.

Top margin. Begin typing either five or six double spaces from the top of the paper, but always allow the same number of spaces on all sheets. This way every page starts at the same place on the paper and has the same number of typed lines.

---

*This section from the book, *The Real Estate Office Secretary's Handbook,* by Lillian Doris. ©1953, 1966, by Prentice-Hall, Inc. Published by Prentice-Hall, Inc., Englewood Cliffs, New Jersey 07632.

Bottom margins. Leave a margin of approximately one inch. Use a backing sheet with a horizontal black line one inch from the bottom or a light pencil mark on the original.

Left margin. On legal cap, begin typing one space to the right of the colored line that indicates the left margin, except for lines beginning a new paragraph.

Right margin. Allow a leeway of seven spaces between the right margin and the colored line (approximately 5/8″ to the left of the colored line). Avoid excessive hyphenation and a ragged right margin. Never type beyond the lines indicating margins.

Line spacing. As a rule, all legal instruments are double spaced. Quotations and land descriptions may be single spaced. Triple space before and after all indicated material. It is permissible to single space an acknowledgment in order to get it on the signature page.

Paragraphs. Indent ten spaces for paragraphs. Never block paragraphs in a legal document. Indent five additional spaces for paragraphing the indented material.

Typing tips and tricks*

Pica type *has 10 digits to 1 horizontal inch.*

Elite type *has 12 digits to 1 horizontal inch.*

There are *6 lines* of typing *to one vertical inch.*

There are *85 horizontal pica spaces on a page 8½″ wide.*

There are *102 horizontal elite spaces on a page 8½″ wide.*

There are *66 vertical lines on a page 11″ long.*

How to center a line horizontally*

1. Assume a 60 space line on a pica typewriter with margins of 12 and 72.
2. Count total digits to be centered and include punctuation and spaces (assume a total of 20).
3. Subtract 2 from 1 (answer is 40).
4. Divide answer to 3 in half (answer is 20).
5. Add answer to 4 to left hand margin in 1 (12 + 20 = 32, which is where to begin typing line to be centered).

---

*Courtesy IBM.

How to justify right margins*

Justify your copy by using the half space lever twice for each letter to be added or removed, as follows:

- Set a right margin.
- Type as close to that margin as possible.
- For each line you type, count the number of characters short of the margin or beyond the margin that the line runs. Use the margin release lever when it is necessary to type beyond the margin.
- For each space short of the margin, add two half spaces. For each space beyond the margin, eliminate two half spaces. Write down the number of spaces you must add or subtract.

For example:

- Set margins at 30 and 60.

Justified copy looks very much	ok	Justified copy looks very much
like the printed material you see	+1	like the printed material you see
everyday in the newspaper or	-2	everyday in the newspaper or
magazines that you read.		magazines that you read.

If you do not have a half space lever on your typewriter, either move the paper manually or move the carriage manually.

How to correct pages bound at the top*

Insert the whole document as if one page.

Pull paper release lever forward.

Flip to desired sheet.

Push paper release lever back.

Align, correct.

How to draw vertical lines*

Put your pen or pencil in the notch of the cardholder.

Hold pen steady, pull line finder lever forward.

Manually turn the platen.

---

*Courtesy IBM.

How to insert a letter*

Erase the incorrect word.

Move the carriage to the space after the last letter of the word just typed.

Depress the half space lever or move the carriage or the paper manually.

Keep the half space lever depressed until you wish to insert a half space (probably at the end of the word) or move the paper or the carriage manually at the time you wish to insert the letter.

How to remove a letter*

Erase the entire word.

Move the carriage to the space after the last letter of the word just typed.

Space once.

Depress the half space lever and hold it until the new word is typed or move the paper or the carriage manually.

Release the half space lever.

Depress the space bar and continue typing.

How to type lines at the very bottom of the page*

As your backing page, use a sheet of paper longer than the one on which you are typing. Be sure they are paper clipped at the top. (You can put a drop of rubber cement at the lower two corners to make sure there is no slippage—when done, the pages will pull apart and the cement will rub off.)

Fit tight column totals by "stair stepping" them*

116,339,247	98,762,941	643,977,521	970,331,699	144,985,889	653,221
741,105,309	34,908,862	67,421,691	894,570,344	966,984,831	985,942
857,444,556					
	133,671,803				
		711,399,212			
			1,864,902,043		
				1,111,970,720	
					1,639,163

*Courtesy IBM.

4

How to Describe Real Property

LAND DESCRIPTIONS

Every parcel of land sold, leased, or mortgaged must be properly and legally identified or described. Every real estate instrument to be recorded must have an adequate description of the physical property—the land. Any improvements upon the property do not have to be described. A good or legal description is said to be one which describes no other piece of property except the one in question, in such a way that the land can be identified.

You have to work with architects, builders, property lessors and lessees, engineers, appraisers, government agencies, construction, community planning, redevelopment, and *more*. You'll need solid knowledge of general methods of property description if you have to explain to someone with no background how to read a map or describe property being bought or sold. You must do the actual typing or dictating of the description, so here are proper typing instructions and some tricks for double-checking your work.

Metes and bounds description is used when the property referred to is not covered by a duly recorded map, or where it is in such shape as to make it impracticable to describe by section, township, and range.

A metes and bounds description starts at a fixed point of beginning and follows, in detail, the boundaries of the land described in courses and distances from one point to another until the point of beginning is reached. If a mistake is made at the point of beginning, the description is worthless.

Metes are measures of length, in units of inches, feet, yards, or rods.

Bounds are measures of boundaries, both natural and artificial, such as rivers and roads. Landmarks (markers), referred to as monuments, are often used in such descriptions and may include trees, boulders, creeks, fences, roads, and iron pipes.

This kind of description should be used as a last resort due to its many disadvantages. Such descriptions are lengthy and unintelligible to anyone but a civil engineer or a surveyor, and they add a great burden to the work of recorders, assessors, and tax collectors.

Figure 4-1 is a simple illustration of a metes and bounds description, describing the dimensions of the front, rear, and sides.

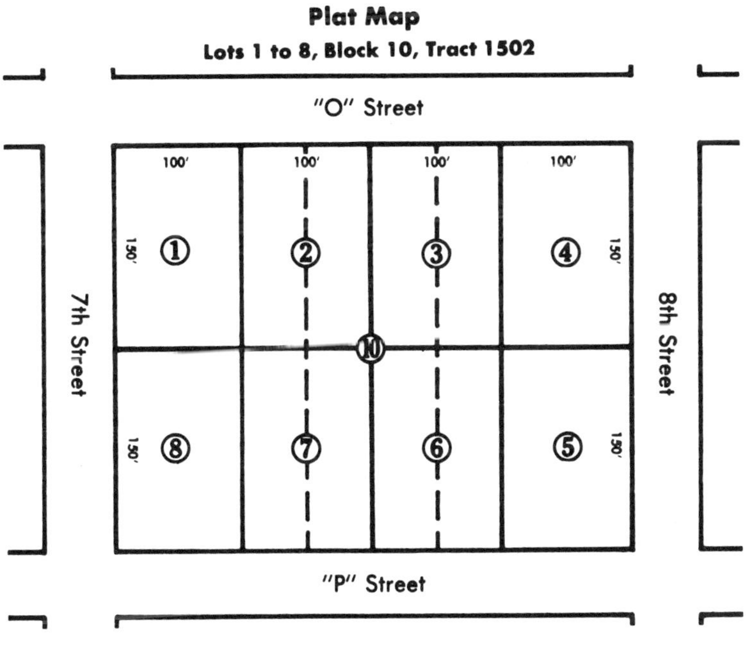

Figure 4-1

> Beginning at a point on the southerly line of "O" Street, 150 feet westerly of the SW corner of the intersection of "O" and 8th Streets; running thence due south 300 feet to the northerly line of "P" Street; thence westerly along the northerly line of "P" Street, 100 feet; thence northerly and parallel to the first course, 300 feet to the southerly line of "O" Street, 100 feet, to the point or place of beginning.

Description by section and township. The United States Surveyor General has jurisdiction over surveys of all public lands. From a prominent starting point, true North and South and East and West lines are run on a true parallel of latitude. The intersection of these lines at this point (or monument) are called the base and principal (prime) meridian, respectively. These proper descriptive names were established in order to locate and describe lands. See Figure 4-2.

MAP OF PRIME MERIDIANS AND THEIR BASE LINES WITHIN THE UNITED STATES

Figure 4-2

Alfred A. Ring, Nelson L. North, REAL ESTATE: Principles and Practices, 6th edition, © 1967, p. 94. Reprinted by permission of Prentice-Hall, Inc.

The public domain is divided into north and south lines, 6 miles apart, called ranges, and into east and west lines, also 6 miles apart, called township lines. The areas between the intersection of these ranges and township lines are called townships. The standard township is 6 miles square and contains 36 square miles.

The intersection of the base line and meridian is the starting point of calculations east or west, north or south, to locate a definite township. Ranges are numbered east or west from a principal meridian, while townships are numbered north or south from the principal base line.

Township 4 North, Range 3 East, would be three (squares of 6 miles each) townships to the east (to the right) of the principal meridian and four (squares of 6 miles each) townships to the north (up) of the principal base line.

Then, Township 5 South, Range 4 West, would be five (squares of 6 miles each) townships south (down) of the principal base line and four (squares of 6 miles each) west (to the left) of the principal meridian. See Figure 4-3.

North and South Meridian Line

T6N R6W	T6N R5W	T6N R4W	T6N R3W	T6N R2W	T6N R1W	T6N R1E	T6N R2E	T6N R3E	T6N R4E	T6N R5E	T6N R6E
T5N R6W	T5N R5W	T5N R4W	T5N R3W	T5N R2W	T5N R1W	T5N R1E	T5N R2E	T5N R3E	T5N R4E	T5N R5E	T5N R6E
T4N R6W	T4N R5W	T4N R4W	T4N R3W	T4N R2W	T4N R1W	T4N R1E	T4N R2E	T4N R3E	T4N R4E	T4N R5E	T4N R6E
T3N R6W	T3N R5W	T3N R4W	T3N R3W	T3N R2W	T3N R1W	T3N R1E	T3N R2E	T3N R3E	T3N R4E	T3N R5E	T3N R6E
T2N R6W	T2N R5W	T2N R4W	T2N R3W	T2N R2W	T2N R1W	T2N R1E	T2N R2E	T2N R3E	T2N R4E	T2N R5E	T2N R6E
T1N R6W	T1N R5W	T1N R4W	T1N R3W	T1N R2W	T1N R1W	T1N R1E	T1N R2E	T1N R3E	T1N R4E	T1N R5E	T1N R6E
T1S R6W	T1S R5W	T1S R4W	T1S R3W	T1S R2W	T1S R1W	T1S R1E	T1S R2E	T1S R3E	T1S R4E	T1S R5E	T1S R6E
T2S R6W	T2S R5W	T2S R4W	T2S R3W	T2S R2W	T2S R1W	T2S R1E	T2S R2E	T2S R3E	T2S R4E	T2S R5E	T2S R6E
T3S R6W	T3S R5W	T3S R4W	T3S R3W	T3S R2W	T3S R1W	T3S R1E	T3S R2E	T3S R3E	T3S R4E	T3S R5E	T3S R6E
T4S R6W	T4S R5W	T4S R4W	T4S R3W	T4S R2W	T4S R1W	T4S R1E	T4S R2E	T4S R3E	T4S R4E	T4S R5E	T4S R6E
T5S R6W	T5S R5W	T5S R4W	T5S R3W	T5S R2W	T5S R1W	T5S R1E	T5S R2E	T5S R3E	T5S R4E	T5S R5E	T5S R6E

East and West Base Line

Figure 4-3

Townships are further divided into sections. Each township contains 36 sections. Each section is 1 mile square and therefore contains 1 square mile of land. The township is six sections long (6 miles) and six sections wide, and therefore contains 36 square miles.

A section may then be divided, for a more specific description, into quarter-sections and fractions of quarter-sections.

The sections along the north and west boundaries of each township are approximately 50 feet shorter than those on the south side due to the spherical shape of the earth. Because of this irregularity, additional lines—guide meridians—are run every 24 miles east and west of the meridian. Other lines—standard parallels—are run every 24 miles north and south of the base line. These guide meridians and standard parallels are also known as correction lines.

Township plat. Figure 4-4 is a township plat showing how each section is numbered, the numbers running from 1 to 36. Each numbered section is divided into quarters of quarter-sections, each small square representing the location of a 40-acre plot of land. Typical descriptions and their respective locations are shown.

1. Beginning at the NE corner of SW ¼ of Section 17, thence southeasterly to the NW corner of the SE ¼ of Section 21, thence southwesterly to the SE corner of the NW ¼ of Section 29, thence northwesterly to the SW corner of the NE ¼ of Section 19, thence northeasterly back to the point of beginning.

2. The SE ¼ of the NE ¼ of the SE ¼, and the S½ of the SE ¼ of Section 10; the SW ¼ of the NW ¼ of the SW ¼, and the SW ¼ of the SW ¼ of Section 11; the E ½ of the NE ¼ of Section 15; and the NW ¼ of Section 14, excepting the SE ¼ thereof.

3. Beginning at the NW corner of the SE ¼ of the NE ¼ of Section 27, thence due east 3,960 feet, thence due south 3,960 feet, then due west 7,920 feet, thence northeasterly in a straight line to the point of beginning.

Figure 4-4

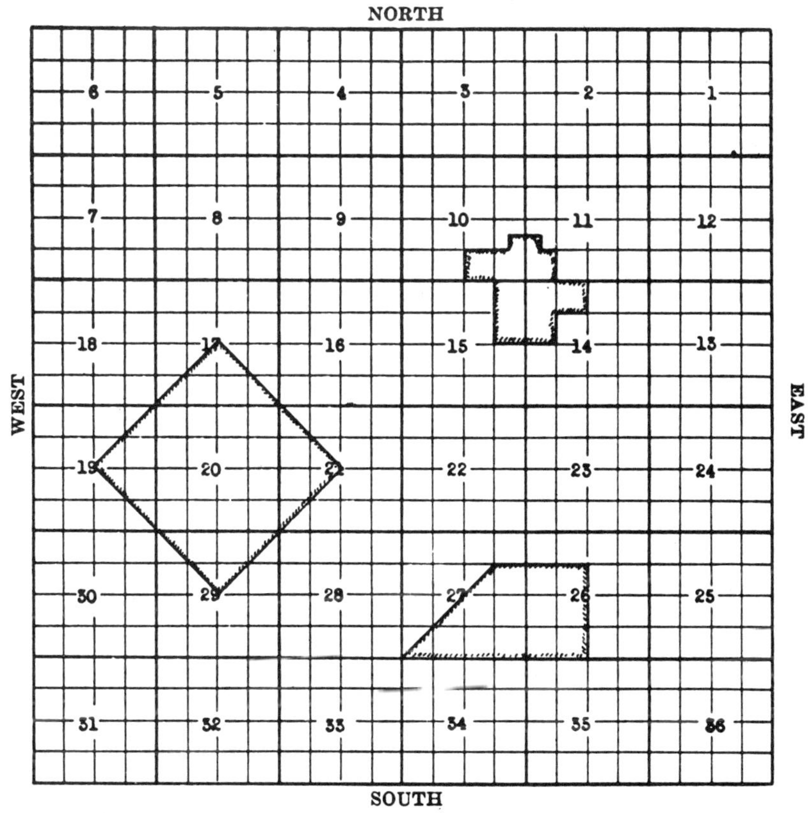

Figure 4-4 (cont'd)

If you have a plat or diagram showing the location of the parcel described, you can check the accuracy of the description against it, especially if the identification is by Government Survey. To compare a government survey description with the map designation, read the parts of the description in reverse order, beginning with the township and range and working backward to the designated plot.

You could also read the description from the beginning on the carbon copy to someone else who follows word for word.

Lot and block descriptions. In certain states all new subdivisions must be mapped or plotted. The map shows the relationship of the subdivision to other lands, and each parcel in the new subdivision is delineated and identified. When accepted by county or city authority, the map is filed in the County Recorder's office and has official status. Afterwards, any parcel in the subdivision is simply described in legal instruments by reference to the tract name or number and block and lot numbers. To this is added, "City of ______, County of ______." For example: "Lot 14, Block B, Parkview Addition (as recorded July 17, 1926, Book 2, Page 49 of maps), City of Sacramento, County of Sacramento, State of California."

Record of survey. Within a certain period after the establishment of points or lines, a land surveyor, or civil engineer who has made a survey in conformity with land surveying practices, files a record of survey relating to boundaries or property lines with the county surveyor in the county in which the survey was made. This record of survey map discloses (1) material evidence of physical change which does not appear on any map previously recorded in the office of the county recorder, (2) a material discrepancy with information of record with the county, (3) any evidence that might result in alternate positions of lines or points, or (4) the establishment of lines not shown on a recorded map which are not ascertainable from an inspection of the map without trigonometric calculations.

The county surveyor, after examining the record of survey map, then files it with the County Recorder.

Assessor's maps. The county assessor prepares and files in his office an accurate map of any land in the county and may number or letter the parcels in a manner approved by the Board of Supervisors or its equal governing body.

Informal methods of land description. In the absence of a title report, it is often convenient to refer to a specific parcel of realty by street number, name, ("The Norris Ranch"), or blanket reference ("my lot on High Street"). These methods are legal, but title companies ordinarily will not insure title derived through such a description. The specific boundaries of the grant must usually be established by one of the formal methods of description before the title insurance can be obtained.

The words "except" and "reserving" as used in descriptions of property are not conclusive in determining whether or not the fee title to the portion in question is being conveyed.

An innocent-looking phrase may be omitted, or the wrong course may be given, either of which may change the entire complexion of the description.

When in doubt about the correct descriptions to be used, you should consult a licensed engineer or surveyor or check with a title company.

How to type real property descriptions.*

1. Single space, with double space between paragraphs.
2. Do not abbreviate Street, Avenue, Road, or Boulevard in the text.
3. Write the words *North, Northeast, South, West, Southwest,* and the like with initial capitals, but do not capitalize the words *northerly, northeasterly,* and the like.
4. Capitalize *Quarter, Township, Section,* and *Range,* and the name or number of a *Prime Meridian.*
5. Write courses as follows: South twenty (20) degrees, thirty-three (33) minutes, forty-five (45) seconds West.
6. Write distances as follows: One hundred thirty-three and twenty-nine one hundredths (133.29) feet.
7. When several courses and distances are given in succession, introduced by a phrase such as "the following three courses and distances," each of the courses and distances is written separately, indented and single spaced, separated one from the other by a double space, and each course and distance is ended with a semicolon. The sentence after the last course and distance is flush with the left-hand margin of the text preceding the itemized courses and distances.
8. It is preferable not to use figures, symbols, and abbreviations, but many law offices use them because of the limited space on a printed form. A description would then be written: "South 20°,33′, 45″ West 30 ft."

Descriptions of tracts of land. In the description of tracts of public land the following abbreviations are used (periods are omitted after abbreviated compass directions that immediately precede and close up on figures):

---

*From the book, *The Real Estate Office Secretary's Handbook,* by Lillian Doris, © 1953, 1966 by Prentice-Hall, Inc. Published by Prentice-Hall, Inc., Englewood Cliffs, New Jersey 07632.

SE¼NW¼ sec. 4, T. 12 S., R. 15 E., of the Boise meridian
lot 6, NE¼ sec. 4, T. 6 N., R. 1 W.
N½ sec. 20, T. 7 N., R. 2 W., sixth principal meridian
Tps. 9, 10, 11, and 12 S., Rs. 12 and 13 W.
T. 2 S., Rs. 8, 9, and 10 E., sec. 26
T. 3 S., R. 1 E., sec. 34, W½E½, W½, and W½SE¼SE¼
sec. 32 (with or without a township number)

If fractions are spelled out in land descriptions, *half* and *quarter* are used (not *one-half* nor *one-quarter*).

south half of T. 47 N., R. 64 E.

In case of an unavoidable break in a land-description symbol group at end of a line, use no hyphen and break after fraction.

5

The Elements of Real Estate Appraisals and Finished Reports

Because proper preparation is as essential as proper typing of the appraisal report, this chapter will give you "behind-the-scenes" knowledge. You will find:

- A discussion of appraisal reports, their purposes and uses
- A fill-in-the-blank form (Standard Residential Appraisal Data Sheet) used for preliminary compilation of information
- Types of appraisal reports
    1. Letter form report—basic information
    2. Short form report—basic information and illustrations
    3. Narrative report—definition and a *complete outline* for a single-family residence report
- Typing, art work, spacing, paging, and binding tips and tricks to make the finished report as attractive as possible

PURPOSE AND USE OF APPRAISALS

1. Transfer of ownership of property
   a. The seller is assured that if he sells at the appraised price, he receives full market value, or that the price offered by the prospective buyer is fair and reasonable. A physical property appraisal may also include its age, remaining life, quality, or authenticity.
   b. The listing agent needs an estimate of value of the property before accepting a listing from the owner. *Generally an owner overvalues his property.* If the agent can show by means of an appraisal what the seller's property is worth, and obtain a listing at that figure, a sale is more likely to result.
   c. When a trade is involved, appraisals tend to offset the opinions of value formed by both parties to the trade.
   d. Valuations are necessary for the distribution of estate properties among heirs.
2. Financing and credit
   a. The lender has an appraisal made of the value of the property to be pledged as security for a mortgage or mortgage loan.
   b. Measuring economic soundness of real estate projects involves feasibility studies in relation to financing and credit.
3. Appraisal for taxation purposes
   a. Appraisals are needed by governmental bodies to establish the proper relationship between land and improvements for real estate taxes (ad valorem taxation).
   b. Properties subject to inheritance taxes must be evaluated for the purpose of levying federal and state inheritance taxes.
   c. Appraisals of income-producing properties are necessary to property owners for the basis of depreciation.

4. Condemnation actions
   a. With the right of eminent domain being vested in governmental agencies, it is important that properties under condemnation be evaluated to set the benefits or damages to the property being affected.
5. Insurance purposes
   a. Appraisals are based principally upon the cost of replacement, important for the purpose of obtaining fire insurance.
   b. Appraisals are useful in settling claims arising from insurance contracts after a property has been destroyed.
6. Miscellaneous reasons for appraisal
   a. Catastrophic damage—establishing fair market value of property before and immediately after the damage
   b. Fair rental value for negotiation of leases
   c. Appraisals for inheritance and gift tax purposes
   d. Fraud cases
   e. Damage cases
   f. Division-of-estate cases—a distribution of property under the terms of a will, in divorce proceedings, or between rival claimants

METHODS OF APPRAISAL

The purpose of the appraisal will have a definite bearing in determining the method of valuation. If the purpose is for sale, purchase, exchange, or condemnation, the market value approach is used. Valuation for property taxation generally results in lower valuation. Appraisals made for mortgage purposes give consideration to long-range income and are usually conservative. FHA or VA mortgage loan appraisals are fully prescribed by these agencies.

The comparison (market value) approach consists of comparing the property with other properties in the area which have already been sold. Since no two properties are exactly the same, adjustments are made by adding to or subtracting from the price to balance out the differences. Dollars are added if the property being compared is worse, and subtracted if it is better, to reach a balance. The formula is, "Comparable Sales plus or minus Adjustments equals Value Estimate." The mechanics of this approach involve the use of market data of all kinds in order to compare. The sources used for determining value include actual sales prices, listings, offers, rents, and leases, as well as an analysis of social and economic factors affecting marketability. (See outline below.) It is used for single residences and vacant land.

The cost (reproduction or replacement) approach is an estimate of the investment which would be required to replace the depreciated investments. The formula is, "Land plus Depreciated Improvement equals Value Estimate." This is used for public and quasi-public properties like government buildings, airports, schools, or churches. A high degree of training and ability is required to use this approach.

The income (capitalization) approach is concerned with the present worth of future benefits which may be derived from the property, and is applied to income-producing property.

THE APPRAISAL PROCESS

The orderly steps and considerations of the appraisal process are outlined below:

A. Define the problem.
   1. Identification of the property to be evaluated.
      a. Complete mailing address (including city and state).
      b. Complete legal description (by lot, block and tract number, including county where recorded; by metes and bounds descriptions; or by the government survey system).
   2. Description of property to be appraised.
      a. Vacant lot.
      b. Single-family residential.
      c. Multiple-family residential.
      d. Miscellaneous property.

3. Interests to be appraised.
   a. Which of the Bundle of Rights are to be evaluated? Rights affect value because they set the limits within which the property may be used.
   b. An appraisal estimates the value of the rights of ownership, not merely the physical land and its improvements.
   c. The extent of the research and the valuation opinion will vary depending upon the rights which are involved:
      1. Fee simple (complete ownership).
      2. Easement across property.
      3. Lessor's or lessee's interest.
      4. Mineral rights.
      5. Miscellaneous interests.
4. Purpose and function of the valuation determine the types of information to be gathered and processed.
   a. Market value for sale of a home.
   b. Value for mortgage loan purposes.
   c. Value for insurance purposes.
   d. Value for condemnation proceedings.
   e. Miscellaneous purposes and functions.
5. Date of the valuation estimate is generally the date of inspection of the property, although it may be for any period of time in the past.

B. Make a preliminary survey.
   1. Determine the highest and best use of the subject property.
      a. Analysis of the site and improvements. Is it a proper improvement? Does the improvement meet the test? Take inventory of important site utilities and building construction features.
      b. Analysis of the neighborhood. Is it stable? Are there adverse influences which must be considered?

2. The type of property determines the variety of data needed.
    a. Single-family home—stress will be placed on data concerning similar lots and improvements.
    b. Four-plex—stress will be placed on data concerning small multiple-family units.
3. A definite plan helps facilitate the gathering of necessary data as indicated from the preliminary survey.

C. Collect other data.

The value of a property is affected by demand and by purchasing power available. Data should be obtained on population trends, income levels, and employment opportunities. A number of sources should be investigated.

1. General data are obtained from governmental publications, newspapers and magazines.
2. Regional data (metropolitan area) are obtained from monthly bank summaries, regional planning commissions, and governmental agencies.
3. Community data (city) are obtained from the Chamber of Commerce, City Planning Commission, City Governmental Agencies, Banks and Savings and Loan Associations, and Real Estate Boards.
4. Neighborhood data are obtained from personal inspections, real estate practitioners, builders active in the area in regard to:
    a. Age and appearance of the neighborhood.
    b. Hazards and adverse influences.
    c. Percentage build-up.
    d. Contemplated development.
    e. Proximity to schools, business, recreation, etc.
5. Comparable market data, such as sales and listing prices on properties are obtained from:
    a. Assessors' Records and County Recorder's Office.
    b. Title Insurance and Trust Companies.

c. Real Estate Boards and local real estate offices.

d. Property owners in the neighborhood.

6. Improvement data regarding subject property should be collected and analyzed.

   a. Sources are:

      1. Assessor's Office for age and size.
      2. City Building Department.
      3. Contractors in area.
      4. Personal inspection of improvements.

D. Analyze the data according to the various approaches to value. The data previously gathered are analyzed in order to arrive at a value conclusion for the property being appraised.

1. Market data approach (comparative).

   a. Analyze subject property as to best use; characteristics of land and improvements; consideration of location, zoning, neighborhood.

   b. Analyze recent comparable sales in relation to the subject by making adjustments to reflect the character of the property being appraised.

   c. Compare sales of comparable properties with the subject to obtain an indication of value.

2. Cost approach (summation).

   a. Determine market value of the land (by comparison).

   b. Determine replacement cost of new improvements.

   c. Deduct all forms of depreciation—functional, physical, and economic.

   d. Land value plus depreciated replacement cost gives an estimate of value for the property.

3. Income approach (gross multiplier).

   a. Obtain sales of properties similar to the subject property.

   b. Determine economic rent of these properties as well as that of the subject property.

c. Determine the ratio of sales price to the monthly rent on the comparable properties (gross monthly multiplier).

d. Apply the derived monthly multiplier to the economic rent of the subject in order to arrive at an estimate of value.

E. Write the report.
After a final value opinion has been obtained, the data and the reasoning are recorded.

THE APPRAISAL REPORT

An appraisal report sets forth the views, experiences, and conclusions of the writer. When set down in writing, it protects both the appraiser and his client. Reports vary in scope and length and depend upon the request of the client. The following information should be included:

1. *A final value conclusion* is expressed in terms of dollars for the property which is being appraised.
2. *The date of the value conclusion* can be made for any date in the past, but not for any period of time in the future. The time of inspection of the physical improvements is generally taken to be the date of valuation unless otherwise informed by the property owner, his attorney, or a court of law. The date of the final writing and delivery of the report is not the date of valuation.
3. *Adequate description of the property.* The street address, including city and state, and a complete legal description as set forth by the deed or County Recorder's office should be shown, and physical structures should be clearly described.
4. *The scope of the reasonings* in determining the value conclusion will depend upon the type of report and the complexity of the appraisal problem.
5. *Market data* and other factual data include information on the city and neighborhood which affects the value conclusion; information gathered on the site, improvements, and the environment of the neighborhood which should be processed by means of one or more of the approaches to value; and the preliminary estimate of value should be correlated by means of logic and

reasoning in order to arrive at one value conclusion for the property.

6. *Signature and certification.* Appraisal reports must be signed by the writer. In most instances the signature is preceded by a statement to the effect that the writer has no present or contemplated interest in the property.

LETTERHEAD

September 6, 19--

Ms. or Mr. or Mrs. ________________,
Secretary
The Real Estate Company
Street Address
Every Town, Every State Zip Code

Dear ________________,

The letter report conveys appraisal data in the form of a business letter. The format should conform with the rules and standards of business correspondence. The appraiser's letterhead may be used for the initial page. Typing should be single-spaced, with adequate margins provided.

The eight essential elements of an appraisal report should be included in the letter report. In addition, the appraiser usually includes a brief description of the improvements, such as type, number of rooms, size, construction, and condition, and some supporting factual data for his value conclusions. The supporting data are often summarized, as a list of the sale properties with pertinent sales data, a reconstructed operating statement and capitalization process, or a depreciated cost study. A brief discussion should follow relating the appraiser's estimate of value to the supporting data.

The letter report usually varies in length from two to six pages. Exhibits such as property or improvement plats and pictures are often attached to and incorporated as part of the letter report. The letter report is very flexible as to format and what data are included.

COMPANY NAME, IF USED

Writer's Name
Title, if used

dictation initials (if appropriate)

enclosure (if appropriate)

Figure 5-1

Text from California Real Estate Appraisal: Residential Properties, 2nd Ed., by Miller, Mercer, and Gilbeau. © 1977. Page 204. Reprinted by permission of Prentice-Hall, Inc., Englewood Cliffs, New Jersey 07632.

COMPETITIVE MARKET ANALYSIS

CALIFORNIA ASSOCIATION OF REALTORS® STANDARD FORM

PROPERTY ADDRESS______________________________ DATE______________

FOR SALE NOW:	BED-RMS.	BATHS	DEN	SQ. FT.	1ST LOAN	LIST PRICE	DAYS ON MARKET	TERMS

SOLD PAST 12 MOS.	BED-RMS.	BATHS	DEN	SQ. FT.	1ST LOAN	LIST PRICE	DAYS ON MARKET	DATE SOLD	SALE PRICE	TERMS

EXPIRED PAST 12 MOS.	BED-RMS.	BATHS	DEN	SQ. FT.	1ST LOAN	LIST PRICE	DAYS ON MARKET	TERMS

F.H.A. ---- V.A. APPRAISALS

ADDRESS	APPRAISAL	ADDRESS	APPRAISAL

BUYER APPEAL / MARKETING POSITION

(GRADE EACH ITEM 0 TO 20% ON THE BASIS OF DESIRABILITY OR URGENCY)

BUYER APPEAL

1. FINE LOCATION______________%
2. EXCITING EXTRAS______________%
3. EXTRA SPECIAL FINANCING______________%
4. EXCEPTIONAL APPEAL______________%
5. UNDER MARKET PRICE__________YES______NO______%

RATING TOTAL ______________%

MARKETING POSITION

1. WHY ARE THEY SELLING______________%
2. HOW SOON MUST THEY SELL______________%
3. WILL THEY HELP FINANCE . . . . .YES______NO______%
4. WILL THEY LIST AT COMPETITIVE MARKET VALUE . .YES______NO______%
5. WILL THEY PAY FOR APPRAISAL . . . . .YES______NO______%

RATING TOTAL ______________%

ASSETS______________________________

DRAWBACKS______________________________

AREA MARKET CONDITIONS______________________________

____

RECOMMENDED TERMS______________________________

____

TOP COMPETITIVE MARKET VALUE . . . . $______________

PROBABLE FINAL SALES PRICE . . . . $______________

SELLING COSTS

BROKERAGE	$
LOAN PAYOFF	$
PREPAYMENT PRIVILEGE	$
FHA ---- VA POINTS	$
TITLE AND ESCROW FEES: IRS STAMPS RECONS RECORDING	$
TERMITE CLEARANCE	$
MISC. PAYOFFS: 2ND T.D., POOL, PATIO, WTR. SFTNR., FENCE, IMPROVEMENT BOND	$
	$
	$
TOTAL	$

TOTAL . . . . $______________

NET PROCEEDS $______________ PLUS OR MINUS $______________

FORM CM 14
REV. 9/64

Figure 5-2

TYPES OF APPRAISAL REPORTS

Letter form report. This type of report is generally used when the client is familiar with the area, and supporting data are not necessary (see Figure 5-1). It consists of a brief description of the property, the type of value sought, the purpose served by the appraisal, the date of the value estimate, the value conclusion, and the signature of the appraiser. One way to collect the necessary information for the letter form appraisal report is to fill out a Competitive Market Analysis (see Figure 5-2).

Short form report. This type of report is normally used by lending institutions, such as banks, insurance companies, saving and loan associations, and government agencies. It consists of simple check sheets or spaces to be filled in by the appraiser. It varies from one to four pages in length and includes pertinent data about the property. This type of report is seldom used for a client who is unfamiliar with the city or neighborhood.

Narrative report. This is a complete document with all pertinent information about the subject property and includes reasons and computations for the value conclusion. The report contains maps, photographs, charts, and plot plans, and it is written for court cases and out-of-town clients who need all the factual data. It gives the complete reasoning of the appraisal as well as the value conclusion.

OUTLINE FOR WRITING THE SINGLE FAMILY RESIDENCE APPRAISAL REPORT*

1. Title Page:
   A. "A fair market value appraisal of the single family residence known as (Address)"
   B. Name of Client
   C. The name and address of the appraiser
2. Table of Contents:
   A. Preface
   B. Body of Report
   C. Addenda Section

*Developed by Independent Study, University of California Extension.

3. Letter of Transmittal:
   - A. Date
   - B. Name and address of addressee
   - C. Salutation
   - D. Authorization
   - E. Legal description or reference thereto
   - F. Purpose of appraisal including type of value estimated
   - G. Date of evaluation
   - H. Reference to the following report of ________ pages including________ exhibits as well as limiting conditions, factors considered and reasoning employed in arriving at the final conclusion of fair market value
   - I. Estimate of value (written and numbered)
   - J. Certification of appraiser
   - K. Signature
4. Summary of Salient Facts and Conclusions:
   - A. Recap of pertinent information such as value estimate, date of value, purpose of appraisal, etc.
5. Premise Section:
   - A. Statement of limiting conditions on which the appraisal is based including full definition of value as estimated in report.
6. Regional, City, and Neighborhood Analysis:
   - A. Pertinent features
   - B. Economic factors
   - C. Significant trends
7. General Property Information:
   - A. Record or legal owner
   - B. Legal Description
   - C. Legal Address
   - D. Location
8. Site Analysis:
   - A. Description of parcel:
     1. Size and shape
     2. Topography and surface drainage

3. Soils including subsoil (foundational)
4. Access
5. Landscaping, etc.

B. Street improvements and utilities
C. Deed restrictions and zoning
D. Assessed Valuation and tax information
E. Current use and adaptability
F. Highest and best use

9. Improvement Analysis:
   A. Basic Description:
      1. Type and Date of construction
      2. Architectural form
      3. Number of rooms
   B. Summary Square Foot Areas:
      1. Residence
         a. Ground floor
         b. Second floor
         c. Porches
      2. Garage
      3. Other structures, walks and drives
   C. General Condition and Remaining Economic Life Estimate
   D. Exterior Description:
      1. Foundation and sub-structure
      2. Exterior treatment
      3. Roof design and cover
      4. Porches
   E. Interior Description:
      1. Room descriptions
         a. Space allotment
         b. Floor, walls and ceiling finish
         c. Built-ins and fixtures
   F. Mechanical Equipment:
      1. Heating and air conditioning
      2. Electrical
      3. Miscellaneous—garbage disposal, etc.

- G. Miscellaneous Improvements:
  1. Outbuildings
  2. Patios and walks
  3. Landscaping

10. Analysis and Valuation:
    - A. Statement of Problem
    - B. Methods of Appraisal
    - C. Investigation

11. Estimate of Land Value:
    - A. By Market Data Approach
    - B. By Sales Abstraction
    - C. Economic Approaches:
      1. As percentage of annual income classification
      2. As percentage of total property value
    - D. Correlation of various approaches
    - E. Final estimate land value

12. The Cost Approach:
    - A. Reproduction Cost Estimate:
      1. Justification
    - B. Estimate of Accrued Depreciation:
      1. Physical deterioration with justification
         - a. Curable
         - b. Incurable
      2. Functional Obsolescence with justification
         - a. Curable
         - b. Incurable
      3. Economic Obsolescence with justification
    - C. Depreciated Reproduction Cost
    - D. Addition of Estimated Land Value
    - E. Value indicated by cost approach

13. The Market Data Approach:
    - A. Market data presentation including statement of source and verification:
      1. Summary of Pertinent Data (Sales and Listings)

   B. Analysis of Market Data:
      1. Factors of Adjustment
   C. Application of adjusted market data factors:
      1. Comparison by various common denominators
         a. Ratio sales price to living area
         b. Ratio sales price to number of rooms
      2. Direct property comparison
   D. Correlation of indications using reliability coefficients
   E. Value indicated by market data approach
14. The Income Approach:
   A. Seldom employed in analysis of single family residential property:
      1. Justified gross multiplier of neighborhood
      2. Justified fair rental estimate for subject
   B. Indicated value by income approach
15. Correlation and Discussion of the Value Estimates:
   A. State values estimated by three separate approaches
   B. Analysis:
      1. Major, but not exclusive, weight to approach that
         a. Is most closely related to purpose of the appraisal.
         b. Is most appropriate for property classification concerned.
         c. Has greatest amount of supporting data.
         d. Most accurately reflects attitude of typical purchaser.
         e. Is most sensitive to current trends.
   C. State of Final Value Conclusions:
      1. Suggest arbitrary separation
         a. Land
         b. Improvements
16. Addenda Section:
   A. Market Data
   B. Market Data Map

C. Plots, maps, pictures, charts, statistical and factual data pertinent to the value estimate and necessary as supporting evidence *not* included in body of report.

17. Appraiser's Qualifications

TIPS FOR TYPING THE FINISHED APPRAISAL REPORT

1. Be sure that the left-hand margin (or top margin, depending on the finished binding) will be wide enough to accommodate a seam or prongs. Leave enough white space for the text to be easily read when the report is opened.
2. Be generous with white space. Wide borders at the top, bottom, and sides make a page easier to read.
3. Start and end each page on exactly the same line. Number every page in exactly the same place.
4. It isn't necessary to justify right-hand margins unless you are so instructed, but you should keep them fairly even.
5. Use white paper with a rag content and a carbon ribbon for typing. Avoid a fancy type face, as these are difficult to read.
6. *Never* use correction paint on an original.
7. Keep art work clean. Clear plastic pages may be obtained which open on the binding side. You can insert a photograph or art work by tucking in and inserting so that the art work falls into proper place on the typed page. Or, you can mount art work as you would in a photo album. Plastic is the better solution for eliminating finger marks and stains.
8. *Never write on art work.* Always label underneath.
9. Reread Chapter 12, which deals with photocopying. One way to do a long report is to type it on 8½″ x 14″ paper, and then reduce it (along with any illustrations). You might get some ideas from a quick printer.
10. Report covers can be purchased or a quick printer can collate and bind.

6

Real Estate Financing Review

THE ROLE OF GOVERNMENT IN REAL ESTATE FINANCE

Federal Housing Administration (FHA) is designed primarily to insure loans made by approved lenders.

Federal National Mortgage Association (FNMA, "Fannie May") is designed to provide a secondary market for home mortgages. Supported more and more by private investors, it buys FHA and VA insured mortgages from private lending institutions and sells second mortgages and trust deeds to individual investors and financial institutions.

Government National Mortgage Association (GNM, "Ginnie May"). Under the Housing Act of 1968, FNMA was made into two corporations. GNMA operates the special assistance functions for federally aided housing programs and has the management and liquidating functions of the old FNMA. It is authorized to issue and sell securities backed by a portion of its mortgage portfolio, with GNMA guaranteeing payment on the securities. It also guarantees similar securities issued by other private issuers where they are backed by FHA, VA, and some Farm Home Administration mortgages or loans.

Community Facilities Administration provides financial assistance to colleges and universities, and to state and local governments in the construction of capital projects, such as student-faculty housing, medical training housing, and public works.

Urban Renewal Administration provides financial assistance to local governments for slum clearance and rehabilitation, provides money for research into slum clearance and rehabilitation, and provides money for research into slum prevention.

Federal Home Loan Bank Board governs the operation of all member savings and loan associations. It provides a reserve credit system or banker's bank for savings and loan association members in almost the same way as the Federal Reserve Bank does for commercial banks.

Federal Savings and Loan Insurance Corporation provides deposit insurance to all depositors of all savings and loan associations that it insures. Current maximum coverage is $40,000. Most (not all) savings and loan associations in the country are insured by this agency.

Federal Reserve Bank serves the same function to commercial banks as the Federal Home Loan Bank does for savings and loan associations. It may seriously influence the flow of money and credit in America through the various activities of its Board (such as open market operation, installment buying regulations, bank reserve, and discount rules).

Federal Deposit Insurance Corporation performs the same service for commercial banks that the Federal Savings and Loan Insurance Corporation does for savings and loans.

Veterans Administration is an agency that, among other things, insures or guarantees loans or portions of loans made to veterans for housing and for farms or businesses.

TYPES OF LENDING INSTITUTIONS

Insurance Companies make conventional loans and supply most loans on properties where large loans are required, such as large commercial properties, shopping centers, industrial properties, and hotels. Operations are governed by the state in which the company is incorporated. Real estate loans placed with life insurance companies are generally for (1) purchase money for occupancy or investment, (2) construction or improvement loans, (3) refinancing of existing indebtedness, (4) consolidation of mortgages, (5) achieving a lower interest rate or longer term, or (6) provision for additional funds.

Savings and Loan Associations account for the greatest share of the home loan market.

Commercial Banks are general purpose lenders. Real estate financing includes (1) long-term mortgage loans for the purchase of real estate already improved or to be improved, (2) construction loans to finance the construction of land improvements, to be repaid when building is completed, (3) interim financing of mortgage companies (business loan to mortgage companies to conduct their mortgage brokerage operations), and (4) home improvement loans for repairing and modernizing existing improvements.

Mutual Savings Banks are located mainly in the northeastern states, where they were first organized, and are important sources of funds to mortgage companies.

Mortgage Companies are privately owned corporations concerned with making various kinds of real estate loans (construction, refinancing, long-term purchase money).

Other types include pension funds, cemetery associations, and college endowment funds.

METHODS OF REPAYING MORTGAGE LOANS

Term (time) mortgages are rarely used; however, there are three kinds you should know about:

A *straight mortgage* is written for a 3- or 5-year term, and at the end of this time must either be repaid or renewed for another 3 or 5 years.

An *open mortgage* is not paid or extended at its due date. The lender can demand payment (which must be paid) at any time. Loan is unrenewed and the borrower can pay it off whenever he wants.

A *closed mortgage* is declared when the mortgagee has advanced the final portion of the loan.

Amortized mortgages are the most widely used today. These incorporate payment of the loan and interest on the loan on an installment basis.

In *straight principal reduction*, the borrower repays the same sum for amortizing each month, and monthly interest on balance due is added. Payments begin high and end low because of decreasing interest as the loan is paid.

In *constant payment amortization*, the borrower pays the same amount in each installment. Monthly payments are always the same. If the monthly payments don't amortize the loan by the time the final payment arrives, the last and larger payment (balloon payment) makes up the difference.

MATHEMATICAL TABLES AND THEIR USE

Amortization tables are commonly available in booklet form from various title companies, escrow companies, and banks. They indicate the monthly payments for various amounts of loans at various interest rates (nominal) and terms. The common format is to have a different set of tables for each rate of interest. A reverse use that may be made of such a table is to determine the amount of money a borrower can afford to borrow. Select the column or row showing the going loan term in years or months. Then go down that column or along that row until you reach the monthly payment the buyer can readily afford. Then read to the other axis and find the amount of loan this monthly payment will pay off.

Discount or present worth tables show how much less a dollar to be paid in one year is worth than it is worth today. It depends on the rate of interest money would normally earn in that year.

Proration tables tell the number of days between various dates.

Depreciation tables tell the amount of depreciation that is deductible each year for properties with varying economic lives.

TYPES OF MORTGAGES AND TRUST DEEDS

Purchase money trust deed (mortgage) is applied to trust deeds or mortgages taken back by the seller as part of the sales transaction, or money borrowed from a third-party lender to purchase the property used as collateral. When "taken back," it is essentially a loan to the buyer by the seller in order to make the sale possible.

Hard money trust deed (mortgage) applies to trust deeds (mortgages) given by a borrower in exchange for actual money received, as opposed to purchase money trust deeds (mortgages).

Package trust deed (mortgage) is a loan on real property that covers more than just the basic structure. It includes fixtures attached to the house (appliances, carpeting, drapes, air conditioning, etc.).

Blanket trust deed (mortgage) covers more than one parcel of property and contains a release clause which provides for release of a parcel upon the payment of a portion of the loan. Typical use is in connection with a tract of homes built on speculation.

Open end trust deed (mortgage) is the term applied to a loan arrangement whereby additional amounts of money may be lent to the borrower in the future under the same trust deed (mortgage).

Wrap-around mortgage (also called the all-inclusive trust deed) is similar to a second mortgage loan in that the existing loan is not disturbed, yet the debtor is able to borrow an additional amount against the property. After the wrap-around mortgage loan has been arranged, the new lender makes the payments that are due on the first loan and receives payments of principal and interest from the debtor on both loans. The debtor no longer has any direct dealings with the first lender.

Federal Housing Administration insured mortgage. The FHA does not loan mortgage funds. It insures lenders against loss, provided the homes involved meet certain requirements. Interest rates change with current rates and are usually lower.

Veterans Administration guaranteed mortgage (GI mortgage). The Veterans Administration will guarantee part of the mortgage for eligible veterans.

Conventional mortgage is the normal loan by the lending institution, made on its terms, and is usually an amortized mortgage.

Budget mortgage includes payments of interest, amortization, and other expenses that a homeowner incurs.

Second mortgage occurs if a buyer can't get a large enough loan to purchase. It is second in lien.

COMPARISON OF MORTGAGE AND TRUST DEED

	Mortgage	*Trust Deed*
Definition	A legal instrument by which property is pledged without transferring possession or title to the lender as specific security for a debt or obligation.	Conveys title of property to a third party or trustee.
Parties	Mortgagor—Borrower Mortgagee—Lender	Trustor—Borrower Trustee—Third party Beneficiary—Lender
Title	Mortgage does not convey title—it creates a lien. Possession of property remains with borrower.	Title is conveyed to a trustee and is a lien. Possession of property remains with borrower.
Statute of Limitations	Action to foreclose is barred when statute has run out on principal obligation (the note).	The rights of the creditor against the property are not ended when the statute has run out on the note, as the trustee has title and can still sell to pay off debt.
Remedy	Only remedy of mortgagee is foreclosure unless mortgage contains power of sale.	There are alternate remedies of trustee's sale or foreclosure.
Redemption	After a mortgage has been foreclosed by court action, right to redeem exists for one year after sale. For mortgage with power of sale, see trust deed provisions of redemption.	Debtor has a limited right of reinstatement after default, but no right of redemption. Sale is absolute.
Satisfaction	When mortgage is satisfied, mortgagee, on demand from mortgagor, must execute and deliver to mortgagor certificate showing that the mortgage has been satisfied, in proper form to enable it to be recorded.	Trustor or his assignee, after final payment, should procure the note, deed of trust, and a request for full reconveyance from beneficiary. These should be given to trustee and reconveyance (later recorded) should be obtained upon payment of trustee's fees.

7

Guidelines for Property Management and Property Management Recordkeeping

The real estate office or building manager plays a key role in rental or property management, as a direct liaison with the owner or accountant through the keeping of records.

The surest way to control papers and their flow through any system is to reduce as much text as possible to its simplest form, as an outline or list. The examples in this chapter consist of lists and forms to show you how to save time and energy:

- Hypothetical files for a large apartment complex with stores
- Sample tenant application form (Figure 7-1)
- Sample lease (Figure 7-2)
- Apartment bill (Figure 7-3)
- 30-day notice terminating tenancy (Figure 7-4) (This Cowdery form is adaptable for use in any state. Remember to use the most current form and to always check your real estate laws before using any form which becomes legal and binding. It is available from Patrick

and Company, 560 Market Street, San Francisco, CA 94104, and other stationery stores.)

- Form for separate record for each property managed (Figure 7-5)
- Summary sheet and POC-IT-FILE (Figures 7-6 and 7-7)

TYPES OF REAL ESTATE MANAGERS

The *property manager* is a member of a real estate office or agency which manages a number of properties for various owners. He may be a member of the firm and devote his time exclusively to management, he may be in business for himself as a managing agent, or he may be one of a number of managers in the management department of a large real estate organization which has many properties and clients under its care. In the latter case he may specialize in the type of building he handles, such as office buildings, loft buildings, and apartment buildings, or a combination, such as apartment buildings and outlying store structures, or office and store buildings in the business district.

An individual *building manager* may be employed by a property manager or directly by the owner and usually manages a single large property.

The *resident manager* is employed by a real estate agency or a managing agent to manage an apartment building property. He lives on the premises. Large buildings with small apartments where the change in tenancy is frequent usually have resident managers.

A *building superintendent* is employed by an agency to supervise an office building and is the agency's representative on the premises. He is concerned chiefly with maintenance and operation. He hires and supervises the work of janitors, elevator operators, and maintenance men.

Among the specific duties of the property manager are to:

1. Establish the rental schedule.
2. Merchandise the space and collect the rents.
3. Create and supervise maintenance schedules and repairs.
4. Supervise all purchasing.
5. Develop a tenant relations policy.

6. Develop employee policies and supervise operations.
7. Maintain proper records and make regular reports to the owner.
8. Qualify and investigate tenants' credit.
9. Prepare and execute leases.
10. Prepare decorating specifications and secure estimates.
11. Hire, instruct, and maintain satisfactory personnel to staff the building(s).
12. Audit and pay bills.
13. Advertise and publicize vacancies through selected media and broker lists.
14. Plan alteration and modernizing programs.
15. Inspect vacant space frequently and periodically.
16. Keep abreast of the times and competitive market conditions.
17. Pay insurance premiums and taxes and recommend tax appeals when warranted.
18. Maintain the duties set forth by the owner of the property.

FILING SYSTEM

The following is a hypothetical property management filing system for a large apartment complex with stores:

Apartments

Accounting
Carpeting
Floor plans
Intercom
Keys
Leases
Mailboxes
Refrigerators
Storage areas
Stoves
Tenant files

Model Apartments

Decorator(s)
Inventory
Suppliers

Commercial

Accounting
Floor plans
General correspondence
Tenant files

General Building

Accounting
Advertising
- newspaper
- radio
- TV

Appliances
Attorney
Building codes
Carpentry
Carpeting
Correspondence

General Building (cont'd)

Drapes
Elevator
Fire
- alarms
- extinguishers

Garage
Garbage
Heating
Insurance
Intercom
Landscaping

General Building (cont'd)

Locks and locksmiths
Maintenance
Office machines
Office supplies
Parking
Personnel
Pest control
Plumbing
Roof
Security
Taxes

TENANT APPLICATION

Property Address: Apt. No.

Name(s) of Applicant(s):

Other Name(s) used within last 3 years:

Names and Age of other Occupants:

Pets (Number & Type):

Present Address:

How long? Reason for leaving:

Name and Address of Owner or Owner's Agent:

Previous Address (Past 3 Years):

How long? Reason for leaving:

Name and Address of Owner or Owner's Agent:

Previous Address (Past 3 Years):

How long? Reason for leaving:

Name and Address of Owner or Owner's Agent:

Employment: Social Security Number Drivers License Number

Present Employer: How long?

Address: Telephone:

Employed as: Salary: $ per

Employment of any other Occupant: Social Security Number Drivers License Number

Present Employer How long?

Address: Telephone:

Employed as: Salary: $ per

Other Income: $ Source:

Credit References (2):

Credit Cards: Issuer Acct. No. Issuer Acct. No.

Automobile License No. State of Registry:

Make & Model: Year: Color:

IN CASE OF EMERGENCY:

Name of Closest Relative: Relationship:

Address: Telephone:

AUTHORIZATION TO VERIFY INFORMATION

I Authorize Landlord or his Authorized Agents to Verify the above information, including but not limited to obtaining a Credit Report and if this application is accepted I agree to execute the residential lease or rental agreement as set forth on the reverse side hereof.

Date 19 Applicant:

Telephone No. Applicant:

RECEIPT FOR DEPOSIT

The undersigned acknowledges receipt of $ in the form of ( ) Cash, ( ) Personal Check or ( ) payable to as deposit on the above described property.

Date Agent

Reprinted by permission, CALIFORNIA ASSOCIATION OF REALTORS®. Endorsement not implied.

Figure 7-1

RESIDENTIAL LEASE

THIS IS INTENDED TO BE A LEGALLY BINDING AGREEMENT – READ IT CAREFULLY

CALIFORNIA ASSOCIATION OF REALTORS® STANDARD FORM

________________________, California ________________________ 19____
____, Landlord, and
____, Tenant, agree as follows:

1. Landlord leases to Tenant and Tenant hires from Landlord those premises described as: ________________________
____
____
together with the following furniture, and appliances, if any, and fixtures: ________________________
____
(Insert "as shown on Exhibit A attached hereto" and attach the exhibit if the list is extensive.)

2. The term of this lease shall be for a period of ________________ months; ________ years commencing ________________ 19______ and terminating ________________ 19____.

3. Tenant is to pay a total rent of $________________, payable as follows: ________________
____
____
____
____
The rent shall be paid at ____
or at any address designated by the Landlord in writing.

4. $________________ as security has been deposited. Landlord may use therefrom such amounts as are reasonably necessary to remedy Tenant's defaults in the payment of rent, to repair damages caused by Tenant, and to clean the premises upon termination of tenancy. If used toward rent or damages during the term of tenancy, Tenant agrees to reinstate said total security deposit upon five days written notice delivered to Tenant in person or by mailing. Balance of security deposit, if any, together with a written itemized accounting shall be mailed to Tenant's last known address within 14 days of surrender of premises.

5. Tenant agrees to pay for all utilities and services based upon occupancy of the premises and the following charges: ________________
____
____
except ____
which shall be paid for by Landlord.

6. Tenant has examined the premises and all furniture, furnishings and appliances if any, and fixtures contained therein, and accepts the same as being clean, in good order, condition, and repair, with the following exceptions: ________________
____

7. The premises are leased for use as a residence by the following named persons: ________________
____
No animal, bird, or pet except ________________________________
shall be kept on or about the premises without Landlord's prior written consent.

8. Any holding over at the expiration of this lease shall create a month to month tenancy at a monthly rent of $________________ payable in advance. All other terms and conditions herein shall remain in full force and effect.

9. Tenant shall not disturb, annoy, endanger or interfere with other Tenants of the building or neighbors, nor use the premises for any unlawful purposes, nor violate any law or ordinance, nor commit waste or nuisance upon or about the premises.

10. Tenant agrees to comply with all reasonable rules or regulations posted on the premises or delivered to Tenant by Landlord.

11. Tenant shall keep the premises and furniture, furnishings and appliances, if any, and fixtures which are leased for his exclusive use in good order and condition and pay for any repairs to the property caused by Tenant's negligence or misuse or that of Tenant's invitees. Landlord shall otherwise maintain the property. Tenant's personal property is not insured by Landlord.

12. Tenant shall not paint, wallpaper, nor make alterations to the property without Landlord's prior written consent.

13. Upon not less than 24 hours advance notice, Tenant shall make the demised premises available during normal business hours to Landlord or his authorized agent or representative, for the purpose of entering (a) to make necessary agreed repairs, decorations, alterations or improvements or to supply necessary or agreed services, and (b) to show the premises to prospective or actual purchasers, mortgagees, tenants, workmen or contractors. In an emergency, Landlord, his agent or authorized representative may enter the premises at any time without securing prior permission from Tenant for the purpose of making corrections or repairs to alleviate such emergency.

14. Tenant shall not let or sublet all or any part of the premises nor assign this lease or any interest in it without the prior written consent of Landlord.

15. If Tenant abandons or vacates the premises, Landlord may at his option terminate this lease, and regain possession in the manner prescribed by law.

16. If any legal action or proceeding be brought by either party to enforce any part of this lease, the prevailing party shall recover in addition to all other relief, reasonable attorney's fees and costs.

17. Time is of the essence. The waiver by Landlord or Tenant of any breach shall not be construed to be a continuing waiver of any subsequent breach.

18. Notice upon Tenant shall be served as provided by law. Notice upon Landlord may be served upon Manager of the demised premises
____
at ________________________________. Said Manager is authorized to accept service on behalf of Landlord.

19. Within 10 days after written notice, Tenant agrees to execute and deliver a certificate as submitted by Landlord acknowledging that this agreement is unmodified and in full force and effect or in full force and effect as modified and stating the modifications. Failure to comply shall be deemed Tenant's acknowledgement that the certificate as submitted by Landlord is true and correct and may be relied upon by any lender or purchaser.

20. The undersigned Tenant acknowledges having read the foregoing prior to execution and receipt of a copy hereof.

Landlord ________________________ ________________________ Tenant

Landlord ________________________ ________________________ Tenant

NO REPRESENTATION IS MADE AS TO THE LEGAL VALIDITY OF ANY PROVISION OR THE ADEQUACY OF ANY PROVISION IN ANY SPECIFIC TRANSACTION. A REAL ESTATE BROKER IS THE PERSON QUALIFIED TO ADVISE ON REAL ESTATE. IF YOU DESIRE LEGAL ADVICE CONSULT YOUR ATTORNEY.

For these forms, address – California Association of Realtors®
505 Shatto Place, Los Angeles, California 90020
 LR-14

Figure 7-2

Figure 7-3 is a simple form which can be adapted to an apartment building. In areas where the power bills go to the building management, the space can be filled in and the bill stapled to the form. The bills can either be mailed, or placed in the tenant's box or under the door.

building name
street address
city, state, zip code

Date ______________
Apt. # ______________

Rent $ ______________
From ______________
To ______________

Utilities $ ______________
From ______________
To ______________

Garage $ ______________
From ______________
To ______________

Other $ ______________

____
TOTAL $ ______________

Figure 7-3

If the real estate company is the property manager for different owners, a form like the one in Figure 7-4 should be kept for each and the money collected should be recorded as shown.

30 DAYS NOTICE TERMINATING TENANCY

To: .... , *Tenant in Possession:*

YOU WILL PLEASE TAKE NOTICE that the tenancy under which you hold possession of the property under tenancy from month to month, situate in the City of ....*County of* ....*State of California, and described as follows, to-wit:* ....

....

....

Designated and known by the No. ....
is by this notice terminated and you are hereby further notified to remove from said premises on or before the .... *day of* .... *, 19* ....

....
Owner

....
Agents

This document is only a general form which may be proper for use in simple transactions and in no way acts, or is intended to act, as a substitute for the advice of an attorney. The publisher does not make any warranty, either express or implied, as to the legal validity of any provision or the suitability of these forms in any specific transaction.

Cowdery's Form No. 780 – 30 Day Notice

Figure 7-4

SEPARATE RECORD FOR EACH PROPERTY MANAGED

Owner	Fridolph Gazze	Deposit	
Address		Monthly Rent	$355.00
Property	Morgan Arms Apts.	Commission:	
Tenant's Name	Marsh #1, Hacker #2	Leases	
Units		Collection	10%
Remarks		Management	Included

Date	Received From or Paid To	Description	Receipt or Check No.	Amount Received	Date Deposited	Amount Disbursed	Balance
4/8/–	Troy Marsh	April Rent Apt. #1	Rcpt. #2	175.00	4/8/–		$175.00
4/8/–	Mildred Hacker	April Rent Apt. #2	Rcpt. #3	180.00	4/8/–		$355.00
4/9/–	City Water Co.	March Water Bill	CK. #1			$25.00	$330.00
4/10/–	Paul Hill	Collection & Mgmt. Fee	CK. #2			$35.50	$294.50
4/10/–	Fridolph Gazze	Apt. Rental Proceeds	CK. #3			$294.50	–0–

Figure 7-5

SUMMARY

	Prop.A	Prop.B
Rental Income	$	$ ....
Total Income	$	$ ....
EXPENSES		
Maintenance and Repairs	$	$ ....
Cleaning—Rubbish Removal—Snow Removal	$	$ ....
Heat, Light, Utilities	$	$ ....
Gardening	$	$ ....
Insurance	$	$ ....
Interest	$	$ ....
Painting & Paper	$	$ ....
Taxes	$	$ ....
Miscellaneous	$	$ ....
Total Expense	$	$ ....
Improvements or Capital Investments	$	$ ....

NOTES

Figure 7-6

This POC-IT-FILE gives you a record of all Rental Income Received and all Rental Expenses Paid. In addition it also gives you File Pockets in which you can keep all bills, receipts, notes, etc. All in one portfolio.

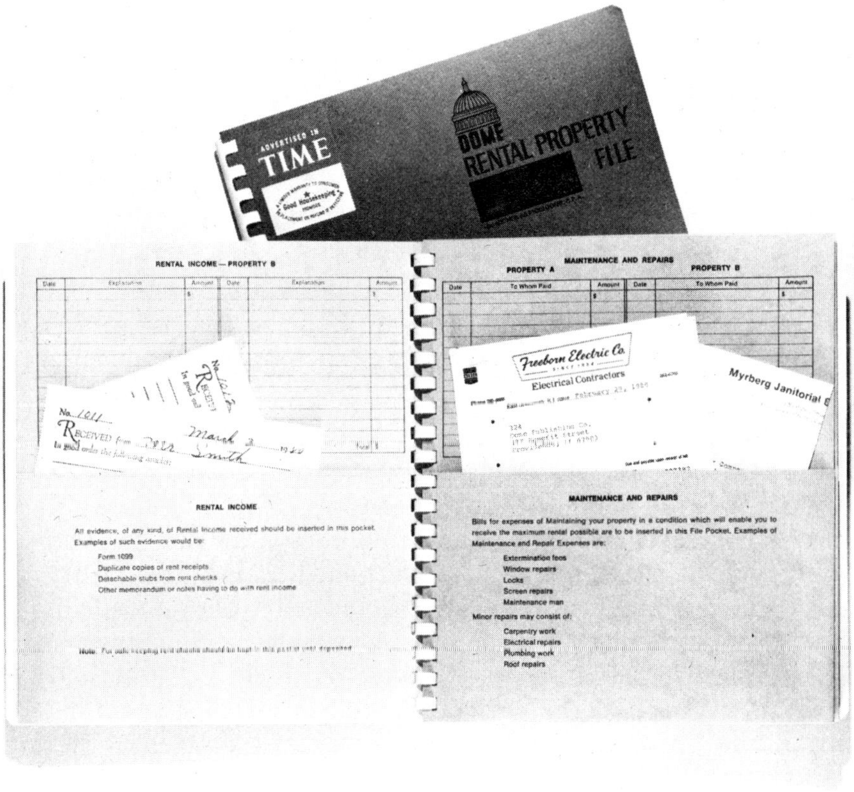

Courtesy Dome Publishing Co., Inc., The Dome Building.
Providence, Rhode Island 02903.

Figure 7-7

8

How to Keep Real Estate Trust Fund and Accounting Records

The moneys in a real estate office may be divided into two main categories: (1) dollars taken in from real estate transactions (commissions) and the dollars paid out for the running of the office (expenses or overhead), and (2) trust fund moneys (money taken on behalf of a principal as deposit on property), which must be treated separately in accounting.

The volume of business will determine the number and complexity of bookkeeping records needed to run the office. Many firms employ an outside accountant to whom the secretary must turn over records periodically. To give you a sound foundation for the knowledge you need to either handle the books yourself or get them ready to turn over to the accountant, a simple recordkeeping method is illustrated here, showing you the proper way to post income and expenses. (The complete system, entitled Real Estate Business Bookkeeping and Tax Record, is put out by Dymo Visual Systems, Inc., Augusta, Georgia, publishers of **ideal™ Business Accounting Systems,** and is available at most stationery stores. See Figures 8-1 to 8-4.) You might be called upon to prepare a profit and loss statement and a balance sheet, so you are given the proper format in Figures 8-5 and 8-6. Petty cash can become a very easy transaction if the money and the receipts are kept *inside* the envelope shown in Figure 8-7 and the transaction written on the format as it takes place.

THE IDEAL SYSTEM
REG U S PAT OFFICE

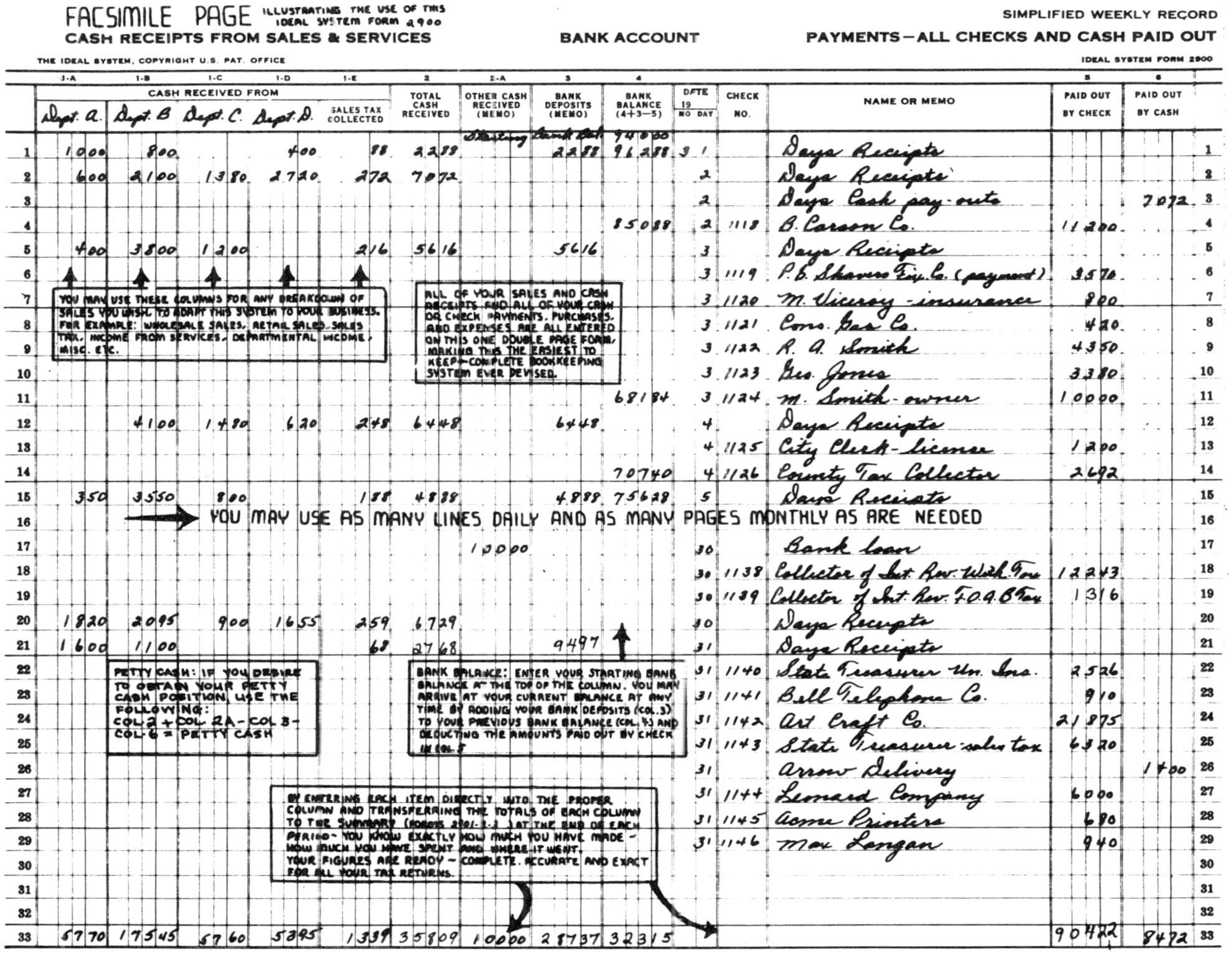

FACSIMILE PAGE ILLUSTRATING THE USE OF THIS IDEAL SYSTEM FORM 2900
CASH RECEIPTS FROM SALES & SERVICES — BANK ACCOUNT — SIMPLIFIED WEEKLY RECORD — PAYMENTS—ALL CHECKS AND CASH PAID OUT

THE IDEAL SYSTEM, COPYRIGHT U.S. PAT. OFFICE — IDEAL SYSTEM FORM 2900

	1-A	1-B	1-C	1-D	1-E	2	2-A	3	4				5	6	
	CASH RECEIVED FROM					TOTAL CASH RECEIVED	OTHER CASH RECEIVED (MEMO)	BANK DEPOSITS (MEMO)	BANK BALANCE (4+3−5)	DATE 19 MO DAY	CHECK NO.	NAME OR MEMO	PAID OUT BY CHECK	PAID OUT BY CASH	
	Dept. A.	Dept. B	Dept. C.	Dept. D.	SALES TAX COLLECTED										
							Starting	Bank Bal.	94000						
1	1000	800		400	88	2288		2288	96288	3 1		Days Receipts			1
2	600	2100	1380	2720	272	7072				2		Days Receipts			2
3										2		Days Cash pay-outs		7072	3
4									85088	2	1118	B. Carson Co.	11200		4
5	400	3800	1200		216	5616		5616		3		Days Receipts			5
6										3	1119	P. B. Shaws Eq. Co. (payment)	3570		6
7										3	1120	M. Viceroy - insurance	800		7
8										3	1121	Cons. Gas Co.	420		8
9										3	1122	R. A. Smith	4350		9
10										3	1123	Geo. Jones	3380		10
11									68184	3	1124	M. Smith - owner	10000		11
12		4100	1480	620	248	6448		6448		4		Days Receipts			12
13										4	1125	City Clerk - license	1200		13
14									70740	4	1126	County Tax Collector	2692		14
15	350	3550	800		188	4888		4888	75628	5		Days Receipts			15
16	YOU MAY USE AS MANY LINES DAILY AND AS MANY PAGES MONTHLY AS ARE NEEDED														16
17							10000			30		Bank loan			17
18										30	1138	Collector of Int. Rev. With. Tax	12243		18
19										30	1139	Collector of Int. Rev. F.O.A.B. Tax	1316		19
20	1820	2095	900	1655	259	6729				30		Days Receipts			20
21	1600	1100			68	2768		9497		31		Days Receipts			21
22										31	1140	State Treasurer Un. Ins.	2526		22
23										31	1141	Bell Telephone Co.	910		23
24										31	1142	Art Craft Co.	21875		24
25										31	1143	State Treasurer - sales tax	6320		25
26										31		Arrow Delivery		1400	26
27										31	1144	Leonard Company	6000		27
28										31	1145	Acme Printers	690		28
29										31	1146	Max Langan	940		29
33	5770	17545	5760	5395	1339	35809	10000	28737	32315				90422	8472	33

YOU MAY USE THESE COLUMNS FOR ANY BREAKDOWN OF SALES YOU WISH, TO ADAPT THIS SYSTEM TO YOUR BUSINESS. FOR EXAMPLE: WHOLESALE SALES, RETAIL SALES, SALES TAX, INCOME FROM SERVICES, DEPARTMENTAL INCOME, MISC. ETC.

ALL OF YOUR SALES AND CASH RECEIPTS AND ALL OF YOUR CASH OR CHECK PAYMENTS, PURCHASES, AND EXPENSES ARE ALL ENTERED ON THIS ONE DOUBLE PAGE FORM, MAKING THIS THE EASIEST TO KEEP—COMPLETE BOOKKEEPING SYSTEM EVER DEVISED.

PETTY CASH: IF YOU DESIRE TO OBTAIN YOUR PETTY CASH POSITION, USE THE FOLLOWING: COL 2 + COL 2A - COL 3 - COL 6 = PETTY CASH

BANK BALANCE: ENTER YOUR STARTING BANK BALANCE AT THE TOP OF THE COLUMN. YOU MAY ARRIVE AT YOUR CURRENT BALANCE AT ANY TIME BY ADDING YOUR BANK DEPOSITS (COL. 3) TO YOUR PREVIOUS BANK BALANCE (COL. 4) AND DEDUCTING THE AMOUNTS PAID OUT BY CHECK IN COL. 5

BY ENTERING EACH ITEM DIRECTLY INTO THE PROPER COLUMN AND TRANSFERRING THE TOTALS OF EACH COLUMN TO THE SUMMARY (FORMS 2901-2-3) AT THE END OF EACH PERIOD—YOU KNOW EXACTLY HOW MUCH YOU HAVE MADE—HOW MUCH YOU HAVE SPENT AND WHERE IT WENT. YOUR FIGURES ARE READY—COMPLETE, ACCURATE AND EXACT FOR ALL YOUR TAX RETURNS.

Courtesy Dymo Visual Systems, Inc., Augusta, Georgia.

Figure 8-1

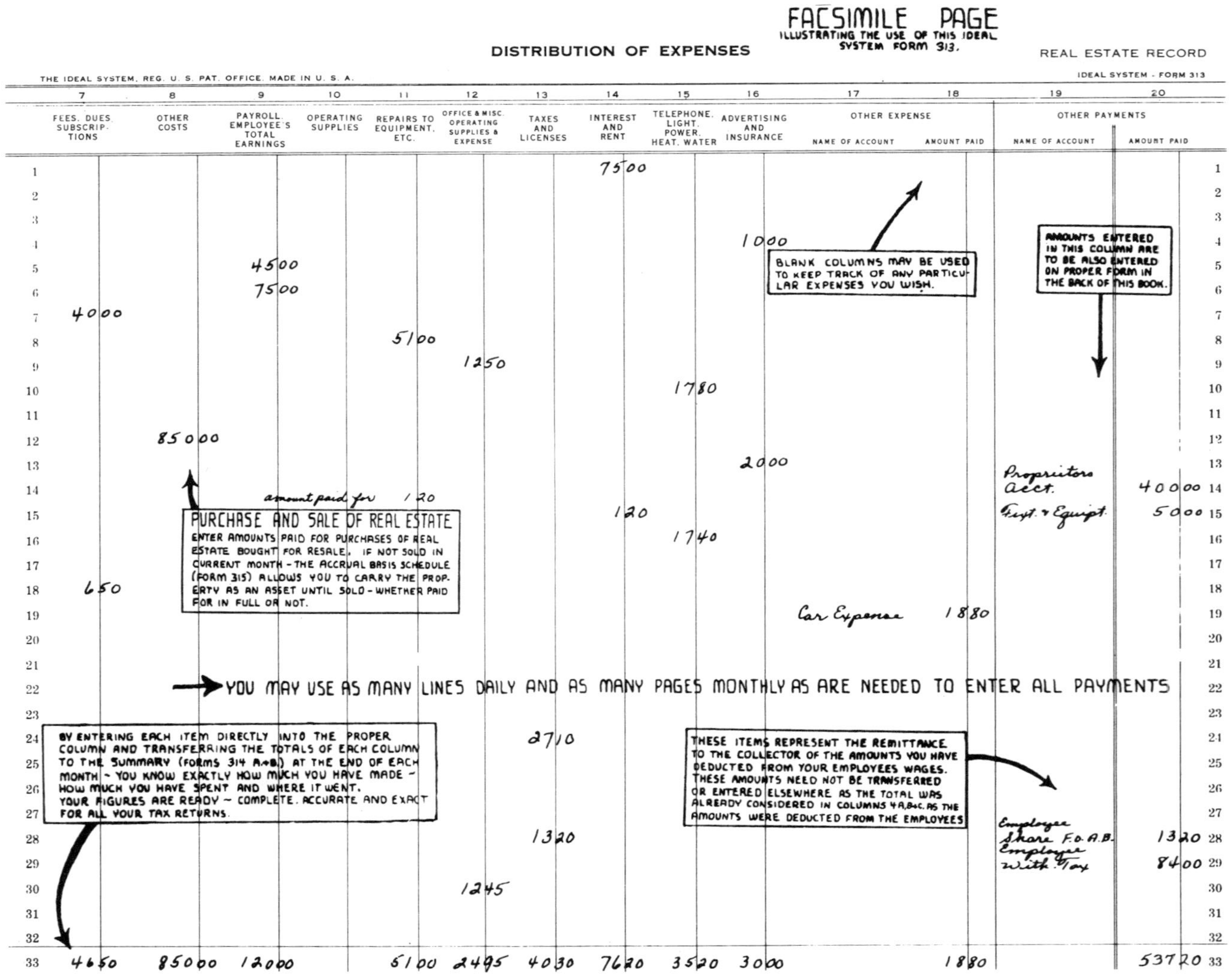

FACSIMILE PAGE
ILLUSTRATING THE USE OF THIS IDEAL SYSTEM FORM 313.

DISTRIBUTION OF EXPENSES

REAL ESTATE RECORD

THE IDEAL SYSTEM. REG. U. S. PAT. OFFICE. MADE IN U. S. A.

IDEAL SYSTEM - FORM 313

	7 FEES. DUES. SUBSCRIP-TIONS	8 OTHER COSTS	9 PAYROLL. EMPLOYEE'S TOTAL EARNINGS	10 OPERATING SUPPLIES	11 REPAIRS TO EQUIPMENT. ETC.	12 OFFICE & MISC. OPERATING SUPPLIES & EXPENSE	13 TAXES AND LICENSES	14 INTEREST AND RENT	15 TELEPHONE. LIGHT. POWER. HEAT. WATER	16 ADVERTISING AND INSURANCE	17 OTHER EXPENSE NAME OF ACCOUNT	18 OTHER EXPENSE AMOUNT PAID	19 OTHER PAYMENTS NAME OF ACCOUNT	20 OTHER PAYMENTS AMOUNT PAID	
1								75 00							1
2															2
3															3
4										10 00					4
5			45 00												5
6			75 00												6
7	40 00														7
8					51 00										8
9						12 50									9
10									17 80						10
11															11
12		850 00													12
13										20 00			Proprietors		13
14			amount paid for		1 20								Acct.	400 00	14
15								1 20					Fixt. + Equipt.	50 00	15
16									17 40						16
17															17
18	6 50														18
19											Car Expense	18 80			19
20															20
21															21
22															22
23															23
24							27 10								24
25															25
26															26
27															27
28							13 20						Employee Share F.O.A.B.	13 20	28
29													Employee With. Tax	84 00	29
30						12 45									30
31															31
32															32
33	46 50	850 00	120 00		51 00	24 95	40 30	76 20	35 20	30 00		18 80		537 20	33

BLANK COLUMNS MAY BE USED TO KEEP TRACK OF ANY PARTICULAR EXPENSES YOU WISH.

AMOUNTS ENTERED IN THIS COLUMN ARE TO BE ALSO ENTERED ON PROPER FORM IN THE BACK OF THIS BOOK.

PURCHASE AND SALE OF REAL ESTATE
ENTER AMOUNTS PAID FOR PURCHASES OF REAL ESTATE BOUGHT FOR RESALE. IF NOT SOLD IN CURRENT MONTH - THE ACCRUAL BASIS SCHEDULE (FORM 315) ALLOWS YOU TO CARRY THE PROPERTY AS AN ASSET UNTIL SOLD - WHETHER PAID FOR IN FULL OR NOT.

→ YOU MAY USE AS MANY LINES DAILY AND AS MANY PAGES MONTHLY AS ARE NEEDED TO ENTER ALL PAYMENTS

BY ENTERING EACH ITEM DIRECTLY INTO THE PROPER COLUMN AND TRANSFERRING THE TOTALS OF EACH COLUMN TO THE SUMMARY (FORMS 314 A+B) AT THE END OF EACH MONTH - YOU KNOW EXACTLY HOW MUCH YOU HAVE MADE - HOW MUCH YOU HAVE SPENT AND WHERE IT WENT. YOUR FIGURES ARE READY - COMPLETE. ACCURATE AND EXACT FOR ALL YOUR TAX RETURNS.

THESE ITEMS REPRESENT THE REMITTANCE TO THE COLLECTOR OF THE AMOUNTS YOU HAVE DEDUCTED FROM YOUR EMPLOYEES WAGES. THESE AMOUNTS NEED NOT BE TRANSFERRED OR ENTERED ELSEWHERE AS THE TOTAL WAS ALREADY CONSIDERED IN COLUMNS 4 A,B&C AS THE AMOUNTS WERE DEDUCTED FROM THE EMPLOYEES

THE IDEAL SYSTEM
REG. U. S. PAT. OFFICE

Courtesy Dymo Visual Systems, Inc., Augusta, Georgia.

Figure 8-2

FACSIMILE PAGE
ILLUSTRATING THE USE OF THIS IDEAL SYSTEM FORM 313.

BANK ACCOUNT — PAYMENTS – ALL CASH AND CHECKS PAID OUT — REAL ESTATE RECORD

THE IDEAL SYSTEM, REG. U. S. PAT. OFFICE. MADE IN U. S. A. — IDEAL SYSTEM - FORM 313

	1	2					3	4	4A	4B	4C	5	6	
	BANK DEPOSITS	BANK BALANCE (2+1−3)	DATE 19__	CHECK NUMBER	TO WHOM PAID	MEMORANDA	PAID OUT BY CHECK	PAID OUT BY CASH	DEDUCTIONS FROM EMPLOYEE'S EARNINGS: F.O.A.B. & UNEMP. INS.	WITHHOLD-ING TAX	OTHER DEDUCTIONS	SUPPLIES, MAPS AND SIGNS	COMMISSIONS PAID OTHERS	
1	bg. bal.	1963 50	Apr. 1	165	Allied Investment Co.	Rent	75 00							1
2			1		Benton Printing Co.			21 00				21 00		2
3			1	166	R. L. Brown		49 00						49 00	3
4			2	167	City Directory		10 00							4
5			2	168	Mrs. R. C. Steel	Steno	39 92		68	4 40				5
6			3	169	Mr. Robert Allen	Agent	66 77		1 13	7 10				6
7			4	170	City Escrow Co.-escrow & title Fees		40 00							7
8			5	171	Elliott Plumbing Serv.		51 00							8
9	225 45	1844 76	5	172	Allard Stationery		12 50							9
10			8	173	Power & Light Co.		17 80							10
11			8	174	Ralph Greene-Purchase of vacant									11
12					lot at 1000 High St.		850 00							12
13			8	175	Aetna Insurance		20 00							13
14			8	176	B. James-owner		400 00							14
15			8	177	Office Fixture Co.		51 20							15
16			8	178	Bell Telephone		17 40							16
17			8		Association Periodical			6 50						17
18			9	179	Adson Co.		18 90					18 90		18
19			10	180	Independent Service		18 80							19
20														20
21														21
22														22
23	→ YOU MAY USE AS MANY LINES DAILY AND AS MANY PAGES MONTHLY AS ARE NEEDED TO ENTER ALL PAYMENTS													23
24			28	210	County Tax Collector		27 10							24
25	42 00	1860 76	28											25
26	50 00	1910 76	29											26
27			30	211	Collector of Int. Revenue	Qtrly Pmt.								27
28					F.O.A.B. Employees Share 13.20 Employers Share	13.20	26 40							28
29			30	212	Collector of Int. Revenue With. Tax		84 00							29
30	27 35	1827 71	30		Petty Cash-misc. payouts			12 45						30
31														31
32														32
33						TOTALS	39 95	1915 79	1 81	11 50		39 90	49 00	33

ENTER THE DETAILS OF EACH EMPLOYEES EARNINGS AND DEDUCTIONS ON THE EMPLOYEES INDIVIDUAL COMPENSATION RECORD (FORM Q-812) IN THE BACK OF THIS BOOK, THUS SIMPLIFYING THE PREPARATION OF YOUR VARIOUS PAYROLL TAX RETURNS.

ACCOUNTS FOR ALL CHECKS AND FOR ALL CASH PAID OUT.

USE TWO LINES WHEN NECESSARY.

AT THE END OF EACH MONTH -- ENTER THE ENTIRE MONTHS TOTALS OF EACH COLUMN ON THE LAST LINE - AND ALSO ENTER UNDER THE PROPER MONTH ON FORMS S-313 (LAST PAGES IN THIS SECTION) AND ON FORMS 314 R.&B. SUMMARY OF BUSINESS AND STATEMENT OF INCOME.

THE IDEAL SYSTEM
REG. U. S. PAT. OFFICE

Courtesy Dymo Visual Systems, Inc., Augusta, Georgia.

Figure 8-3

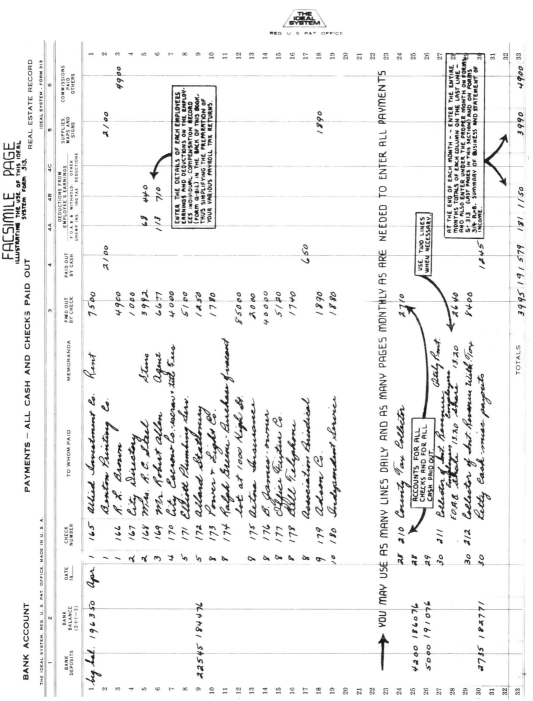

FACSIMILE PAGE
ILLUSTRATING THE USE OF THIS IDEAL SYSTEM FORM 311.

THE IDEAL SYSTEM. REG. U. S. PAT. OFFICE. MADE IN U.S.A.

INCOME FROM COMMISSIONS AND SALES

REAL ESTATE RECORD
DISTRIBUTION OF INCOME
IDEAL SYSTEM - FORM 311

DATE 19__	MEMORANDA	1 PAID IN CASH	2 CHARGED ON ACCOUNT	3 TOTAL (1+2)	4 CASH RECEIVED ON CHARGED ACCOUNTS	5 OTHER CASH RECEIVED	6 TOTAL CASH RECEIVED (1+4+5)	7 SALES COMMISSION	8 RENTAL COMMISSION	9 INSURANCE COMMISSION	10 SALES	11	12
Apr 1	Days total income	4050	1400	5450	1000		5050		4500	950			
2	" " "	3860		3860	1650		5510		3860				
3	" " "	4250		4250	925		5175		4250	1200			
4	" " "	2100	825	2925	2650		2100		1725				
5	" " "	6810	1600	8410			6810		8050	360			
6	" " "	4120		4120			6770		4120				
8	" " "	4750		4750			4750		4750				
9	" " "	4800	2000	6800	1250		6050		5800	1000			
9	Sale of vacant lot												
	at 1000 High St.	120000		120000			120000				120000		
10	Deposit Refund rec'd Gas Co.					2500	2500						
	Days total income	4100		4100			4100		3400	700			
11	Charge to M. Viceroy		2110	2110					2110				
	" " L. Warren		1000	1000					1000				
	Collected for Conrad Co.											4000	
	Charge to Mrs. Morgan		350	350					350				
12	Days total income	5500		5500			5500		4900	600			
	Charge to J. Brown		1650	1650					1650				
	" " T. Jones		1810	1810					1810				
	Escrow - Smith property	42000		42000			42000	42000					
	YOU MAY EITHER SUMMARIZE THE ENTIRE DAYS CHARGES AND CASH RECEIPTS ON ONE LINE EACH DAY - IN WHICH CASE YOUR ENTIRE MONTHS ENTRIES WILL BE ON ONE PAGE - OR YOU MAY USE AS MANY LINES DAILY AND AS MANY PAGES MONTHLY AS ARE NEEDED TO ITEMIZE EACH TRANSACTION EACH DAY.												
Apr 25	Days total income	1100	1100	2200			1100		2200				
26	" " "	3450	1650	5100	2450		5900		5100				
27	" " "	6200		6200			6200		5600	600			
28	" " "	4200	810	5010			4200		4260	750			
29	" " "	4100	925	5025	900		5000		5025				
			925	925					925				
	TOTALS	225390	18155	243545	10825	2500	238715	42000	75385	6160	120000	4000	

COLUMNS WITH BLANK HEADINGS MAY BE USED TO KEEP TRACK OF ANY PARTICULAR CLASS OF INCOME YOU WISH.

THIS AMOUNT WOULD BE KEPT IN A SEPARATE TRUST ACCOUNT SO AS NOT TO COMMINGLE FUNDS.

TRANSFER ALL OF THE MONTHLY TOTALS TO FORM S-311 SUMMARY (LAST PAGE OF THIS SECTION) AND ALSO TO FORMS 314 A+B. SUMMARY OF BUSINESS AND STATEMENT OF INCOME (UNDER THE PROPER MONTH) THIS GIVES YOU A MONTH BY MONTH COMPARISON OF YOUR INCOME AND SHOWS YOU - AT A GLANCE - EXACTLY HOW YOU ARE PROGRESSING.

THE IDEAL SYSTEM
REG. U. S. PAT. OFFICE

Courtesy Dymo Visual Systems, Inc., Augusta, Georgia.

Figure 8-4

SIMPLIFIED

PROFIT AND LOSS STATEMENT

January 1, 19____
to
December 31, 19____

RECEIPTS		$40,000.00
COST OF SALES		
Beginning Inventory	$ 3,500.00	
Purchases	22,000.00	
	$25,500.00	
Less: Ending Inventory	2,000.00	
TOTAL COST OF SALES		23,500.00
GROSS PROFIT		$16,500.00
EXPENSES		
Payroll	$10,000.00	
Advertising and promotion	1,000.00	
Accounting	500.00	
Insurance	800.00	
Taxes	500.00	
Repairs and maintenance	800.00	
Supplies	1,000.00	
TOTAL EXPENSES		$14,600.00
OPERATING PROFIT		1,900.00
LESS DEPRECIATION		500.00
NET PROFIT		$ 1,400.00

Reprinted with permission from The Real Estate Examination Prep Book, 35th Edition, Anthony Schools, 4401 Birch Street, Newport Beach, California 92663.

Figure 8-5

BALANCE SHEET

YEAR 19____

ASSETS AND LIABILITIES AT BEGINNING OF YEAR

ASSETS

CURRENT ASSETS:
- Cash on Hand .... ________
- Cash in Bank .... ________
- Notes Receivable .... ________
- Accounts Receivable .... ________
- Inventory Stock on Hand .... ________

TOTAL .... ________

FIXED ASSETS:
- Land .... ________
- Buildings .... ________
- Equipment .... ________
- Furniture and Furnishings .... ________
- ________ ...... ________

TOTAL .... ________

OTHER ASSETS:
- ________ ...... ________
- ________ ...... ________
- ________ ...... ________

TOTAL .... ________

TOTAL ASSETS .... ________

LIABILITIES

CURRENT LIABILITIES:
- Notes Payable .... ________
- Accounts Payable .... ________
- ________ ...... ________
- ________ ...... ________

TOTAL .... ________

FIXED LIABILITIES:
- Mortgages .... ________
- ________ ...... ________

TOTAL .... ________

TOTAL LIABILITIES .... ________

NET WORTH (Deduct Total Liabilities from Total Assets and enter the difference here) .... ________

TOTAL LIABILITIES AND NET WORTH .... ________

ASSETS AND LIABILITIES AT END OF YEAR

ASSETS

CURRENT ASSETS:
- Cash on Hand .... ________
- Cash in Bank .... ________
- Notes Receivable .... ________
- Accounts Receivable .... ________
- Inventory Stock on Hand .... ________

TOTAL .... ________

FIXED ASSETS:
- Land .... ________
- Buildings .... ________
- Equipment .... ________
- Furniture and Furnishings .... ________
- ________ ...... ________

TOTAL .... ________

OTHER ASSETS:
- ________ ...... ________
- ________ ...... ________
- ________ ...... ________

TOTAL .... ________

TOTAL ASSETS .... ________

LIABILITIES

CURRENT LIABILITIES:
- Notes Payable .... ________
- Accounts Payable .... ________
- ________ ...... ________
- ________ ...... ________

TOTAL .... ________

FIXED LIABILITIES:
- Mortgages .... ________
- ________ ...... ________

TOTAL .... ________

TOTAL LIABILITIES .... ________

NET WORTH (Deduct Total Liabilities from Total Assets and enter the difference here) .... ________

TOTAL LIABILITIES AND NET WORTH .... ________

Courtesy Dymo Visual Systems, Inc., Augusta, Georgia.

Figure 8-6

OFFICE FUND VOUCHER

Voucher No.__________

From________________19____to________________19____ Paid by Check No. __________

AUDITED BY	APPROVED BY		

DATE	RECEIPT NO.	TO WHOM PAID	FOR WHAT	ACCT. NO.	AMOUNT
			TOTAL DISBURSED		
			CASH ON HAND		
			AMOUNT OF FUND		

DISTRIBUTION

BURROUGHS CORPORATION TODD DIV. - L PRINTED IN U. S. A. REG. U. S. PAT. OFF. STANDARD OFFICE FUND VOUCHER ENVELOPE FORM C507

Courtesy Burroughs Corporation, Business Forms Division.

Figure 8-7

The moneys involved in a trust fund are twofold: (1) those which go to the escrow, and (2) those which go into the trust fund account (and which are *never* commingled). Detailed records of *all* trust account transactions *must* be kept. Figures 8-8 and 8-9 are some very easy forms to use.

Along with the recording of actual dollar amounts, you are responsible for keeping copies of certain coordinating documents. They are reviewed here and some samples you can adapt are shown.

DOCUMENTS FOR A BASIC RECORD SYSTEM

USE FOR ALL TRUST FUNDS WHICH GO INTO TRUST ACCOUNT

COLUMNAR RECORD OF ALL TRUST FUNDS RECEIVED AND PAID OUT
TRUST FUND BANK ACCOUNT

19___			RECEIVED				PAID OUT				
Date Received	From Whom Received Or To Whom Paid	Description	Amount Received	Cross Ref.	Date of Deposit	XX	Amount Paid Out	Check No.	Date of Check	XX	Daily Balance of Trust Bank Account
(1)	(2)		(3)		(4)			(5)	(5)		(7)
4/5/-	Paul Hill	Cash to open T/A	$100.00	Rcpt. 1	4/5/-						$100.00
4/8/-	Troy Marsh	Jan. Rent	$175.00	Rcpt. 2	4/8/-						$275.00
4/8/-	Mildred Hacker	Jan. Rent	$180.00	Rcpt. 3	4/8/-						$455.00
	City Water Co.	March Water Bill		Acct. 1			$25.00	1	4/9/-		$430.00
	Paul Hill General Acct.	Coll. & Mgmt. Fee					$35.50	2	4/10/-		$394.50
	Fridolph Gazze	Apt. Rental Proceeds					$294.50	3	4/10/-		$100.00
	Donald Carlson	Deposit on Saunders Pty.	$1500.00	Rcpt. 4	4/16/-						$1600.00
1/15/-	Title Escrow Co.	Deposit on Saunders Pty.					$1500.00	4	4/18/-		$100.00

Figure 8-8

RECORD OF ALL TRUST FUNDS RECEIVED—NOT PLACED IN BROKER'S TRUST ACCOUNT

TRUST FUNDS INCLUDING UNCASHED CHECKS RECEIVED					
Date Received	Received From	Amount	Description Property or Identification	Disposition of Uncashed Checks or Other Funds Forwarded to Escrow or Principal	Date Forwarded
4/25/-	William Stevenson	$2,000	Deposit on Dunn Property, 100 Joyce Ln	Title Escrow Co (R-116)	4/25/-

Figure 8-9

Purchase contract and receipt for deposit

Most brokers use a standard form of deposit receipt and offer to purchase. In addition to the copies given to those who sign, the broker must keep a copy on file for a certain period of time. This receipt will show the date, the amount, from whom, and for what transaction the money is received. See Figure 8-10.

REAL ESTATE PURCHASE CONTRACT AND RECEIPT FOR DEPOSIT

THIS IS MORE THAN A RECEIPT FOR MONEY. IT MAY BE A LEGALLY BINDING CONTRACT. READ IT CAREFULLY.

SACRAMENTO, California, APRIL 25, 19—

Received from WILLIAM STEVENSON herein called Buyer,
the sum of TWO THOUSAND Dollars ($2000.00)
evidenced by cash ☐, personal check ☒, cashier's check ☐, or ______ as deposit on account of
purchase price of TWENTY THOUSAND Dollars, ($20,000.00)
for the purchase of property, situated in SACRAMENTO, County of SACRAMENTO,
California, described as follows: 105 JOYCE LANE

Figure 8-10

Collection receipt

All moneys received from a real estate sale, or which have been collected as a result of a real estate transaction, should be recorded in the receipt book. This includes all initial down payments (earnest money) and subsequent down payments. Explanations on receipts must be in sufficient detail to completely identify the item. All receipts are to be used in

COLLECTION RECEIPT

Date 4/25/— No. 5

Received from William Stevenson
Address 100 Armstrong Blvd.
Two Thousand & 00/100 Dollars
For Account of Gerald Dunn (Deposit on Dunn Property, 105 Joyce Ln.)
Received by Paul Hill

Cash ______ Check ✓

Figure 8-11

numerical order and accounted for. The receipt book is to be used only for the receipt of moneys pertaining to real estate transactions. See Figure 8-11.

An additional control can be included by indicating on all receipts that the checks must be made payable to the brokerage concern's trust fund and not to the salesman.

Bank deposit slips

Bank deposit slips are furnished by the bank (see Figure 8-12). Ideally, bank deposit slips should be filled out in duplicate and one copy retained by the broker. The teller will stamp the carbon copy, if presented with the original deposit and deposit slip. If separate deposit slips or other deposit records are furnished by the bank, as in the case of mail deposits, they should be stapled to the carbon copies to which they apply.

DEPOSIT SLIP		
Home Bank	Dollars	Cts.
Silver		
Currency	$355	—
Checks		
Receipt #2 Troy Marsh		
Receipt #3 Mildred Hacker		
Morgan Arms Apts Acct. #1		
Total	$355	—
For credit of: Paul Hill, Trust		
Account # 00-001 200 North St., Sacramento		
Date: April 8, 19—		
Duplicate		

Figure 8-12

The bank deposit slip provides a convenient record to indicate the content of deposits to the trust account. The date of deposit of trust funds can then be entered in the cash receipts register or transaction record.

On the left or detail side, the bank number and the purpose of the receipt can be shown on the deposit slip. If more space is needed, the back of the slip may be used. It is desirable for the deposit slip to include the numbers of the collection receipts, or to identify the transactions which are included in the deposit.

Escrow receipt

If the customer's deposit is placed in escrow, a receipt should be obtained from the escrow or title company and kept on file.

Cancelled trust account check

By the use of a description space on the trust account check, a brief accounting can be given to the principal. However, the use of a description column is limited and it may be necessary to forward a separate accounting statement with the check.

All trust account checks should be pre-numbered, and all voided checks retained.

9

How to Properly Prepare Real Estate Newspaper Advertising

The real estate secretary is the intermediary between the salespeople, who write the ads, and the newspaper. The information in this chapter will familiarize you with all phases of real estate newspaper advertising, so that you will be able to apply what you need to your particular situation.

See that there is essential, current data (rate cards or contract information; type sizes and counts per line; borders; copy and cancellation deadlines; direct line phone numbers to advertising salespeople; cut, mat, and art work information; column size and widths) for *each* newspaper in which your firm advertises. Use a three-ring binder with tabs. Keep the art work in envelope files. *Label everything.*

You can call your local library for additional information. Standard Rate and Data Services, Inc., supplies informational directories, including *Newspaper Circulation Analyses, Newspaper Rates and Data*, and *Weekly Newspaper and Shopping Guide Rates and Data*. N.W. Ayer & Son's *Directory of Newspapers and Publications* provides data about newspapers and periodicals, and information about the states, cities, towns, and marketing areas in which these publications circulate. The Newspaper Advertising Bureau, 555 Madison Avenue, New

York, New York 10022, publishes the *Newspaper Advertising Plan Book.*

The National Association of Realtors, 430 N. Michigan Avenue, Chicago, Illinois 60611, publishes *Clip-Art Insights,* a quarterly publication, with each issue containing ads complete with copy and illustrations and an "Insights" page with public relations information and suggestions. They also publish an *Energy Conservation Issue,* eight energy conservation ads complete with illustrations and copy and an "Insights" page, offering public relations suggestions and information on energy.

George Putz, Classified Advertising Manager of the *San Francisco Examiner and Chronicle,* tells of three monthly publications which give examples of real estate classified ads and ideas. They are:

> *Classified Real Estate Idea Exchange,*
> published by MacDonald Classified Services,
> Harrison C. MacDonald & Sons Inc.,
> P.O. Box 225, Lafayette, Indiana 47902
> Offices: 1202 Columbia. Phone: (317) 742-9012
>
> Gives examples of classified line and display ads and classified promotions held by newspapers across the country.
>
> *Real Estate Showcase,*
> published by SCAN Corporation
> Box 806
> Peoria, Illinois 61652
>
> Gives examples of line and display classified ads and a column of real estate sales tips. The art shown is reduced 43 percent from actual size; the full-size reproducible art is available from your newspaper.
>
> *Classified Real Estate Display Ideas,*
> published by Classified International Advertising Services, Inc.
> 1345 East Tenth Avenue
> Hialeah, Florida 33010
> Phone: (305) 885-4526
>
> Publishes a monthly booklet of classified line ads. Included in the booklet are copywriting tips and trends, original

headings, and suggested copy for condominiums, commercial property, farms and ranches, homes for sale, income property, rentals, and waterfront property. Their monthly display ad booklet has a "Tips 'n Trends" column, Realtor copy, townhouses, new homes, condominiums and an ad series.

For additional help, Prentice-Hall, Inc., Englewood Cliffs, New Jersey 07632, has published the *Lifetime Encyclopedia of Real Estate Classified Advertising* (1977), by E. Turner.

Mary Ann France, Classified Advertising Manager, tells of an advertising presentation developed at *The News American* in Baltimore, Maryland, which is presented to real estate agents throughout the area. The following sections, Elements of Successful Ads, Principles of Effective Classified Advertising, Headline Ideas to Get Your Real Estate Ads Off to a "Selling Start," and the Elements of a Real Estate and a Rental Ad, are a part of that program. The complete "course" includes coordinating slides. It would be an interesting idea to start up with a newspaper and/or other real estate firms in your area.*

ELEMENTS OF SUCCESSFUL ADS

The headline is the single most important element in your classified ad. People frequently scan the columns, so you must catch the reader's eye. A few ways to attract attention are (1) heavier type, (2) bigger type, and (3) quite a bit of white space around the headline. If you don't stop them with the headline, the copy won't get read. Good rules are:

1. Try, above all else, to get a self-interest appeal into the headline. The headline should suggest to the reader that here is something he really wants.
2. Get news into the headline if it is in any way possible. The very fact that the listing is on the market is news to most of your readers.
3. Avoid headlines which rely solely on the reader's curiosity. If you can combine self-interest with curiosity, or news with curiosity, or all three, you may have a really good headline, but never rely on curiosity by itself.

---

*Courtesy *The News American*, Baltimore, Maryland.

4. Avoid the gloomy or negative approach. Stress the cheerful, positive side of the story.

Most readers want to know, "What's in it for me?" So, the headline should point out the main benefit and the supporting facts should be in your first line of copy. Use white space top and bottom, left and right. Body copy should be easy and interesting to read, without complex abbreviations. Last, but certainly not least, the advertiser's name and phone number should be easy to find and easy to read.

Before you start putting these principles to work, the following steps will make the job easier for the secretary or salesperson.

Gather the facts. Ask the seller questions. What was the primary feature of this property that made you buy it? What do you feel the best sales point of this property is?

Write the ad as you would talk. The best way to accomplish this is to pretend you are talking to a prospect and tape record what you are saying. This way, there will be a natural flow to your thoughts, and they won't be stiff and choppy when you put them down on paper. Type the material and edit your copy to strengthen it. Be specific and eliminate all weak statements.

Be certain you advertise to live prospects. Urge them to buy right now!

PRINCIPLES OF EFFECTIVE CLASSIFIED ADVERTISING

1. Make your ads easily recognizable.
2. Use a simple layout.
3. Use a dominant element.
4. Use a prominent benefit headline.
5. Let your white space work for you.
6. Make your copy complete.
7. State price or range of prices.
8. Specify branded merchandise.
9. Urge your readers to buy now.

To illustrate some of these pointers, here are line and display ads from a booklet mentioned earlier, *Classified Real Estate Display Ideas.*

THE ELEMENTS OF A REAL ESTATE AD

REAL ESTATE

Location
Construction (frame? brick?)
Architecture, landscaping
Number of rooms, description
Number of bedrooms
Condition, age
Possession date
Convenience to stores,
  schools, and transportation
Lot size, zoning
Garage
Bathrooms
Kitchen (disposal?)
Basement, recreation room
City sewer, utilities
Heating
Fireplace
Plumbing
Built-ins, closets
Features for children
Price, terms, how much down?

Courtesy The News American, Baltimore, Maryland.

Figure 9-1

THE ELEMENTS OF A RENTAL AD

RENTALS

Location
Number of rooms
Closets
Bath, shower
Garage
Heating
Air conditioning
Furnishings
Utilities furnished
Elevator
Neighborhood
Convenience to stores, schools and transportation
Children accepted
Pets allowed
Privileges— phone, kitchen, laundry, television, etc.
When available
Price

Courtesy The News American, Baltimore, Maryland.

Figure 9-2

Ad Breakdown

COUNTRYSIDE SETTING

It is a delight to see a home that is this clean and this well cared for. Beautiful hardwood floors, an elegant formal dining room, first floor laundry, a truly country style kitchen with fireplace and informal dining room, full basement with 2nd fireplace, 2½ baths, 4 spacious bedrooms, electronic air purifier and a beautiful countryside setting. Price reduced to $63,900. This executive home has just about everything you could ask for including a lovely decor. Call Bill Ziegler, 344-2341.

don CAIN inc.
Realtors 382-5563

Appealing headline, aimed at your type of prospect.

Copy that determines the main points of the property, showing the desirable qualities the prospect is going to be looking for.

A good ad always contains the price; it helps to locate the right buyer.

Identifiable logo, telephone number, address and hours are important items.

REAL ESTATE INVESTMENT OPPORTUNITY

Baird & Warner is now offering eight unit income apartment buildings, fully rented, near Clarendon Hills and Hinsdale. These apartment buildings may be purchased for investment or for owner/occupied and managed income properties. These properties are located in a park-like setting which includes a recreational pavillion with game and party room, swimming pool, and clubhouse with gym facilities for basketball, volleyball and badminton. A fulltime recreational director plans and organizes activities. Each building contains 4 one and 4 two-bedroom apartments with indivdually controlled central heat and private patio or second floor balcony. Wall-to-wall carpeting, ceramic baths with separate vanity room, spacious closets, color coordinated kitchen appliances, air conditioning, garbage disposal, master TV antennas, walk-in storage lockers, parking all highlight the individual apartment.

8 Unit Apartment Buildings
from $189,500
to $224,500

Directions:
Take I-55 (Stevenson) to Rte. 83, North to first stoplight and left onto Frontage Road to:

STRATFORD GREEN APTS.

Sales Office
Open Daily 10AM to 5PM
Call 986-8370

Baird & Warner

Investment Div.
115 S. LaSalle Street
Chicago, Il 60603

CROWN CENTER

LUXURY CONDOMINIUMS

Weather-protected living: covered walkways to Crown Center shops, restaurants, hotels, offices. Affordably priced from $41,650.

You've got style.
We've got style.

SAN FRANCISCO TOWER
2510 Grand
474-3333

Open 9-6 Mon. thru Fri., 10-5 Sat. & 12-5 Sun. Other times by appointment. Charles F. Curry Real Estate Company, exclusive sales agent.

10 ACRE RANCH WITH GUEST QUARTERS/ 3 B.R.

10 acres of usable ranch land with 4 years young ranch home with 3 B.R.'s & 1½ baths, plus separate guest quarters with 1 B.R. & bath. Large living room with fireplace and lots of storage, with gas built-ins, fireplace, & covered patio. Municipal water to houses. Well on property with new pump that handles all irrigation. Delicious apple orchard in front of house. Zoned A1. $65,000. Call now for appointment to see.

MARCUS W. REALTORS
MEAIRS

684-2211 3600 Central
684-5212 6734 Brockton

TRI-PLEX

Close to hospitals and college. One bedroom units make ideal student rentals. 2 units have new paint and carpeting. Priced at $66,900. For showing, call Judy Towlerton at 652-2410 or 259-5036.

HORIZON

From Classified International Advertising Services, Inc.
1345 East Tenth Avenue, Hialeah, Florida 33010.

Figure 9-3 (cont'd)

A successful ad should begin with an outstanding headline to catch the reader's eye. It should be interesting and different enough to make him read further.

The art layout and descriptive copy should be appealing, yet easy on the eye. Well written, easy flowing copy is an essential in describing dimensions, special features, brand names and styling to appeal to the reader.

Be sure to include a distinctive logo with the address, phone number and a map for easy reference and directions. Also remember to include the most important factor of any successful ad—the price. Research proves that ads are 48% more effective if the price is mentioned.

From Classified International Advertising Services, Inc.
1345 East Tenth Avenue, Hialeah, Florida 33010.

Figure 9-3 (cont'd)

HEADLINE IDEAS TO GET YOUR REAL ESTATE ADS OFF TO A "SELLING START"*

For the Love of Living See...
Try This For Sighs.
It needn't be so Humble.
Be it ever so Humble, Own Your Own Home.
Mom's House at Dad's Price.
Blue Chip Home Environment.
Kitchen Sink Included.
A Friendly Little House.
For the Choosy Family.
Not Fancy ... Just Homey.
Needs Elbow Grease and Your Talents.
The World looks Brighter from Your Own Windows.
Gold and Silver melt away ... Real Estate is here to Stay.
The Busy Man's Haven.
Do You get a Headache when You Write Your Rent Check?
Perfect Homes in the Perfect Location.
Give Your Family the Best.
Go Where the Good Life is.
Built for a Heap of Living.
Children Need a Big House.
Every Room is an Invitation.
This Home is Child Proof.
A Home is a Savings Account.
Country Boy at Heart? You'll Love This.
Live a Country Club Life All Year Long.
Now Your Family can Live in Luxury.
You'll have Room to Play Ball Here.
Neighborhood Conscious?
... Where Life Begins at 55.
Your Bankbook won't Blink an Eye.
Children Wanted to Enjoy This ...
Right Neighbors, Right Value.

---

*Courtesy *The New American*, Baltimore, Maryland.

Planned for Important People.
Your Money couldn't Buy More Happiness.
Should I buy Now or Wait till Prices go UP?
Happy is the Home Hunter who Sees These Homes First.
We Hate to Rave, But ...
Help Yourself to Leisurely Luxurious Living.
If Where You Live is Important ...
A Home of Space and Comfort.
One Visit Will Convince You.
Unsurpassed Elegance ... In an Unsurpassed Location.
Living at its Level Best.
Wife Wanted ... With Family and Charming Husband to Occupy this ...
Wanted Unhappy Renters.
A House that Dared to be Different.
Your Rent Dollars Will Buy this Home.
Homes with a Future, Your Future.
Move One More Time ... To Your Own Home.
The Birds and Bees Enjoy a Home ... Why Not You?
A Home is a Woman surrounded by a Good House.
Pampers Your Purse.
Open for Inspiration.
Modest but Cute.
Don't Let These Homes Pass You Up.
The Address You Give with Pride.
If You Think of Your Family ...
Designed to Delight ... Built to Endure ... Priced to Please.
The Nicest House on the Nicest Street.
For the Woman Who has Everything, but a Home.
To See it is to Love it.
Where Your Children Build Happy Memories.
Homes with a Priceless Look.
Petted and Pampered by Particular People.
Undeniably Lovely ... Infinitely Livable.
... And This could be for you.
Charm and Dollar Value You haven't Seen in Years.

Away from the Hub Bub of City Living.
Is Living near School important to You?
Designed to Delight the Young at Heart.
Have You Seen this Superb New Suburb?
The Wife you Save may be Your Own.
How Many Ways are there to Say "Perfect."
Fourteen Karat Look.
Woman to Woman ... Don't Settle for less.
New Paint Sparkles on the Beauty.
What a Wonderful Way to Live.
This House is More than a Home.
Tired of "Look Alike" Homes.
Decorator Designed with the Family in Mind.
A Take-It-Easy House.
A Fine Home Says a Great Deal.
Near-New Homes with the Brand-New Look.
This Home Puts You Up where Your Ambitions Are.
Good Neighbors for Sale.
Like It? Golfers Will!
The Greatest Thrill is Rent Money invested in Your Own Home.
Your Address is Important.
Your Home is You.
Count Your Blessings in your Own Home.
A Half Acre of Heaven.
One of these Should be Your Home for Keeps.
It's Good House Sense.
Apple Pie Condition.
See the Quiet Home in beautiful ...
Bring Your Bathing Suit to ...
Go Fishing across the Street.
Needs Paper and Paint But ...
Out where it is Cool.
Such a Wonderful World of Difference.
When Spacious Living Matters.
The Door to Happiness is the Door to Your Own Home.
When you own a Spot of Land you own a Portion of the World.

It's a Great World if you Live in the Right Place.
Back Yard Full of Park.
If You Like Individuality ... Here it is.
Where Happy Folks Live.
An Older Home with Young Ideas.
Now it can be Sold.
An invitation to Spacious Living.
Styled with You in Mind.
Stop Supporting Landlords!
Talk about Clean ... This Home Sparkles!
Live Better for Less in ...
Tree Lovers, Have You Seen ...
Where it's Fun for the family to Live.
A Pure White Gem in a Setting of Pines.
Shattered City Nerves?
Rocking Chair Kitchen.
A Masterpiece in Planning.
A Big Little House.
Twenty-First Century Living.
A Man's House that Women Like.
The Perfect Marriage of Land and House.
Live like the Joneses, But for less Money.
Most Everybody is Moving to ...
Your Whole Family will Live Better in ...
Trade up to Elegance.
Dutch Cleanser Bright.
Happiness and Good Luck For Sale.
Jet Age Efficiency.
All Weather House.
Put your Heart and Whole Family in this Happy Home.
Homes don't Grow but Families do.
Young Family? Growing Children? See This.
For the Wife of an Executive.
Don't Put Off Life's Greatest Thrill.
You've Seen the Rest ... Now ... See the Best.
Building Happiness into a home.
The Community with Prestige ...
Rent Donor— ... or Home Owner?
Do You have Countryitis?

For a Successful Man.
How Sweet it is for You and the Kids.
It's Wife Approved.
Enjoy the New Sound of a Happy Family.
Think Twice ... Can you Pass Up This Home?
Get a Whopping Income Tax Refund next Year.
A Prettier Home is Mighty Hard to Find.
We're Looking for a Special Kind of Family ...
Be sure the House You Buy will be a Home.
The View Goes On and On.
Where Everything is New but its Trees.
The Years and the Tenants have been Good to this House.
A Rare and Serene Beauty.
Live—Where You want to Live ...
Don't be Chained to an Old House.
Paradise for You and Your Children.
The Measure of Your Success ... Your Home.
Join the Happy Move to ...
Room to Room.
Will Outlast Your Grandchildren.
A Home with a Warm Heart.
Love a Gracious Setting.
Crying on the Outside .. Laughing on the Inside.
For the Tired or Retired.
Plush as a Palace.
The House with Everything.
Kitchen of Beauty and Joy Forever.
Not Just a New Home, but a New Way of Life.
Pride of Ownership Sparkles in Every Home.
Where You Live Makes a Difference in How you Live.
Custom Designed with Your Type of Living in Mind.
Heaven on Earth for Your Girl and Boy.
Good to the Last Nail.
The Theme Here is Roominess.
To Make a House a Home ... Own it.
Stop that Leak in Your Bankroll.

House Gourmet?
Love ... At Purse Sight.
A Planned Community of Titled Charm.
Genteel Country Living ...
New Beauty Outside ... New Comfort Inside.
Dramatic Homes for People who want the Finest.
It's the Cheeriest House.
Built like Gibraltar.
It ain't Fancy but This Home is Flawless.
Just Right ... For Family Comfort!
Move-In-Able.
A Career Woman's House.
What are You doing about Inflation?
Easy, Carefree Way of Living.
Does Your Family Deserve a Promotion?
Designed with the whole family in mind.
An old home that reflects sensibility and charm.
A doll house, painted white, trimmed in (color) and set off in an expanse of green lawn.
Compact modern cottage with the neat, clean lines that only brick can give.
No ups and downs in this compact bungalow.
Sleek-lined contemporary design for an expanding young family.
Proud Colonial with graceful pillars bespeaks your preference for elegance.

An easy way to cut down on paper work and recordkeeping is to make a master of the form in Figure 9-4 on 8½″ × 14″ paper for long ads, and have it printed at the instant printer.

The original will go the newspaper as the advertising order and one carbon copy goes to the salesperson to use as a record of calls. The secretary keeps the second carbon copy as the record of advertising run and ordered for the month (by date in a three-ring binder), and uses it to check against the statement of the newspaper at the end of the month. If you clip out the ad from the paper and paste it on the bottom, you will have a perfect double-check as well as an actual copy which you can reproduce and use if you have to order the ad again.

ADVERTISER ____________ KIND OF AD ____________ CLASSIFICATION ________ SIZE ________

DATE(S) OF PUBLICATION ____________________ OR T.F. (till forbidden) ______________

CONTRACT OR RATE INFORMATION ____________ CUT INFORMATION ______________

PICK UP FROM ISSUE OF ____________________ AUTHORIZED BY ______________

PROSPECT NAME, ADDRESS, PHONE	DATE OF CALL	ADDITIONAL INFORMATION

]HOW TO PREPARE[center - all caps

\#

]LINE ADS[center - all caps

\#

Set typewriter to width of column. For every type size, use proper character count (newspaper will advise). Type ad EXACTLY as it should appear.

\#

]Use[center - caps and lower case

flush left caps and lower case — [Margin Notes] — flush right - caps + lower case

\#

File carbon chronologically in notebook. Clip ad when published and paste. Check off dates above as ad runs.

\#

Call newspaper as soon as possible if there is error.

Figure 9-4

HOW TO PROPERLY PREPARE DISPLAY ADVERTISING

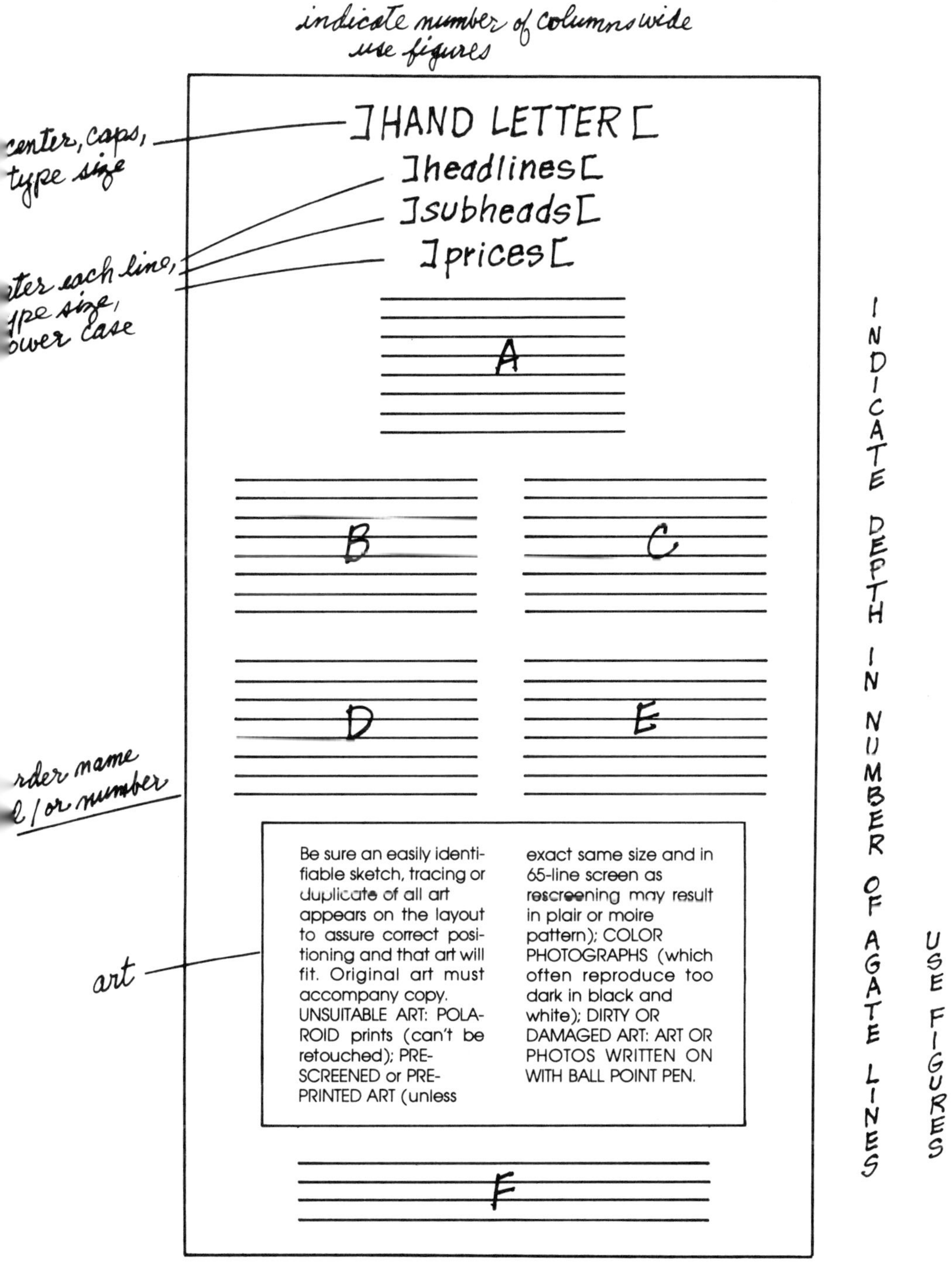

indicate number of columns wide
use figures
center, caps, type size
]HAND LETTER[
]headlines[
]subheads[
]prices[
A
B
C
D
E
art
Be sure an easily identifiable sketch, tracing or duplicate of all art appears on the layout to assure correct positioning and that art will fit. Original art must accompany copy. UNSUITABLE ART: POLAROID prints (can't be retouched); PRESCREENED or PREPRINTED ART (unless exact same size and in 65-line screen as rescreening may result in plair or moire pattern); COLOR PHOTOGRAPHS (which often reproduce too dark in black and white); DIRTY OR DAMAGED ART: ART OR PHOTOS WRITTEN ON WITH BALL POINT PEN.
F
INDICATE DEPTH IN NUMBER OF AGATE LINES
USE FIGURES

Text courtesy The New York Times.

Figure 9-5

HOW TO PROPERLY LABEL AND SET UP COPY BLOCKS FOR DISPLAY ADVERTISING

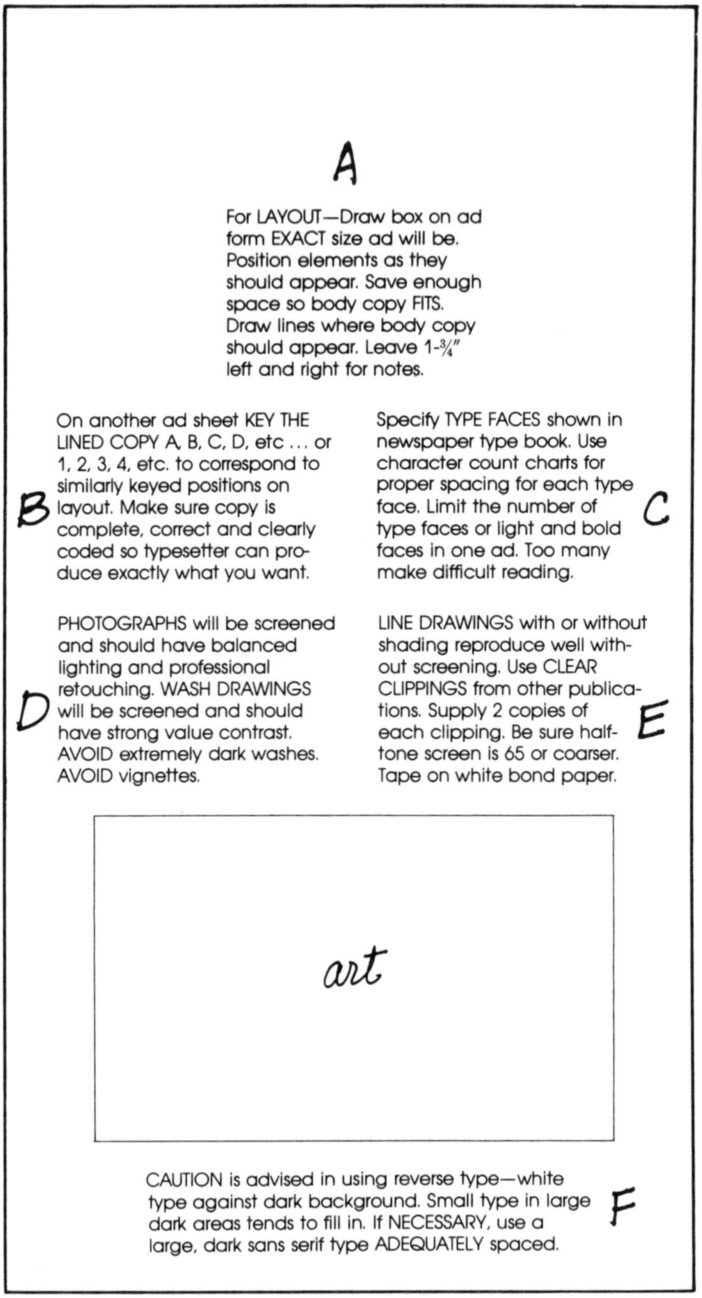
A
For LAYOUT—Draw box on ad form EXACT size ad will be. Position elements as they should appear. Save enough space so body copy FITS. Draw lines where body copy should appear. Leave 1-¾" left and right for notes.
B
On another ad sheet KEY THE LINED COPY A, B, C, D, etc ... or 1, 2, 3, 4, etc. to correspond to similarly keyed positions on layout. Make sure copy is complete, correct and clearly coded so typesetter can produce exactly what you want.
C
Specify TYPE FACES shown in newspaper type book. Use character count charts for proper spacing for each type face. Limit the number of type faces or light and bold faces in one ad. Too many make difficult reading.
D
PHOTOGRAPHS will be screened and should have balanced lighting and professional retouching. WASH DRAWINGS will be screened and should have strong value contrast. AVOID extremely dark washes. AVOID vignettes.
E
LINE DRAWINGS with or without shading reproduce well without screening. Use CLEAR CLIPPINGS from other publications. Supply 2 copies of each clipping. Be sure halftone screen is 65 or coarser. Tape on white bond paper.
art
F
CAUTION is advised in using reverse type—white type against dark background. Small type in large dark areas tends to fill in. If NECESSARY, use a large, dark sans serif type ADEQUATELY spaced.

Text courtesy The New York Times.

FIGURE 9-6

The following list contains abbreviations used in real estate, rental, and business opportunity classified advertisements in newspapers across the United States. Abbreviations are valuable for saving space, but should be used with discretion. If the ad is not easily readable, the message and the potential customers will be lost.

accounts	accts
acres	ac
adjacent	adj
afternoon	aft
agent	agt
air conditioner	AC
all electric kitchen	AEK
aluminum	al
and	&
apartment	apt
appliance	appl
appointment	appt
assumption	assum
available	avail
back	bk
back yard	bk yd
business	bus
basement	bsmt
bath	ba
bedrooms	bdrms
between	bet
black top road	blk tp rd
blocks	blks
brick	brk
boulevard	blvd
building	bldg
built ins	blt in
business	bus
business opportunity	bus opp
busy	bzy
cabinet	cab
carpet	cpt
cathedral ceiling	cath ceil
ceiling	ceil
cellar	clr
central air conditioning	ctl air

closet	clos
colonial	colon
commercial	comm
combination windows	combo winds
condominium	condo
convenience	conv
corner	cor
country	ctry
couple	cpl
crossing	Xing
custom,-ized	cust
deck	dk
deep water	dp wtr
delicatessen	deli
deluxe	dlxe
den	dn
department	dept
detached	det
development	dev
dining	din
directions	dir
double	dbl
down	dn
downtown	dwntn
drapes	drp
dryer	dry
easy	E-Z
electric	elec
elementary	elem
elevator	elev
enclose,-ed,-ure	enc., encl.
equipment	equip
established	est., estab.
excellent	exc., xlnt
extras	xtras
east	E
facilities	facil
familiar	fam
family room	f r, fam rm
finance,-d	fin, finc
fireplace	frpl

floor	flr
forced hot water heat	fhw heat
formal	form
frontage	frntg
furnished	furn
garage	gar
garden	grdn
good	gd
greenhouse	grnhse
grocery	groc
gross	gr
hardwood	hdwd
heat	ht
heavy	hvy
heights	hgts
high rise	hi riz
highway	hwa., hwy
hospital	hosp
hot water heat	HW Heat
immediate	immed
including	incl
industrial	indus
insulate,-ion	insul
interest	int
inventory	invty
investment	invest
irrigated	irrig
kitchen	kit
land contract	LC
lane	ln
large	lg
laundry	lndry
lease	lse
library	lib
location	loc
luxury	lux
maintain	mtn
maintenance	maint
manufacturing	mfg

marble	mbl
marine	mar
market	mkt
maximum	max
medical	med
miles	mi
minutes	mins
mobile home	M.H.
modern	mod
month	mo
mortgage	mtg
mount	mt
national	nat'l
natural	nat
near	nr
new	nu
newly decorated	nu dec
neighborhood	nbrhd
north	N
occupancy	occup
offer	ofr
opportunity	oppty
opposite	opp
original	orig
overhead	O.H.
package	pkg
paint	pnt
panoramic	pano
parking	pk, prkg
penthouse	pent
phone	ph
porch	prc
possession	poss
power	pwr
principal	prin
private	pvt, priv
professional	prof
property	prop
quarters	qtrs

Realtor	Rltr
reasonable	reas
recreation	rec
redwood	rdwd
reference	ref
refrigerator	refrig
regular	reg
remodeled	remod
restaurant	rest
route	rte
security deposit	sec dep
separate	sep
shower	shr
shopping	shop
single	sgle
small	sm
south	S
spacious	spac
sprinklered	sprklrd
square	sq
stove	stv
suite	ste
system	syst
terrace	terr
thousand	M
townhouse	twnhse
trailer	trlr
transportation	trans
trust deed	TD
unfinished	unfin
unfurnished	unfurn
university	univ
utilities	utils
underground	undgrnd
upper	upr
valley	vly
veranda	ver
Victorian	vict
view	vu

wall-to-wall	w/w
warehouse	whse
weekend(s)	wknd(s)
west	W
with	w
woodburning	wdbrng
yard	y
year	yr

The Wall Street Journal, because of its regional, national, and international coverage, offers real estate advertisers a unique marketplace for classified line and display ads of one column inch or more in its "Friday Real Estate Corner." Also available is "The Mart," the daily classified section, which offers a real estate classification.

Here buyers and sellers nationwide of commercial and industrial real estate, industrial parks, shopping centers, downtown office buildings, investment and development sites, apartment property, resorts, motels, restaurants, warehouses, and manufacturing plants are brought together, as are buyers and sellers of farms, farm land, dairy farms, cattle ranches, horse ranches, acreage for subdivision, timberland investments, ski areas, waterfront property, country estates, mountain retreats, luxury townhouses, condominiums, and other residential properties.

Advertising can be placed in one, in a combination, or in all of the four United States editions Monday through Friday.

Eastern Edition: Circulates mainly throughout New York and other Middle Atlantic states, New England, and Southwestern states, eastern Tennessee and West Virginia. Published at Chicopee, MA; South Brunswick, NJ; Silver Springs, MD; and Orlando, FL.

Midwest Edition: Circulates throughout Illinois, Indiana, Iowa, northern Kansas, Kentucky, Michigan, Minnesota, Missouri, Nebraska, the northwest portions of New York and Pennsylvania, Ohio, North Dakota, South Dakota, and Wisconsin. Published at Chicago and Highland, IL; Cleveland, OH.

Western Edition: Circulates through California, Alaska, Arizona, Colorado, Hawaii, Idaho, Montana, Nevada, New Mexico, Oregon, Utah, Washington, and Wyoming. Published at Palo Alto and Riverside, CA; Federal Way, WA; and Englewood, CO.

Southwest Edition: Circulates throughout Texas, Arkansas, southern Kansas, Louisiana, Mississippi, Oklahoma, and Western Tennessee. Published at Dallas, TX.

Advertising for the Asian edition, published at Hong Kong on Monday through Friday, and which circulates throughout all of Asia, can be placed through the New York office.

Information about rates, contracts, copy deadlines and specifications, mechanical measurements, box numbers, and copywriting help can be obtained by writing or calling a classified advertising office located in: Atlanta, GA; Boston, MA; Chicago, IL; Cincinnati and Cleveland, OH; Coral Gables, FL; Dallas, TX; Englewood (Denver), CO; Detroit, MI; Federal Way, WA; Bellaire (Houston), TX; Los Angeles, CA; Milwaukee, WI; Minneapolis, MN; New York, NY; Philadelphia and Pittsburgh, PA; Palo Alto, CA; Silver Springs, MD; St. Louis, MO; International Press Center, 76 Shoe Lane, London, E.C. 4, England; and 6 Frankfort/Maine, Savigny Strasse 29., West Germany.

10

Successful Real Estate Sales Aids

Everything which transpires in a real estate office ultimately has to do with making money—with sales.

Listings are the merchandise of the real estate office. They are the authorizations to sell property. Since each real estate operation is different, the procedures vary. It is important for the secretary to file the listings so that everyone in the office can find them. She should be sure to label everything.

The stationery store may carry clever notebooks for the salespeople's listings. A filing cabinet with trays and plastic pockets is a good way to file the listing cards. All you have to do is flip through the drawer and you will have the picture and the information readily available.

Perhaps it is easiest to keep the information on each property in a file folder. Design a form for the outside of the manila folder which will give the data on the property. Take the folders to the quick printer and have the form printed directly on the folder so that all you will have to do is fill in the blanks and the details will be visible right away. If you want to paste a picture of the property on the front, use transparent tape in strips to cover the whole picture so that it won't tear when you put it back in the file cabinet. You will make things easier for yourself if you ask, "How can I make three steps into one?"

LISTINGS

A listing is an employment contract between the principal and the agent, authorizing the agent to perform services for the principal involving the principal's property. Listings are also termed "authorizations to sell," binding the agent holding a listing under the law with certain obligations to his principal. These must be in writing if a broker is to be assured of collecting his commission.

In a *net listing*, the compensation is not definitely determined, but a clause in the contract usually permits the agent to retain as compensation all of the money received in excess of the selling price set by the seller.

An *open listing* is a written memorandum signed by the party to be charged (usually the seller of the property) which authorizes the broker to act as agent for the sale of certain described property. A time limit is not usually specified, although it can be. This kind of listing may be given to more than one agent at the same time, and the seller is not usually required to notify the other agents in case of a sale by one of them. The sale of the property is considered to cancel all outstanding listings.

An *exclusive agency listing* is a contract containing the words "exclusive agency." The commission is payable to the broker named in the contract and if the broker or any other broker finds the buyer and makes the sale, the broker holding the exclusive listing is entitled to the commission.

An *exclusive right to sell listing* is one in which commission is due to the broker named in the contract if the property is sold within the time limit by the said broker, by any other broker or by the owner. Frequently, such contracts also provide that the owner shall be liable to pay a commission, if the sale is made within a specified time after the listing expires, to a buyer introduced to the owner by the listing broker during the time of the listing.

The *Multiple Listing Service* is a cooperative listing service conducted by a group of brokers, usually members of a real estate board. The group provides a standard Multiple Listing form which is used by the members. It is usually an "Exclusive Authorization Right to Sell" listing form, and provides among other things that the member of the group who takes the particular listing is to turn it in to a central bureau. From there it is distributed to all participants in the service and all have the right to work on it. Commissions earned on such listings are shared among the cooperating brokers, with the listing broker providing for the division of commission in his listing sent to other participants.

Some boards of Realtors use computers. Each week the real estate company receives a computer printout showing the status of their listings. They have a computer terminal in their office which they can program for information.

Penny Denney, secretary at Evans Pacific Corporation in San Francisco, California, offers the following ideas.

Keep a large ledger, paged day by day. Use rubber stamps as shown in Figure 10-1 to record information.

OPEN HOUSE
TIME:
ADDRESS:
LISTER:
PRICE:
DESC:

SOLD
PRICE:
ADDRESS:
SALESPERSON:
LISTED:

LISTING
PRICE:
ADDRESS:
DESCRIPTION:
LISTER:
EXCL:

Figure 10-1

Keep a library table for office reference and include the following:

- Real estate atlas of the county
- Area telephone directories
- Reverse telephone directory
- City directories
- Current Multiple Listing
- Folder of fliers about properties from other real estate offices
- Folder of probate sales (investigate subscription services)
- Folder of recordings from Recorder's office (investigate subscription services)
- Area maps
- Any other subscription services or information necessary to your particular office

Figures 10-2 and 10-3 are examples of forms which give the pertinent information on properties available for sale and rent. Triple space between categories and type the title (condominiums, duplexes, etc.) as a heading in the middle of the clear line. The forms can be copied for the salespeople to use as masters to complete for the typist, and the form with the completed information can be copied and distributed to the salespeople. Leave additional copies where they are easily accessible.

Figure 10-4 is a form which can be used as a control in a condominium project.

It is a good idea to keep keys in a locked cabinet. A form like the one in Figure 10-5 can be used to control the keys. For properties where keys are on the premises or can be obtained from outside the real estate office, show the information on the sales sheet under "Other Instructions." A 3″ × 5″ card should serve the purpose.

The form in Figure 10-6 may be reproduced and given to the salespeople. Additional copies should be left in the office for future showings. Photographs can be added.

SALES

Address	Price	Lister	Description	To Show	Comments
			Condominiums		

Courtesy Evans Pacific Corporation,
1405 Sutter Street, San Francisco, California 94109.

Figure 10-2

RENTALS

Price	Description	Lister	Address	Keys	Comments

Courtesy Evans Pacific Corporation,
1405 Sutter Street, San Francisco, California 94109.

Figure 10-3

Apt.	Owner	Lister	Rent	To Show
		Studio		
		JR-1 Bedroom		

Courtesy Evans Pacific Corporation,
1405 Sutter Street, San Francisco, California 94109.

Figure 10-4

Keys in Office

Property Address	Name	Date Key Out	Date Key In

Courtesy Evans Pacific Corporation,
1405 Sutter Street, San Francisco, California 94109.

Figure 10-5

EPC Evans Pacific Corporation, Realtor

1405 Sutter Street • San Francisco, California 94109 • (415) 441-7272

23 - 29 Kendall Road

PRICE:	$229,000 Reduced!
LOCATION:	23, 25, 27 and 29 Kendall Road, between Arleigh and Parkview
DESCRIPTION:	Sunny four unit building. Completely renovated last year. Each unit is a 1 bedroom, 1 bath with a modern kitchen and new bathroom Included in Purchase Price: Dishwashers, garbage disposals, ADT Security System, stoves, refrigerators, all wall to wall carpets and light fixtures in kitchens and living rooms
INCOME:	19-- Gross Income $13,140.00 Rents have been increased to the following effective September 1, 19--: Unit # 23 $ 350.00 # 25 404.90 # 27 433.15 # 29 420.76 $1,608.81 $1,608.81 per month x 12 = $19,305.72
TERMS:	All offers must be subject to Purchasers agreeing to participate in a tax-deferred exchange with Seller at no additional expense to Purchasers
FINANCING:	Present loan is with San Francisco Bank
REAL ESTATE TAXES:	19-- $1,540.00
TO SHOW:	Call Listing Office

Figure 10-6

A new kind of "associated" real estate business, called Home Inspection Services, is on the rise across the country. The report, which can be purchased by either the buyer or the seller, details every part of the structure. It is a very good additional sales point for a listing. The salesperson can show the buyer that a professional has checked out the property and has put the results in writing. It proves the validity of the sales talk. If the salesperson represents the buyer, the suggestion can be made to purchase a Home Inspection Report (see Figure 10-7). It shows what questions should be asked about a piece of property. You must sometimes help someone else get information. If you know what a home inspection requires, you can intelligently handle the customer, the home inspector, and the office salesperson.

Chapter 11 will give you samples of sales letters to prospects which, of course, are potential listings.

Sources of listings can be quite varied, and include business contacts, professional contacts, newspaper stories, mailing lists, social clubs, fraternal and church groups, direct mail, friends, public records, and newspaper and magazine advertising.

Speaking of magazine advertising, Figure 10-8 is an ad from the *Florida Realtor* by Mr. Phillip Baker, President of Bay Crest Realty, Inc., in Tampa, Florida, who has another kind of vision for obtaining listings—from other brokers and from potential buyers and sellers.

A picture *is* worth 1000 words, *if it is properly presented.* For those staff sales meetings, presentations for a potential buyer, and community projects in which your office is involved, 3M tells you, in Figure 10-9, how to prepare and present transparencies for overhead projection with their Tartan system. You can use normal room lighting and prepare the originals on almost any office copying machine. You are limited only by your own ingenuity.

STANLEY HOME INSPECTION SERVICE
ONE ORINDA VISTA DRIVE / OAKLAND, CA. 94605 / (415) 569-8131

Building
Address: ____________________

INSPECTION CHECK LIST

Property Inspected: ______________________________ Date: ____________ Weather: __________

OUTSIDE

DRAINAGE: Good ☐ Satisfactory ☐ Poor ☐ Needs Correction ☐
GRADING: Good ☐ Satisfactory ☐ Poor ☐ Needs Correction ☐
UTILITIES:
Electricity: Overhead ☐ Underground ☐ Number of Wires ____________
Sewers: Installed/city ☐ Cesspool ☐ Other ____________________ Verify Sewer Hook Up ☐
Gas ☐ Water ☐ Wells ☐ Pump ☐ Adequate ☐ Needs Repairs ☐
TERMITES: Evidence of ☐ Not observable ☐ Suspicion of ☐ See Remarks ☐
BUILDING:
Sidewalls: Brick ☐ Wood ☐ Shingle ☐ Stucco ☐ Masonry ☐
Other ____
Condition: Good ☐ Acceptable ☐ Poor ☐
ROOF:
Material: Asphalt shingle ☐ Wood shingle ☐ Slate ☐ Approaching useful life ☐
Rolled Roofing ☐ Other ____________ Will need repairs & replacement
Condition: Good ☐ Acceptable ☐ Poor ☐ Needs Repair ☐
Flashing: Copper ☐ Other ______________________ ____________
LEADERS & GUTTERS:
None ☐ Galvanized ☐ Copper ☐ Wood ☐ Aluminum ☐
Condition: Good ☐ Adequate ☐ Poor ☐ Needs Repair ☐
EXTERIOR PAINT: Good ☐ Acceptable ☐ Needs Repainting ☐
GARAGE: Yes ☐ No ☐ Number of Cars Attached ☐ Detached ☐
Heat ☐ Electric ☐ Storage Space ☐ Water ☐ Suspicion of Termites ☐
WINDOWS:
Putty: Good ☐ Acceptable ☐ Needed ☐ Number Broken
Caulking: Good ☐ Acceptable ☐ Needed ☐
Screens: Yes ☐ No ☐ Good ☐ Acceptable ☐ Needs Repair ☐ Missing ☐
Storm Windows: Yes ☐ No ☐ Good ☐ Acceptable ☐ Needs Repair ☐ Missing ☐
DOORS:
Number ____________ Weather Stripped: Yes ☐ No ☐ Needs Repairs ☐
Putty: Good ☐ Acceptable ☐ Needed ☐
Caulking: Good ☐ Acceptable ☐ Needed ☐
Locks ☐ Working ☐ Needs Repairs ☐
PORCH:
Front: Good ☐ Acceptable ☐ Needs Repairs ☐
Side: Good ☐ Acceptable ☐ Needs Repairs ☐

NOTE: Addition To Building Should Be Filed With Building Department ☐
SIDEWALKS: Condition: Acceptable ☐ Needs Repairs ☐
DRIVEWAYS: Condition: Acceptable ☐ Needs Repairs ☐
PATIO: Yes ☐ No ☐ Condition: Acceptable ☐ Needs Repairs ☐

REMARKS: ____

____

This report of inspection has been prepared at your request for the purpose of ascertaining the present physical condition of the premises and/or equipment. The report covers only these portions of the subject premises and equipment as were capable of being visually inspected and does not include any portion not actually seen or capable of being seen. The report as to present condition is not to be construed as a guarantee or warranty and is not intended for the purpose of fixing a value or as an opinion as to the advisability or inadvisability of purchase.

Figure 10-7

STANLEY HOME INSPECTION SERVICE
ONE ORINDA VISTA DRIVE / OAKLAND, CA 94605 / (415) 569-8131

Building Address: ____________________

KITCHEN Stove ☐ Refrigerator ☐ Sink ☐
CABINETS: Adequate ☐ Inadequate ☐ Condition: Good ☐ Satisfactory ☐ Poor ☐
WORK SPACE: Excellent ☐ Adequate ☐ Poor ☐
CEILINGS:
Plaster ☐ Accous. Tile ☐ Sheet Rock ☐ Water Stains ☐
Cracks: Yes ☐ No ☐ Needs Repairs ☐ Paint ☐ Paper ☐
WALLS: Plaster ☐ Sheet Rock ☐ Other
Cracks: Yes ☐ No ☐ Needs Repairs ☐ Paint ☐ Paper ☐
FLOORS:
Linoleum ☐ Wood ☐ Other ____________________
Condition: Good ☐ Serviceable ☐ Needs Repairs ☐ Floor Sags ☐
WINDOWS:
Number ____________ Weatherstripping ☐ Adequate ☐ Poor ☐
ELECTRIC OUTLETS: Adequate ☐ Inadequate ☐
TRIM: Wood ☐ Miscellaneous ☐ Condition: Good ☐ Adequate ☐ Needs Repairs ☐
HEATING: Radiators ☐ Ducts ☐ Baseboards ☐ None ☐
EXHAUST FAN: Yes ☐ No ☐
EATING SPACE: Excellent ☐ Adequate ☐ Poor ☐ None ☐
DOORS:
Interior: Number __________ Condition: Good ☐ Adequate ☐ Poor ☐ Door bucks square ☐
Exterior: Number __________ Condition: Good ☐ Adequate ☐ Poor ☐
Weatherstripped: Yes ☐ No ☐
HARDWARE: Good ☐ Adequate ☐ Needs Repairs ☐
PLUMBING:
Leaks ____________ Pressure Adequate: Yes ☐ No ☐
Condition: Good ☐ Adequate ☐ Poor ☐ Needs Repairs ☐
Evidence of Rusting: Yes ☐ No ☐ Cleanout: Yes ☐ No ☐

REMARKS: ____

____

ROOM:
CEILINGS: Plaster ☐ Accous. Tile ☐ Sheet Rock ☐ Water Stains ☐
Cracks: Yes ☐ No ☐ Needs Repairs ☐ Paint ☐ Paper ☐
WALLS: Plaster ☐ Tile ☐ Sheet Rock ☐
Cracks: Yes ☐ No ☐ Needs Repairs ☐ Paint ☐ Paper ☐
FLOORS: Linoleum ☐ Wood ☐ Miscellaneous ____________________
Condition: Good ☐ Serviceable ☐ Needs Repairs ☐ Floor Sags ☐
WINDOWS: Number __________ Weatherstripped: Adequate ☐ Poor ☐
ELECTRIC OUTLETS: Adequate ☐ Inadequate ☐
TRIM: Wood ☐ Miscellaneous ☐ Condition: Good ☐ Adequate ☐ Needs Repairs ☐
HEATING: Radiators ☐ Ducts ☐ Baseboard ☐ None ☐
CLOSETS: Number ____________
DOORS: Interior: Number ____________ Condition: Good ☐ Adequate ☐ Poor ☐ Door bucks square ☐
Exterior: Number ____________ Condition: Good ☐ Adequate ☐ Poor ☐
Weatherstripped: Yes ☐ No ☐
HARDWARE: Good ☐ Adequate ☐ Needs Repairs ☐

FIREPLACE: Needs Repairs ☐ None ☐
Needs Cleaning ☐
Damper Not Operational ☐
Get Representation that Fireplace Is Operational ☐

BATHROOM:
PLUMBING: Leaks ____________ Pressure Adequate: Yes ☐ No ☐
Condition: Good ☐ Adequate ☐ Poor ☐ Needs Repairs ☐
Evidence of Rusting: Yes ☐ No ☐ Copper ☐ Brass ☐ Galv. Iron ☐
Adequate tiling behind sinks, bathtubs, showers: Yes ☐ No ☐

REMARKS: ____

This report of inspection has been prepared at your request for the purpose of ascertaining the present physical condition of the premises and/or equipment. The report covers only these portions of the subject premises and equipment as were capable of being visually inspected and does not include any portion not actually seen or capable of being seen. The report as to present condition is not to be construed as a guarantee or warranty and is not intended for the purpose of fixing a value or as an opinion as to the advisability or inadvisability of purchase.

Figure 10-7 (cont'd)

STANLEY HOME INSPECTION SERVICE
ONE ORINDA VISTA DRIVE / OAKLAND, CA 94605 / (415) 569-8131

Building
Address: ____________________

CELLAR AND/OR UTILITY ROOM

TERMITES:
Evidence of ☐ Not observable ☐ Suspicion of ☐ Probe Holes ☐
Termite Protection: Good ☐ Adequate ☐ Poor ☐ None ☐ See Remarks ☐

REMARKS: ____________________

____

WALLS: Concrete ☐ Block ☐ Other ____________________
Condition: Acceptable ☐ Needs Repairs ☐ Cracks ☐ Fine ☐ Large ☐
FLOOR:
Concrete ☐ Wood Finish ☐ Tiled ☐ Other ____________________
Condition: Acceptable ☐ Needs Repairs ☐
GIRDERS:
Steel ☐ Wood ☐ None ☐ Slab on / below grade
Condition: Good ☐ Acceptable ☐ Needed ☐ Non observable ☐
COLUMNS:
Steel ☐ Wood ☐ None ☐
Condition: Good ☐ Acceptable ☐ Needed ☐
FLOOR JOISTS:
Spacing ____________ Size ____________
Condition: Good ☐ Acceptable ☐ Poor ☐
HEATING SYSTEM:
Furnace/Boiler Manufacture: ____________________
Condition Appears to be: Good ☐ Serviceable ☐ Poor ☐
Evidence of rusting: Yes ☐ No ☐ ☐ Approaching useful life
Will need repairs & replacement
Adequate ☐ Inadequate ☐
Gas ☐ Oil ☐ Coal ☐ ☐ Maintain a premium oil service contract covering
Hot Water ☐ Steam ☐ Hot Air ☐ *all parts* such as: oil pump, circulator pump,
Ducting: Adequate ☐ Inadequate ☐ hot water coil, oil tank, relay, etc.
HOT WATER SYSTEM:
Capacity: Gallons ____________ Manufacturer ____________________
Electric ☐ Gas ☐ Instant, with heat system ☐
Condition: Good ☐ Serviceable ☐ Poor ☐
Adequate ☐ Inadequate ☐ Rusting: Yes ☐ No ☐

☐ BOILER NOT OPERATING DURING INSPECTION
Due to Summer ☐ Due to Utilities Turned Off ☐ Other ____________________

☐ Get representation from Seller that Plumbing, Boiler, Burner and Hot Water Heater are in good working order, that no repairs are required, and a list of repairs that have been made (if any) to units.

REMARKS: ____________________

____

____

This report of inspection has been prepared at your request for the purpose of ascertaining the present physical condition of the premises and/or equipment. The report covers only these portions of the subject premises and equipment as were capable of being visually inspected and does not include any portion not actually seen or capable of being seen. The report as to present condition is not to be construed as a guarantee or warranty and is not intended for the purpose of fixing a value or as an opinion as to the advisability or inadvisability of purchase.

Figure 10-7 (cont'd)

STANLEY HOME INSPECTION SERVICE
ONE ORINDA VISTA DRIVE / OAKLAND, CA. 94605 / (415) 569-8131

Building Address: ____________________

CELLAR AND/OR UTILITY ROOM (cont'd.)

ELECTRICITY: **Approximate Service at Panel**
No. of Circuits________ Amps: 30 ☐ 60 ☐ 100 ☐ 125 ☐ Volts: 110 ☐ 110/220 ☐
Adequate: Yes ☐ No ☐ Condition: Good ☐ Serviceable ☐ Poor ☐
Circuit Breakers: Yes ☐ No ☐ Outlets in Cellar ______________
VENTILATION: Good ☐ Acceptable ☐ Poor ☐ Exhaust Fan: Yes ☐ No ☐
CHIMNEY: Yes ☐ None ☐ Condition: Acceptable ☐ Needs Repairs ☐ Cleanout: Yes ☐ No ☐
STAIRS: Condition: Good ☐ Acceptable ☐ Poor ☐ Needs Repairs ☐
HEADWAY OVER STAIRS: Adequate ☐ Inadequate ☐

CELLAR DRAINAGE: Wet Basement Conditions ☐
Sump Pump ☐ None ☐ Adequate Drains ☐
Evidence of Moisture ☐ Leaks ☐ Water ☐
Walls ☐ Floor ☐ Ceiling ☐ Condition Should Be Eliminated ☐

____

PLUMBING:
Copper ☐ Brass ☐ Galv. Iron ☐ Corrosion will decrease water pressure ☐
Condition Appears To Be: Good ☐ Serviceable ☐ Poor ☐ Needs Repairs ☐ Galvanic Action ☐
Sewer Lines: Cleanouts: Yes ☐ None Apparent ☐ None ☐ Water Shutoffs: Yes ☐ None ☐

REMARKS: ____

____

ATTIC OR CRAWL SPACE

ROOF LEAKS: Evidence of: Yes ☐ No ☐
INSULATION:
Roof ☐ Floor ☐ Walls ☐ None ☐
Condition: Good ☐ Acceptable ☐ Poor ☐
FRAMING:
Size ____________________ Spacing ____________________
Good ☐ Acceptable ☐ Below Standard ☐
JOISTS:
Size ____________________ Spacing ____________________
Good ☐ Acceptable ☐ Below Standard ☐
FLOORING: None ☐ Partial ☐ Complete ☐
ELECTRIC WIRING: Installed ☐ None ☐ Adequate ☐ Poor ☐
VENTS (PLUMBING): None ☐ Poor ☐ Adequate ☐
VENTILATION: Adequate ☐ Inadequate ☐
Windows: Number ________ Weatherstripped ☐
Ventilator Fan: Yes ☐ No ☐
CONDENSATION: Evidence of: Yes ☐ No ☐
PLUMBING: None ☐ Provision for Expansion ☐
DOORS: Number ________ Hardware: Good ☐ Adequate ☐ Needs Repairs ☐
CHIMNEY: Yes ☐ No ☐

REMARKS: ____

____

This report of inspection has been prepared at your request for the purpose of ascertaining the present physical condition of the premises and/or equipment. The report covers only these portions of the subject premises and equipment as were capable of being visually inspected and does not include any portion not actually seen or capable of being seen. The report as to present condition is not to be construed as a guarantee or warranty and is not intended for the purpose of fixing a value or as an opinion as to the advisability or inadvisability of purchase.

Figure 10-7 (cont'd)

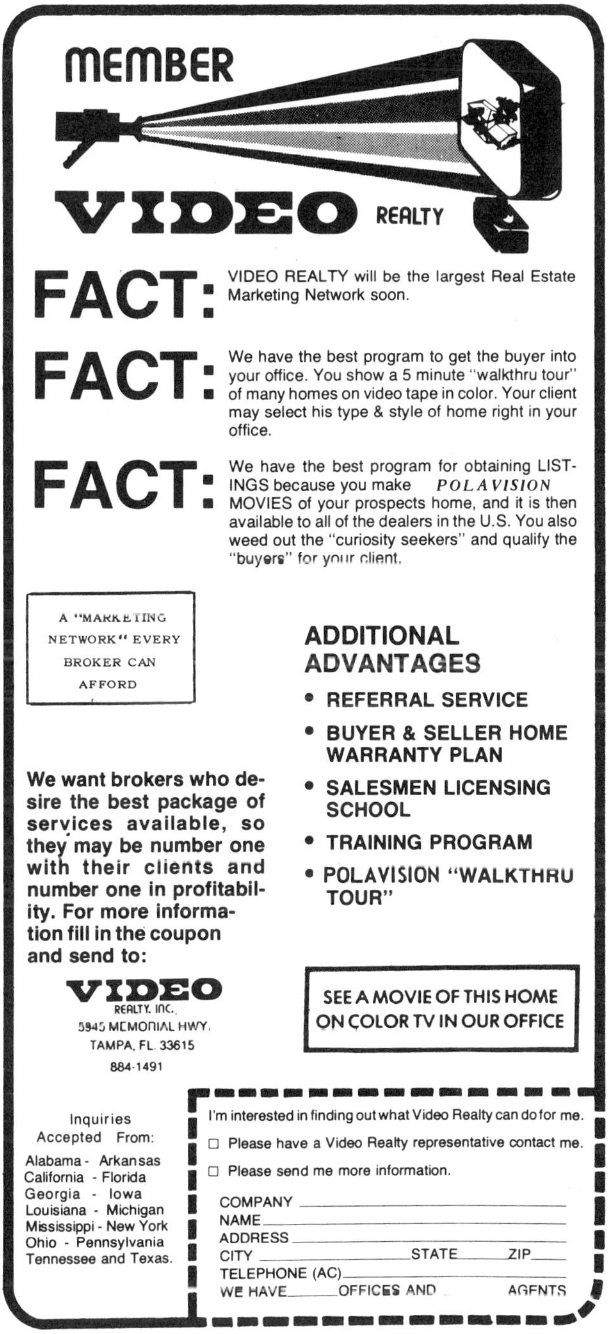
MEMBER
VIDEO REALTY
FACT: VIDEO REALTY will be the largest Real Estate Marketing Network soon.
FACT: We have the best program to get the buyer into your office. You show a 5 minute "walkthru tour" of many homes on video tape in color. Your client may select his type & style of home right in your office.
FACT: We have the best program for obtaining LISTINGS because you make POLAVISION MOVIES of your prospects home, and it is then available to all of the dealers in the U.S. You also weed out the "curiosity seekers" and qualify the "buyers" for your client.
A "MARKETING NETWORK" EVERY BROKER CAN AFFORD
ADDITIONAL ADVANTAGES
• REFERRAL SERVICE
• BUYER & SELLER HOME WARRANTY PLAN
• SALESMEN LICENSING SCHOOL
• TRAINING PROGRAM
• POLAVISION "WALKTHRU TOUR"
We want brokers who desire the best package of services available, so they may be number one with their clients and number one in profitability. For more information fill in the coupon and send to:
VIDEO
REALTY, INC.
5945 MEMORIAL HWY.
TAMPA, FL 33615
884-1491
SEE A MOVIE OF THIS HOME ON COLOR TV IN OUR OFFICE
Inquiries Accepted From:
Alabama - Arkansas
California - Florida
Georgia - Iowa
Louisiana - Michigan
Mississippi - New York
Ohio - Pennsylvania
Tennessee and Texas.
I'm interested in finding out what Video Realty can do for me.
☐ Please have a Video Realty representative contact me.
☐ Please send me more information.
COMPANY
NAME
ADDRESS
CITY STATE ZIP
TELEPHONE (AC)
WE HAVE OFFICES AND AGENTS

Figure 10-8

How to prepare and present transparencies for overhead projection.

A good presentation depends on the quality of the visuals. Good visuals start with properly prepared originals. For preparation of good originals always remember the following steps in preparation.

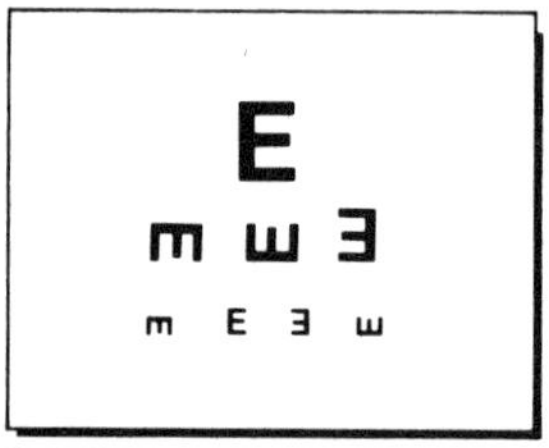

Visibility—Write, print or type large. Letter must be ¼" to be read at a distance of ten feet in presentations.

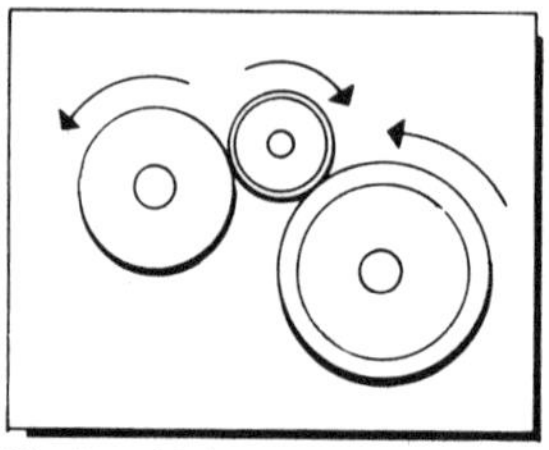

Clarity—Make everything instantly recognizable. If it isn't, label it. Use color, it's attention getting.

Simplicity—One point per original. Use a maximum of six or seven lines with six or seven words per line.

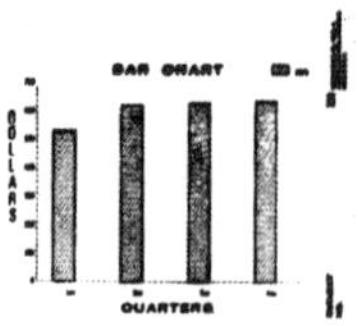

Image area—Tartan transparency film is 8½ x 11". Mounting takes ¼" on all sides, limit your image area to 7½ x 10" so that you will have sufficient room for the border.

Preparing the original—When preparing the original remember the size of your audience. Letters must be ¼" on the original to be legible for an audience ten feet from the screen. This is an excellent guide to follow with all images.

Paper—Hard surface paper is best overall for originals because it will reproduce in all of the imaging processes. Sources for this type of paper are Tartan design-a-visual pads, copy machine paper.

You can use liquid or chalk cover-ups to correct mistakes on originals. Or, erase completely or cut out and replace. You need clear, clean originals.

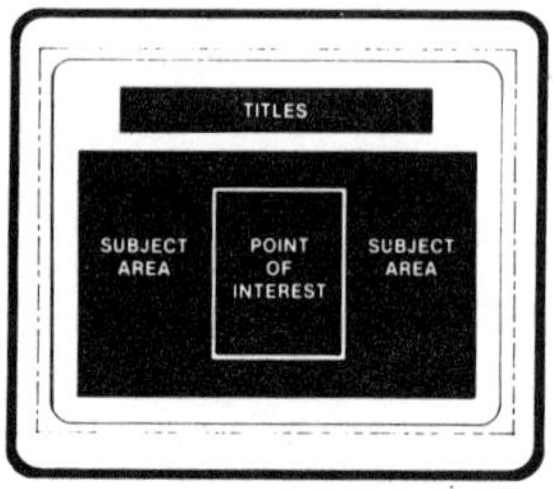

Standard image format—The horizontal format is the best to facilitate easy audience viewing. But, you may use the format that fits your specific purpose. Keep the title at the top, and other information in the upper two-thirds for best visibility.

Headline—The Tartan print shop in a box provides an inexpensive, practical way to produce visual original copy. The kit includes a magnetic headliner, a 8½ x 12" magnetic preparation board and two trays of reuseable headline size letters and numerals in Futura and Cartoon type styles. Place your original on the magnetic board, spell out the headline by magnetically affixing the metallic letters and numerals, place the completed board face down on your plain paper copier and push the print button. The result will be a sharp, bold visual original that is ready for imaging.

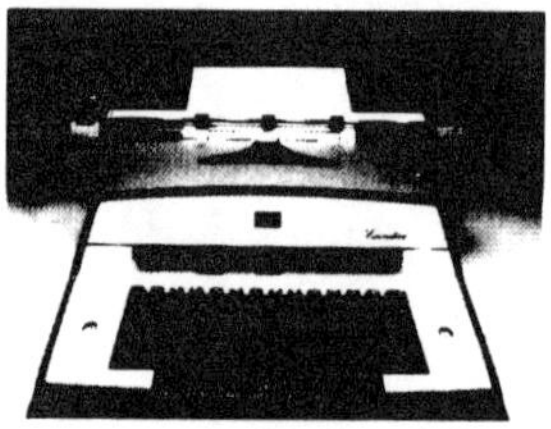

Typewriter—Typewriters can be used for visual original copy, although most typewriter faces are too small to be really effective. Larger faces, such as the IBM "Orator" and other speech type faces work very well. Typewriters do have the advantage of quick access and easy composition.

Making the transparency—Tartan plain paper copier transparency film works in most office plain paper copiers. To make a transparency for overhead projection, load the Tartan transparency film on top of the existing paper supply. Place your original art work face down on the copier as if you were making a regular paper copy, press the copy button and your plain paper copier will produce a transparency of

Reprinted by permission of 3M Company.

Figure 10-9

your original art work. For complete imaging guide information see enclosed PPL Transparency Imaging Guide.

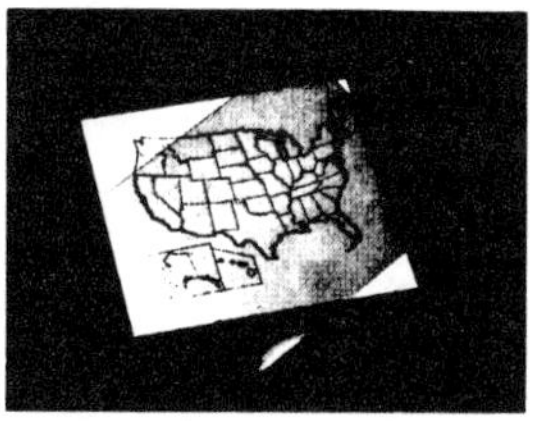

Adding impact to image transparencies.

Tartan color transparency film—This is the simplest and quickest way to add interest and eye appeal to a program without using special processes in making the original. Combinations (Tartan clear and color film) add impact to a visual. Additional colors can be produced by placing an unimaged sheet of one color over a sheet of imaged color. Unimaged blue over imaged red will produce black images on a purple background, for instance.

Color pens—
A variety of specially made pens offers another effective way to add color to transparencies. Both permanent and water-soluble colors are non-fading and project beautifully.

Billboarding—This technique highlights a specific area on a visual. A sheet of imaged or unimaged color film is taped to the mounting frame over the imaged visual. Then the section is cut out of the color film and removed. Be careful to cut only the color film.

Overlays—This method helps simplify difficult concepts and also lets the presenter build the visual's story in a meaningful way. It involves two or more overlays and different colors for each other. Using no more than two overlays and different colors for each makes this a very effective way to present step-by-step information. Overlays are "hinged" to the frame on one side with tape to allow the base visual to be presented first, then the overlay is flopped over it to complete the message.

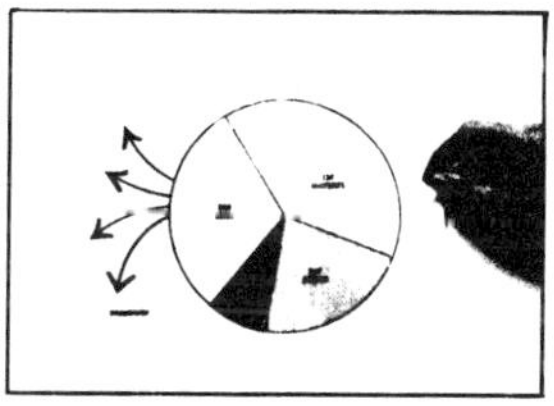

Framing the completed visual.

An overhead projection visual can be projected unframed, but there are good reasons why you should use frames. The frame blocks light around the edge of the visual; it adds rigidity for handling and storage; and provides a convenient border for writing notes. To frame your visuals simply follow these easy steps.

1. Lay frame upside-down on a flat surface.
2. Center transparency face down on the frame.
3. Tape all four corners to secure transparency. For added security, tape all four sides.

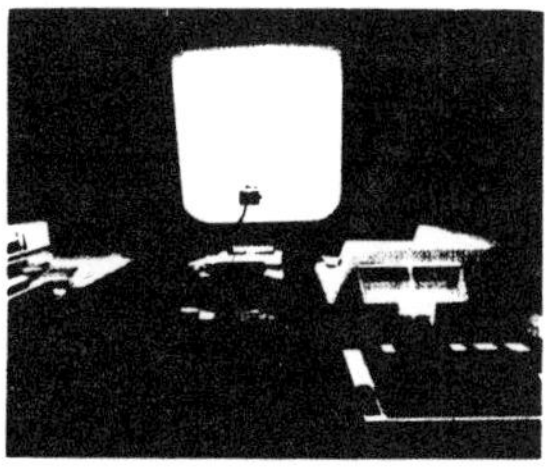

Checklist For Professional Presentations

1. Consider the size of your audience, then choose a meeting place that best accommodates them.
2. Make sure everyone in the audience knows the purpose of the meeting, then make sure your presentation fulfills this purpose.
3. Adjust the size and height of the projected image (on screen or wall) so everyone has a "front row" seat.
4. Keep the room lights on. The Tartan overhead projector produces bright images even in a fully-lighted room.
5. Always face your audience. With overhead projection, there is no need to turn your back to look at the screen.
6. Use the projector's on-off switch to control and direct your audience's attention.
7. When appropriate, invite questions and comments from the audience, and turn these into discussions.
8. Keep your visuals simple, concise and uncluttered so they can be easily read from the back of the room.
9. Make sure the meeting runs no longer than absolutely necessary to achieve its purpose.
10. For fast, easy preparation of visuals, for maximum flexibility during your presentation and for easy, trouble-free operation, use the Tartan Brand Visual Presentation Products System.

Figure 10-9 (cont'd)

11

Guidelines for Model Real Estate Sales Letters and Examples of Styles

Much of real estate involves handling correspondence. In this chapter, you will find examples of the following:

- Letters seeking listings
  A letter to neighboring families to help find buyers (Figure 11-1)
  A letter to "Wanted to Rent" advertisers (Figure 11-2)
  A letter congratulating a betrothed person (Figure 11-3)
  A letter congratulating a married couple (Figure 11-4)
  A letter for birth announcements (Figure 11-5)
- Adaptable form letters for increasing sales
  A letter to notify "cold" prospects of new listings (Figure 11-6)
  A letter to accompany a brief sent to prospects (Figure 11-7)
  A letter to weed out prospect files (Figure 11-8)
  A letter to follow up a property inspection (Figure 11-9)
  Letters announcing sales calls (Figures 11-10 and 11-11)

- Adaptable goodwill letters
  Greetings on the anniversary of purchase of a home (Figure 11-12)

Make carbon copies of all form letters and keep them in a three-ring binder. Invent your own categories and letters.

Because everyone's stationery is different, and because certain styles of letters are used for particular situations, you will find illustrated examples of:

- The *advertising style letter*, which omits the inside address because it is usually mass mailed and preprinted. It is flexible, adaptable to situation and letterhead, and may or may not be dated, indented, and signed (Figure 11-13).

A letter to neighboring families to help find buyers

Dear ____________________:

The Home Near You

At ____

Has New Owners

It was sold through our office to some folks we are sure you are going to like as neighbors.

If your home or some neighboring homes you know about might also be for sale, we would appreciate knowing of it. We have some more people who would like to locate in your neighborhood.

Why not give us a ring or drop in and tell us about it?

Yours very truly,

Courtesy of Hamline Twin City Real Estate Co., St. Paul, Minnesota.

Figure 11-1

- The *block style letter* indents the date and the complimentary close at the same tab. All else is flush left (Figure 11-14).
- The *indented style letter* indents the date and complimentary close at the same tab, and indents paragraphs (Figure 11-15).
- The *official style letter* indents the date and complimentary close at the same tab, but has the inside address flush left under the salutation. This is one of the most formal letter styles (Figure 11-16).
- The *press release* (Figure 11-17).
- A *news release checklist* (Figure 11-18).

A letter to "Wanted to Rent" advertisers

Dear ____________________:

May I suggest that you consider purchasing property instead of renting? The same dollars can buy you equity and possible profit potential.

Our office has many different kinds of listings from single-family residences to income property. There are situations where little or no down payment is needed or where newly established credit is acceptable.

Please give us the chance to help you spend your money as wisely as possible by calling for an appointment very soon.

Sincerely,

Figure 11-2

A letter congratulating a betrothed person

Dear ____________________:

Congratulations on your engagement!

We would be pleased to have a part in making your life together more pleasant by helping you find a place to rent or buy.

Please give us the opportunity of discussing your requirements by calling or stopping in.

Sincerely,

Figure 11-3

A letter congratulating a married couple

Dear New Mr. and Mrs.:

CONGRATULATIONS!

We would like to assist you in your search for a place to live—now and in the future.

Please let us suggest property.

With good wishes,

Figure 11-4

A letter for birth announcements

Dear Mom and Dad:

We wish your family happiness.

As the years pass and your living requirements change, please check with us.

Cordially,

Figure 11-5

A letter informing a "cold" prospect of a new listing

Dear ______________________:

I have not been able to reach you by telephone so I am writing to tell you that we have just listed a house with **reasonable** financing that meets your requirements for size and location.

Let's get together to discuss the property and details.

Please contact my secretary for an appointment.

Sincerely,

Figure 11-6

A letter to accompany a brief sent to prospects

Dear Sir:

We are pleased to present for your consideration the home located at

287 Blenheim Road
Columbus, Ohio

owned by Mr. and Mrs. Clarence L. Weaver.

Mr. and Mrs. Weaver are moving out of the city. They expect to be in their new nome by November 1, and possession can be given on the property at about that time.

All estimates, statements, and descriptions in the enclosed brief are correct to the best of our knowledge and, while not guaranteed, were obtained from sources we deem reliable.

We shall appreciate your courtesy if, when this brief has served its purpose, you will return it to us.

Thank you for your interest in this property.

Cordially yours,

Courtesy of Henry E. Worley, Columbus, Ohio.

Figure 11-7

A letter to weed out prospect files

Dear ______________________:

We saw you in September when we looked at the duplex on Telegraph Hill, and the 4-plex in the Marina.

Income properties of all sizes and prices (as well as estate sales) are always being listed.

If you (or friends) are still in the market, stop by or call to talk type, location, financing, and appointments.

Sincerely,

Figure 11-8

A letter to follow property inspection

Dear ____________________:

When I returned to the office after we inspected the property at ____________________________________
____,
I made the following list so we could get a complete picture.

PROS	CONS
______________	______________
______________	______________
______________	______________
______________	______________

After you have had a chance to evaluate and add or subtract ideas, please call me to discuss these topics.

If this turns out not to be for you, we can look at other properties.

Sincerely,

Figure 11-9

A letter announcing a sales call

Dear ______________________:

Recently I drove an out-of-town couple around your neighborhood to house-hunt. We saw your "For Sale by Owner" sign and rang the bell but there was no answer.

Please call me to discuss particulars.

If it is out of the scope of these buyers, possibly other purchasers would be interested.

Please contact our office.

Sincerely,

Figure 11-10

A letter announcing a sales call

Dear ____________________:

It has been some time since we had the pleasure of talking to you about your personal housing problems.

According to our files, we last saw you at our office when you inquired about the house at 269 Van Buren Street—the one with the large landscaped yard and the outdoor fireplace.

As we recollect, there were a few things about that house that did not quite come up to your family's needs. Since it is our wish to be of service to those who consult us, we are always on the alert to satisfy individual requirements. We now have a listing that will interest you, I am sure.

I would like to drop by your home Thursday evening around 7:30 to tell you about this outstanding home. Please phone me if this time is not convenient and we'll fix a more suitable hour.

Sincerely,

Courtesy of Donald J. Dockry, Green Bay, Wisconsin.

Figure 11-11

Greetings on the anniversary of purchase of a home

Dear Mr. and Mrs. ________:

Birthday Greetings! You bought your home one year ago today.

We hope you have been happy and wish you a pleasant future.

Please call if you decide to purchase other property.

Cordially yours,

Dear Mr. ________:

It has been almost a year since you purchased your home at ________ Street. By this time you have had extended opportunity to appraise the wisdom of your investment, and we sincerely trust that you continue satisfied with our recommendation.

We appreciate the confidence you placed in our office. Whenever we can be of further service to you or any of your friends, we shall be pleased to have you call us.

Sincerely yours,

Courtesy of W. Kelton Evans, Inc., Madison, New Jersey.

Figure 11-12

Advertising style letter

LETTERHEAD

This newsletter is to familiarize you with certain aspects of property insurance with which we feel you should be well versed.

Key to the purchase is that the owner of the property understands the co-insurance clause and the difference between property coverage on the replacement cost or actual cash value basis. Insurance values deal with what it would cost today to replace or repair damaged property in the event of an insured loss. This figure is usually different from the market value, which is the selling price.

Replacement cost coverage reimburses for repair or replacement of the damaged property without deduction for depreciation.

Actual cash value contracts reimburse, with a deduction for depreciation.

To further clarify, I'll suggest the following example. A 7.5-year-old roof is blown off a house by windstorm. The bill to replace the roof is $3500. An insurance contract on a replacement cost basis will reimburse for replacing the roof—$3500 less applicable deductible.

On the actual cash value basis, the contract will reimburse $1,750 less any applicable deductible. Reason: The average life of any residential roof is 15 years. This one was 7.5 years old and the owner only had 7.5 years left. The depreciation factor is 50%. This principle is the same for commercial and residential property.

Basically, all one has to do is purchase enough coverage for replacement at today's construction levels for the replacement cost coverage.

The co-insurance clause is the most misunderstood clause in the insurance industry. It's difficult to explain, but I'll try. The standard co-insurance clause is 80%. A property owner must purchase an amount of insurance equal to 80% of the value of his property; if he does, losses will be paid in full up to the limit of liability purchased. Coverage can be either on the replacement cost basis or actual cash value basis; whichever, 80% of the value must be purchased.

Example: Property worth $50,000. Minimum amount of insurance purchased is $40,000. If

Figure 11-13

2

purchaser buys a lower limit he will suffer a penalty in the event of a loss. Assume \$20,000 purchased as limit on the property valued at \$50,000. Now a \$10,000 loss occurs. Adjustment is as follows:

$$\frac{\text{Amount of Insurance Carried}}{\text{Amount Required}} \times \$\text{ loss} = \text{Payment}$$

$$\frac{\$20{,}000}{\$40{,}000} \times \$10{,}000 = \$5000$$

As one can see, the penalty for non-compliance with the co-insurance clause can be brutal.

Now that we're aware of the two basic facts, we can proceed further. Residential owners normally protect their property under a homeowners contract. There are a number of different forms available with different insuring agreements providing varying degrees of protection. The homeowners contract provides both property and personal liability insurance coverages and should be designed by a professional insurance agent or broker to meet specific needs. This type of policy is generally considered a package policy providing coverage for the dwelling, personal property, additional living expense, and liability. Normally, flood and earthquake coverage are not included and must be purchased separately.

Similar types of contracts are available to meet commercial needs.

The forms and types of coverage are numerous and cannot be explained satisfactorily in a one- or two-pagé typewritten document. Each individal case is different, with programs designed to meet those needs.

Suffice it to say that every property owner needs to purchase public liability insurance to protect him from suits arising from negligent acts. Today, liability judgments can be astronomical and substantially impair one's financial condition.

Please call us if we can be of assistance.

Figure 11-13 (cont'd)

The block style letter

Ridgewood Development, Inc.

August 23, 19--

Mr. Jim Corbett
Pacific Federal Savings
690 Newport Center Drive
Newport Beach, California 92660

Dear Jim:

Pursuant to your request I have prepared a brief historical summary of Ridgewood Development, Inc.

Ridgewood Development, Inc. was incorporated in April of 19-- and immediately started construction of Tract 31273 which was part of a 64 acre acquisition from Umark, Inc. The Company was founded by Harriet Frizelle and Bill Harris and had gross sales of approximately $1.8 million in its first full year of operation. During its second year sales increased to approximately $9.6 million with a gross pre-tax profit of $1.2 million. For the year ended March 31, 19--, sales were a record $13.3 million with a pre-tax profit of $1.7 million.

Ridgewood Associates, Ltd. was started in July of 19-- for the purpose of acquisition and development of approximately 85 acres in West Covina of which Tract 33663, 33664, 33665, 34894 and 34895 are a part. In this partnership, Ridgewood Development, Inc. is a 63% general partner and Housing Capital Corporation, Washington D.C. is a 35% limited partner. The other 2% is held 1% by Harriet Frizelle and 1% by Fred Armstrong, but only for the legal convenience of the partnership. Those 1% interests were signed over to Ridgewood Development, Inc. in 19--.

In addition to the above Ridgewood has recently acquired Tract 9565 in Riverside. Sixty two single family detached units, including three models, will be built on this property. Construction of these units will commence in September 19-- with final deliveries in early July 19--.

We trust this information will answer any questions you may have about Ridgewood. If additional information is required, please do not hesitate contacting me.

Very truly yours,

Michael J. Bibin
Vice President

MJB:kk

3187 C Airway Avenue, Costa Mesa, California 92626

Figure 11-14

The indented style letter

CENTURY 21

CLEVENGER REALTORS®
4225 Park Blvd.
Oakland, California 94602
(415) 530-4373

Glenn D. Fink, Broker

Sales Associates
Marilyn Armstrong
Alice Clark
Joe Cohan
Mayme Cohan
Milt Cole
Eleanore Farrell
Jack Farrell
Anita Holland
Lani Junas
Jini Kelley
Julie Marchman
Margit Muck
Bette Pennington
Cindi Viale
Jane Yoon

Dorothy Hanft, Secy

May 15, 19--

Mrs. Carol Johnson
Personnel Manager
Universal Company
127 Industrial Way
Anytown, TX 17397

Dear Mrs. Johnson:

Thank you so much for the opportunity to meet with you to offer our services in transferring your employees. Our vast network of independently owned CENTURY 21 offices can save your company people time and money by easing their relocation and house hunting problems.

Enclosed is literature on our company and CENTURY 21, along with some of my business cards.

We would be glad to give information about the San Francisco Oakland Bay Area to those employees who are definitely moving here as well as those who are considering relocation.

We look forward to assisting your employees in a smooth transition with our professional manner.

Sincerely,

CENTURY 21
Clevenger Realtors

Lani Junas
Sales Associate

LJ:dh

encs.

REALTOR® "Each office is independently owned and operated"

Figure 11-15

The official style letter

THE HIBERNIA BANK
MAIN OFFICE
201 CALIFORNIA STREET AT FRONT
SAN FRANCISCO, CALIFORNIA 94111

WRITER'S DIRECT DIAL NUMBER

(415) 565-7416 May 1, 19--

Dear Mr. Davis:

With great pride, I wish to advise you that I have joined The Hibernia Bank as head of our newly formed Construction Lending Division.

In developing a Construction Lending Division at Hibernia, we recognize our ability to offer the expertise and responsiveness you deserve in meeting your needs. Whether these needs are in the area of tract or commercial real estate lending, Hibernia will provide quick and effective service.

Because we recognize that we are a regional bank and we desire to grow with quality developers with whom we can relate, we would make a great team.

I look forward to visiting with you soon and discussing specific ways we can benefit each other. In the meantime, should a need arise, please call me at the above number.

Very truly yours,

Michael W. Kelly

Michael W. Kelly
Vice President
Construction Lending Division

Mr. John Davis
President
The Builders, Inc.
1005 Bay Street
San Francisco, CA 90109

Figure 11-16

The press release*

TO: RELEASE DATE:

FROM: PERSONAL CONTACT:

The Press Release can begin as above on plain paper, but general use is letterhead with information under and/or a cover letter. Always double space. If there are many pages, end all but the last with -MORE- alone on a line 1 inch from the bottom and number each page. Always indicate the end of the release—the usual end is # # # alone on the line below the last line of typing.

The release should contain the who, what, where, when, how and why of real estate news which is interesting to the public. This form from Jackson Cross is used for pertinent information when a piece of property changes hands.

Topics which make interesting press releases include (but certainly are not limited to)*:

Real estate firm enlarges its office
President of real estate firm makes rental vacancy study
Real estate firm reports volume of total sales
Broker's client begins to build unusual houses
Dozen dwellings to be ready in May
Two exhibit homes now open for inspection
Managers appointed for three buildings
Broker rents apartment to prominent person
Mortgage broker arranges for refinancing of property
Appraiser's opinion aids court in reducing assessment
Historical site, held by one family for many years, is sold
1,000 trees planted in a housing project
Store building scheduled for prominent street
Real estate company to give solar energy seminars
Developer plans 10 acre low rent housing project

# # #

Figure 11-17

*Topics from the book, *The Real Estate Office Secretary's Handbook*, by Lillian Doris, © 1953, 1966, by Prentice-Hall, Inc. Published by Prentice-Hall, Inc., Englewood Cliffs, New Jersey 07632.

A news release checklist

When a property has been leased or sold, this form is sent to the salesperson involved. He/she completes the requested information and returns it to Marketing. This form is then handed over to our advertising agency for a written release.

Industrial - Office - Commercial

1. State whom Jackson-Cross represented.
2. Name of Lessor or Seller.
3. Name of Lessee or Buyer.
4. Complete description of premises sold or leased.
5. Scope of planned alterations.
6. Nature of Lessee's or Buyer's business (get from him if unknown, usually very cooperative for the free publicity).
7. Where moving from, if new to Philadelphia area.
8. Price or gross rent, if substantial ($100,000+).
9. Cooperating broker, if any.
10. For industrial—size of building, square feet, number of floors.
11. Financing (PIDC, etc.).

Courtesy
Jackson-Cross
JACKSON-CROSS COMPANY • **REALTORS®**
2000 Market Street, Philadelphia, PA 19103

Figure 11-18

12

How to Prepare Real Estate Forms and Mailers

"Preparation" falls into three categories in this chapter.

1. The idea stage and setting it down on paper, showing:

- Design tricks (Figure 12-1)
- Space savers, problems and solutions (Figure 12-2)
- Two-sided printing (Figure 12-3)
- Ways to assemble self-mailers (Figure 12-4)
- Ways to fold a form (Figure 12-5)

2. The coordination stage, showing:

- Photo order form (Figure 12-6)
- Form used for computer company when requesting mailing labels (Figure 12-7)

3. The concretizing of the idea—the printing—showing:

- How to prepare camera ready copy for either the final copier original or printer's original (Figure 12-8)
- What to use for best photocopier reproduction (Figure 12-9)
- Tips for running special photocopier originals (Figure 12-10)

- Special applications on copy machines (Figure 12-11)
- Possible copier machine end results (Figure 12-12)
- How to work with crystal film stencils (Figure 12-13)

These are basic "how-to's." An idea for a file is to keep a separate folder for each project step—including art work in an envelope inside the file or in an envelope file between cardboard—and copies of invoices for comparison if more of the same are needed or a similar project must be priced. Most printers and quick print shops give price lists describing kinds of printing and deadlines.

In many large cities there are wholesale paper companies which will establish an account for a minimum purchase. Some even have art departments with salespeople who will call on your office to show you their lines of appropriate papers for special projects. There is a possible price differential at the printer if you supply your own paper.

Some of the uses of forms and brochures include:

- Announcements (new project open for inspection, open house, open apartment, model apartment redecorated, new real estate company office)
- Lecture series or slide presentation being offered by real estate company
- Descriptions of properties (farm land catalogs, business opportunity listings, new developments, commercial and industrial properties, rentals)
- Space available in new complex (residential, apartment, business, shopping malls, arts and cultural center)
- For listings
- To pre-sell properties before a specific appointment
- To follow up a sales presentation
- To create an image
- In response to inquiries about signs on properties or businesses
- In answer to a newspaper or magazine ad

Many of these presentations are shown at the property or at the real estate office.

If the project is prepared by an advertising agency, the work order and, most likely, the mailing responsibility will go through the secretary. If the project is prepared by your office, the secretary will be involved either directly or as a liaison in the planning and coordination of typing and/or typesetting, art work and/or photographs, layout, printing, and distribution. The mechanics are illustrated here as a guide along with a bibliography of postal source material, texts, advertising, and mail order directories and periodicals for ideas and statistics. There is also a list of ways to save postage on mailers and a list of tips for creating and maintaining mailing lists.

DESIGN TRICKS

BOX DESIGN

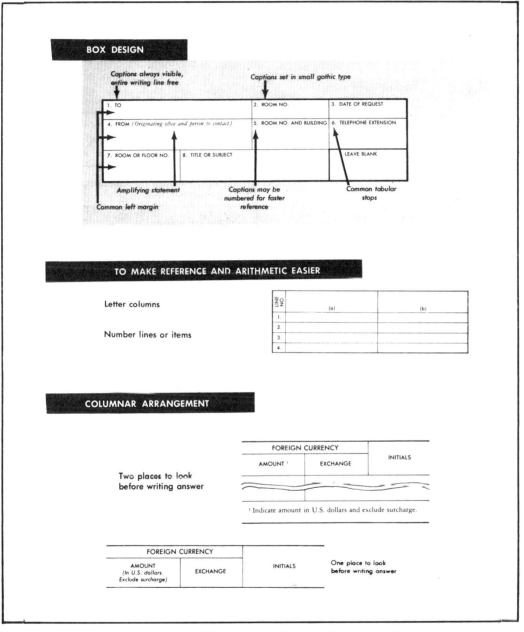

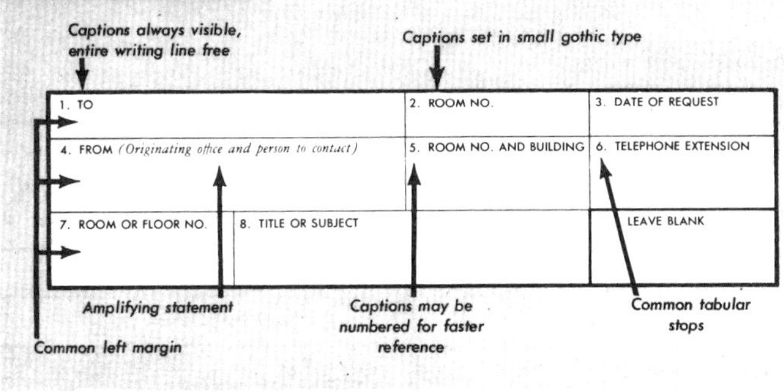

TO MAKE REFERENCE AND ARITHMETIC EASIER

Letter columns

Number lines or items

LINE NO.	(a)	(b)
1.		
2.		
3.		
4.		

COLUMNAR ARRANGEMENT

Two places to look before writing answer

FOREIGN CURRENCY		INITIALS
AMOUNT [1]	EXCHANGE	

[1] Indicate amount in U.S. dollars and exclude surcharge.

FOREIGN CURRENCY		INITIALS
AMOUNT (In U.S. dollars. Exclude surcharge)	EXCHANGE	

One place to look before writing answer

From U.S. Government Records Management Handbook: Forms Design.

Figure 12-1

SPACE SAVERS

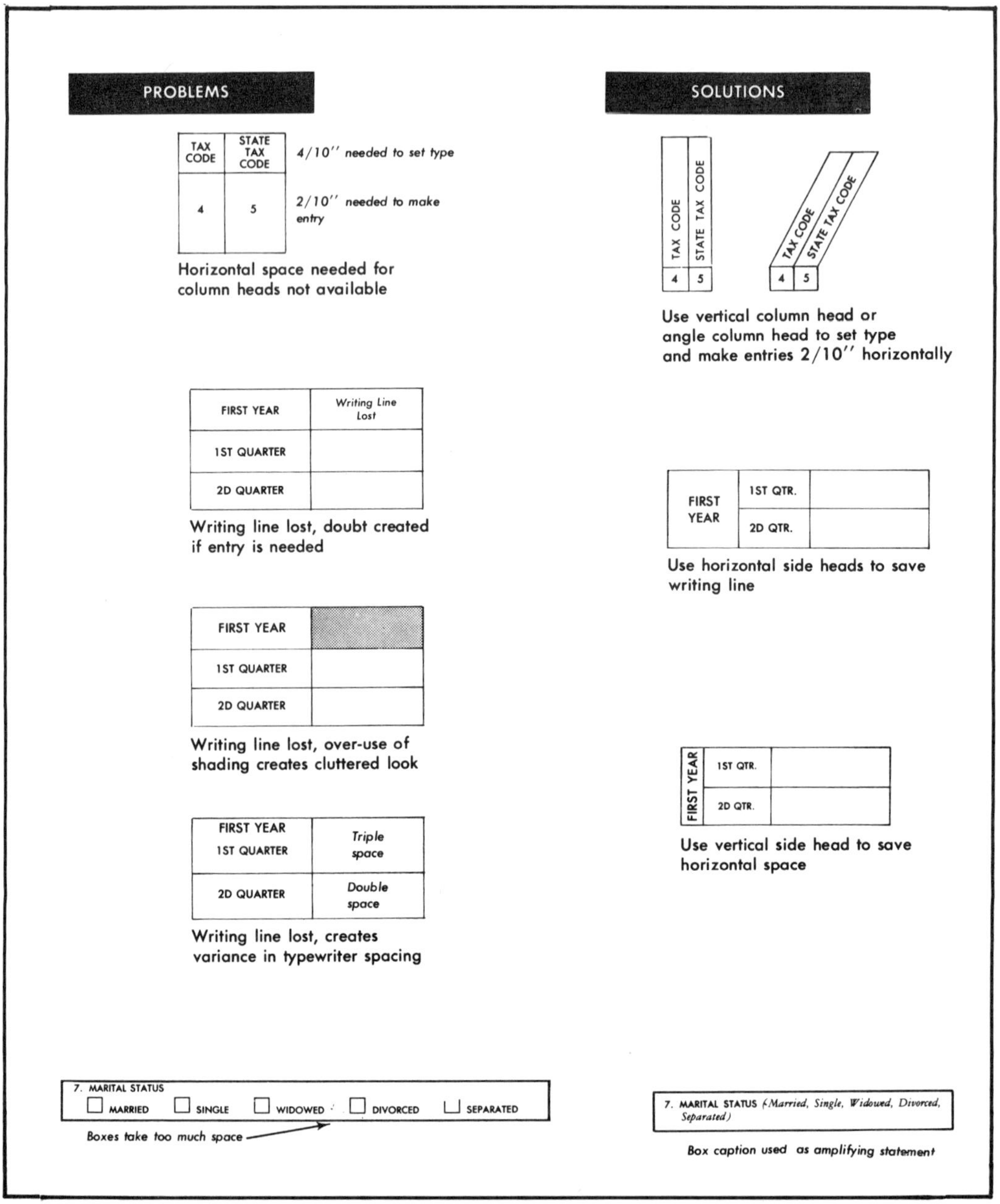

From U.S. Government Records Management Handbook: Forms Design.

Figure 12-2

TWO-SIDED PRINTING

HEAD TO HEAD

- Head (top) of front to head (top) of back

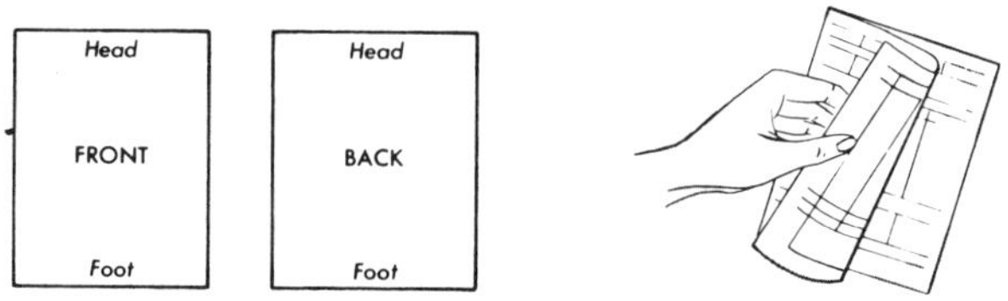

HEAD TO FOOT

- Head (top) of front to foot (bottom) of back

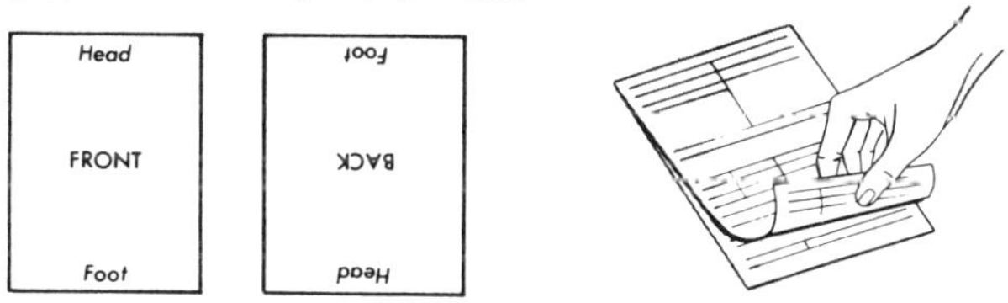

HEAD TO SIDE

- Head (top) of front to right of back

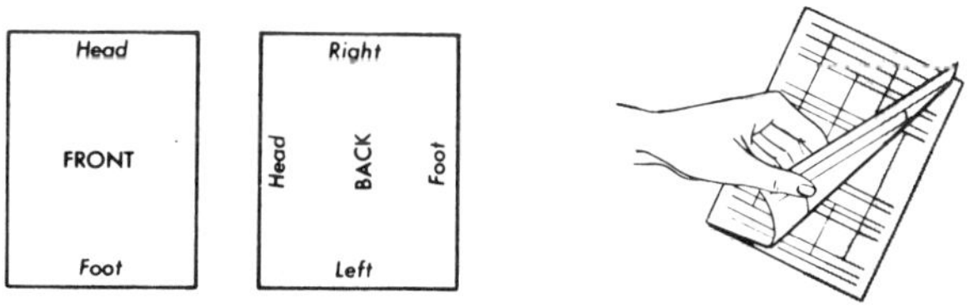

- Head (top) of front to left of back

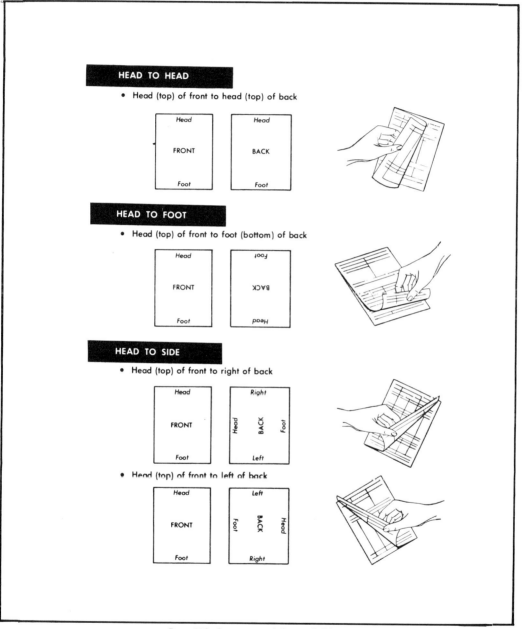

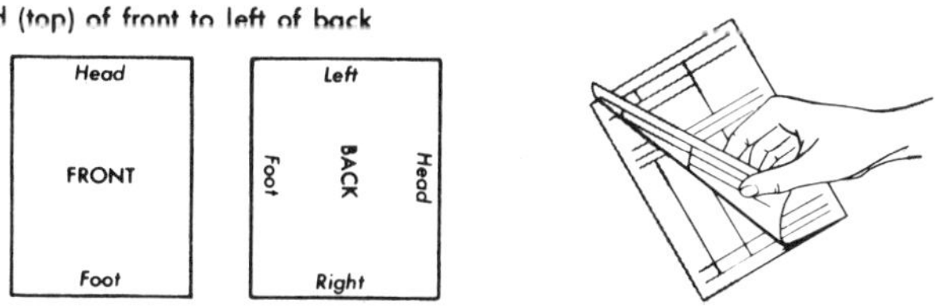

From U.S. Government Records Management Handbook: Forms Design.

Figure 12-3

WAYS TO ASSEMBLE SELF-MAILERS

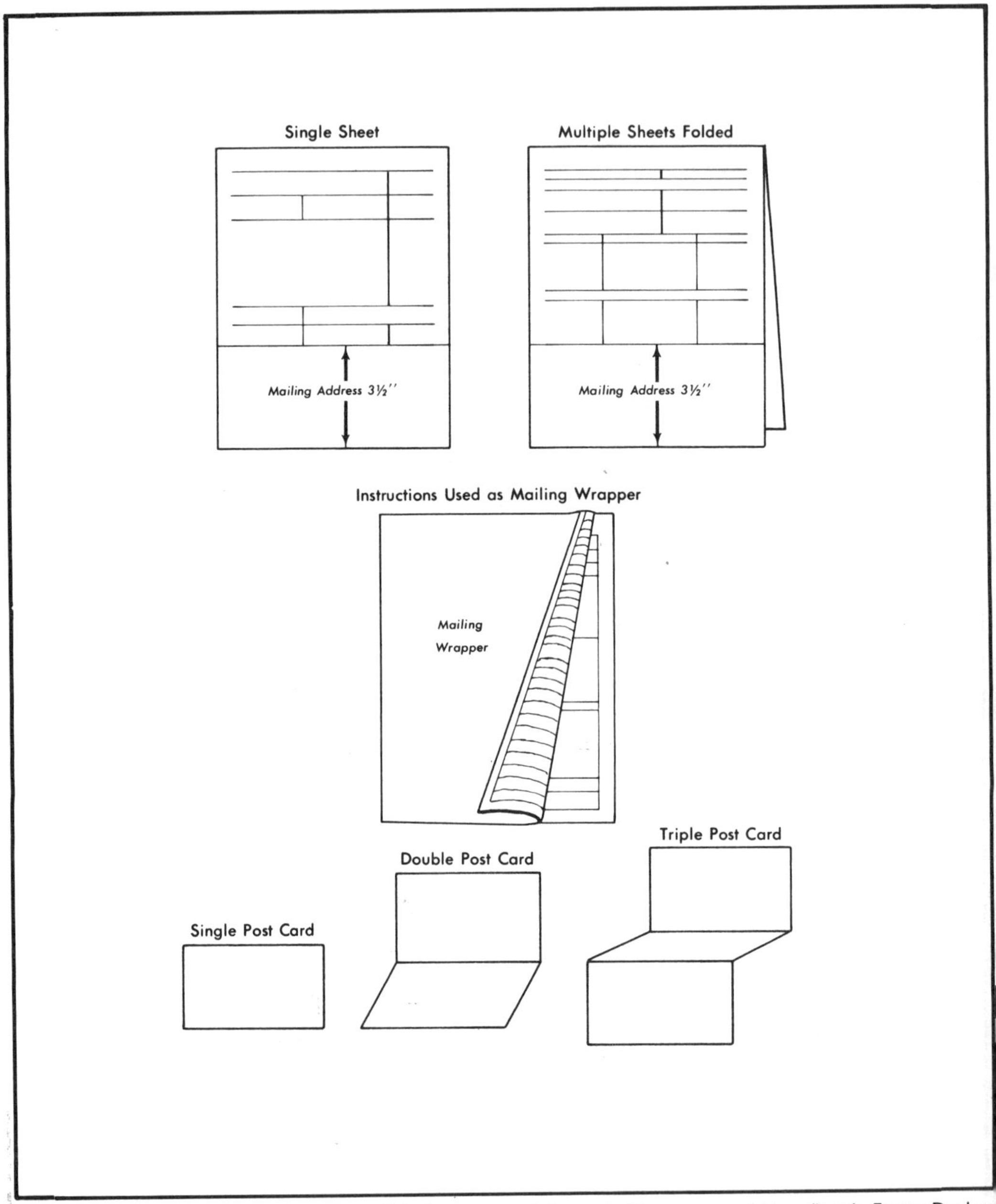

From U.S. Government Records Management Handbook: Forms Design

Figure 12-4

WAYS TO FOLD A FORM

TOP AND BOTTOM

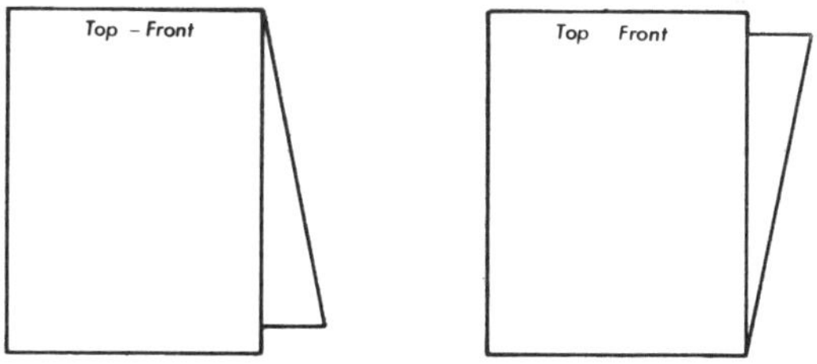

- Facilitates typing
- Generally printed head to foot
- May be folded allowing for binding
- May be used for duplicate forms by identical printing on pages one and three. Perforation on fold for separation

OTHER FOLDS

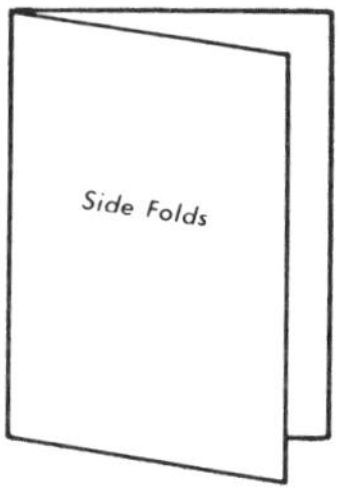

- Not recommended for typing since it is bulky
- Hard to insert carbons
- Used for handwritten forms, when only an original is needed
- Printed head to head

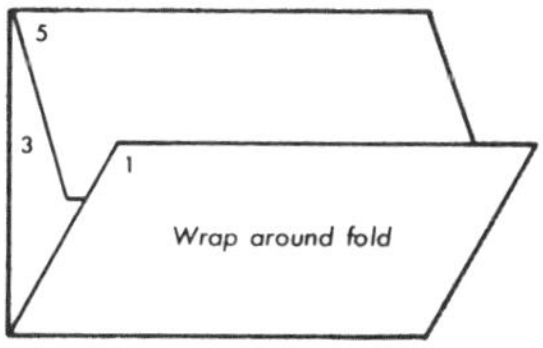

- Used for six page forms
- Facilitates typing
- Printed head to foot

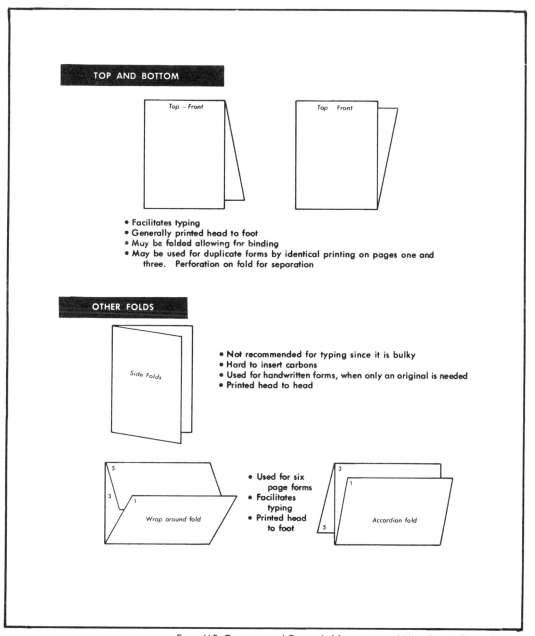

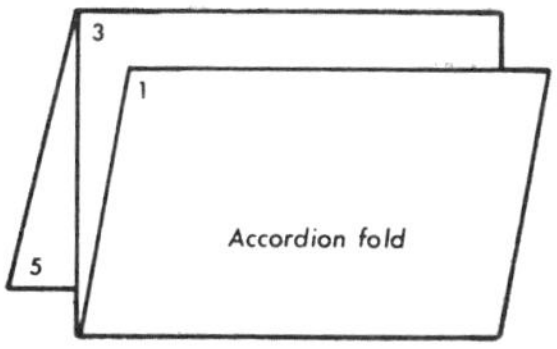

From U.S. Government Records Management Handbook: Forms Design.

Figure 12-5

Listing No. ________

Salesperson ________

№ 0019

PHOTO ORDER FORM

Date ____________ Date Due ____________

Client ____

Building Name ____

Address ____

Client Location (if within the building) ____________________

Name of Contact at Building ____________________________

Do employees know building is for sale? ____________________

Photos: Interior (Number ________ B&W ______ Color ______)

Exterior (Number ________ B&W ______ Color ______)

Aerial (Number ________ B&W ______ Color ______)

Slides (Number ________)

Final Use of Photos ____________________________________

Unusual features of property to be included in photo __________

____

____

When is sun on building ? ____________________________

Should J-C sign be kept out of photo? ____________________

Directions to building (from Center City) ____________________

____

____

____

____

____

Do Not Write Below This Line

- -

Amount Approved ____________

Charge To ____________

When a photograph is needed for a brochure to be printed, the salesperson handling the property must fill out this form and coordinate the photography through Marketing. After the form is completed by the salesperson, the original is sent to our photographer (after negotiating a price with him), and a copy is put into our "tickler" file for follow-up. When the photographs are received, the copy is retained in our files.

Courtesy
Jackson-Cross
JACKSON-CROSS COMPANY • **REALTORS®**
2000 Market Street, Philadelphia, PA 19103

Figure 12-6

JACKSON-CROSS COMPANY
2000 MARKET STREET
PHILADELPHIA, PENNSYLVANIA 19103

Nº 299

DATE________/DATE DUE________

LISTING______________________ SALES PERSON ______________________

SEND TO: ____

1. ______________________________ 7. ______________________________

2. ______________________________ 8. ______________________________

3. ______________________________ 9. ______________________________

4. ______________________________ 10. ______________________________

5. ______________________________ 11. ______________________________

6. ______________________________ 12. ______________________________

****

FOR Jackson-Cross OFFICE USE ONLY

BROCHURE: _____(NO)______(YES - DESC.)-______________________________

____

____

ENCL: (NO) ______________ POSTAGE: (BULK)________ SIZE: (SELF-MAILER)__________

(LTR.)______________ (1st) ________ (9 x 12)__________

(MEMO)______________ (#10)__________

TOTAL # ______________________ DATE DUE: ______________________

W/P - $______________________ COMPLETED______________________ W P

SENT OUT ON - ______________________ M L

Mlg. Hse. - $______________________ SENT OUT TO - ______________________ H S

P.O. # - ______________________ E

Postage - $______________________ DATE MAILED - ______________________ W P

(1st Class Postage - $_________)

Misc. - $____

Courtesy
Jackson-Cross
JACKSON-CROSS COMPANY • REALTORS®
2000 Market Street, Philadelphia, PA 19103

Figure 12-7

HOW TO PREPARE CAMERA READY COPY

If you use a typewriter to prepare your copy, make sure you get a dark, even impression on white paper. A carbon or mylar ribbon will give the best results. A new, or relatively new, ink type ribbon will also produce a good job.

Typewriter keys must be clean. However, if your typewriter still does not give you a sharp image, reverse a piece of carbon paper in order to get two images: one in front and the other in back of the sheet of paper.

When original copy is made from paste-ups, position the paste-up onto a white sheet of paper. If guide lines are used to position paste-ups, use a very light green, blue, or yellow pencil as these colors drop out of the picture and do not show on the printed copy.

Rubber cement, glue stick, or cellophane-type "double-stick tape" should be used when pasting up. A small amount of cement or a small piece of tape under the paste-up is sufficient and facilitates repositioning of paste-up if needed. It is not necessary to seal edges down.

Copy in black or red will photograph and print best. All other colors, when deep and dark enough, will reproduce with good results.

Newspaper clippings: Although not ideal, these will give satisfactory results. The paper from these clippings may cause a slight background to appear on the printed copies. Magazine clippings give better results.

Quality in reproducing black and white photographs clipped from newspapers, magazines, etc., will depend on their density or contrast. Avoid colors which are too deep if using preprinted color photos from these two sources.

Unscreened photographs, not previously broken into dots, either black and white or color, will give very poor results. A screened print, velox, must be made from the original before attempting to print it.

Use a white correction fluid, available at most graphic arts supply shops or stationery stores, to get rid of unwanted marks, smears, smudges, shadow lines, etc.

If still in doubt . . . ask your printer before preparing your material.

Courtesy PIP—Postal Instant Press of San Francisco.

Figure 12-8

For Best Reproduction, Use	Additional Information
• Smooth bond paper	Rough paper may produce shadows on the copies. (Avoid erasable papers.)
• 20-80 pound paper for originals	
• Originals unwrinkled, torn or folded, without bent corners, and undamaged from staples	
• Clean corrections	If you use correction fluid, be sure it is completely dry before typing over it. Add thinner to the liquid if it does not spread easily.
• Non-reproducible blue pencil	Should be used for notes on your originals which you don't want to appear on your copies.
• Avoid yellow highlighter	It will appear very dark on your copies.
• Correction tape with beveled edges	
• Uniform page numbering	Each page should be numbered in the same place. Always number your two-sided originals so that the fronts are odd-numbered and the backs are even.
• Adequate margins	At least ¼″ on all sides. If you will place your copies in a binder, leave 1¼″ margins.
• Originals all same size	If machine feeds automatically.

Figure 12-9

Running Special Originals	Additional Information
• Copies can be made from colored originals	Except goldenrod.
• Light pencil copy, color-on-color materials, carbonless blue impressions, and weak carbon copies	Can be reproduced to make good, legible copies.
• 3-dimensional objects	Can be copied.
• Bound volumes	Can be copied.
• Oversize originals	Reduce/duplicate large bulky documents down to a more easily handled size (Charts, Diagrams, Computer Printouts, Ledger Sheets).
• Any original up to 14″ × 18″	One big original, a grouping of smaller originals, or a 14″ × 18″ segment of any size original.
• Type lengthy documents on oversize paper	11″ × 14″ instead of 8½ × 11″—then reduce duplicate down to standard 8½″ × 11″; giving more data on fewer sheets (a 100 page report becomes 64 pages).
• Use overlays to add, delete, or change information on your originals	
• Documents with printing to the edge of the page	Request "98% reduction."
• Use blank paper for originals which will be copied on letterhead	

Figure 12-10

Special Applications	Additional Information
• Copy machines which operate either off-line from magnetic tape or on-line directly from computers	
• Computer output can be reproduced on ordinary 8½″ × 11″ paper	
• Overlay capability is available	Permits simultaneous printing of the output data and the form on which it appears. An overlay providing any type of fixed-format information—headings, logos, vertical and horizontal lines—solves the problem of maintaining an expensive inventory of preprinted forms.
• A microfiche printer	Copies and enlarges directly from standard 4″ × 6″ microfiche onto ordinary paper at the rate of nearly a page a second. The microfiche film sheets each contain up to 98 images and any number of images can be selected for copying.
• An engineering print system	Automatically reproduces bulky engineering drawings and other technical information directly from originals, reduces them to easy-to-handle sizes, and folds and sorts them into complete packages ready for immediate distribution.
• There is a printer which fills a variety of engineering needs	From engineering drawing reproduction and old drawing restoration to the creation of completely new drawings from paste-up originals.
• There is a microfilm enlarger printer	Designed primarily to enlarge and print engineering drawings automatically from aperture cards.
• There is also a printer used for engineering	Can take any original as wide as 36″, as long as 120″ or more, and up to ⅛″ thick. Originals can be single sheets or board mounted. Copies can be made on paper up to 18″ × 60″ and it reproduces copies same size by dialing in a choice of reduction ratios ranging from 95% down to 45% of original size.
• And a companion engineering printer	Accepts all types of microfilmed originals as intermediates for producing prints.

Figure 12-11

Possible End Results	Additional Information
• Position of writing on copies can be raised or lowered	
• Preprinted forms	
• Any paper stock between 16-110 lbs. and between 5″ × 8″ and 8½″ × 14″	
• Mixed weights	Card stock can be used for durable covers.
• Colored paper	Dividers can be copied on colored paper.
• Documents (charts, forms, etc.) can be copied onto oversize paper	
• Two-sided copying	Be sure to run the second side within one half-hour after running the first side, to avoid wrinkles.
• Your job can be run on paper that is punched, perforated, reinforced, and on gummed labels	
• Your job can be made into tear-aways to your specifications after being printed	
• Use a copy sorter	Automatically collate up to 50 sets of multi-page reports that are ready for binding and distribution.
• Documents can be fan folded by machine	
• The finished copies can be stapled and stacked by machine	

Used with permission of Xerox Corporation.

Figure 12-12

HOW TO WORK WITH CRYSTAL (FILM) STENCILS

HOW TO WORK WITH CRYSTAL (FILM) STENCILS

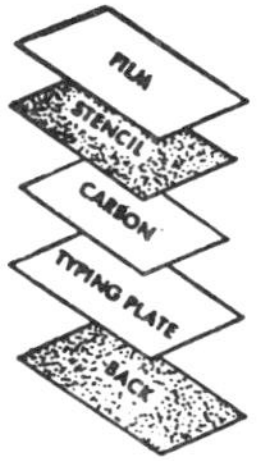

1. MEDIUM COPY

Remove interleaving sheet between stencil and film. *Insert carbon (coated side up) directly under stencil. Place typing plate between carbon and stencil back.

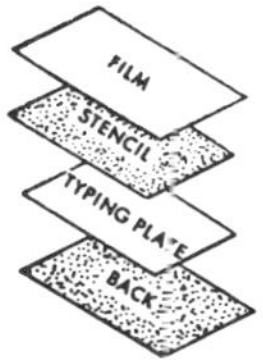

2. LIGHT COPY

(best for bond paper duplicating) Remove interleaving sheet between stencil and film. *Insert typing plate only, directly under stencil.

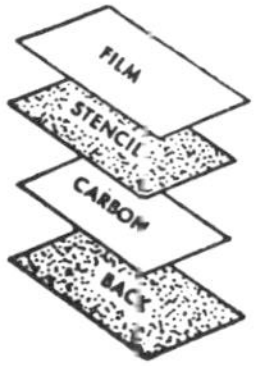

3. HEAVY COPY

Remove interleaving sheet between stencil and film. *Insert carbon only (coated side up) directly under stencil.

- CORRECTIONS

Do not remove stencil from typewriter. Detach film from top of stencil. Apply correction fluid on stencil and allow to dry. Reattach film to stencil. Then type over corrected spot.

- STYLUS WORK

Remove top film, then insert a drawing plate directly under stencil. Write or draw directly on the stencil itself.

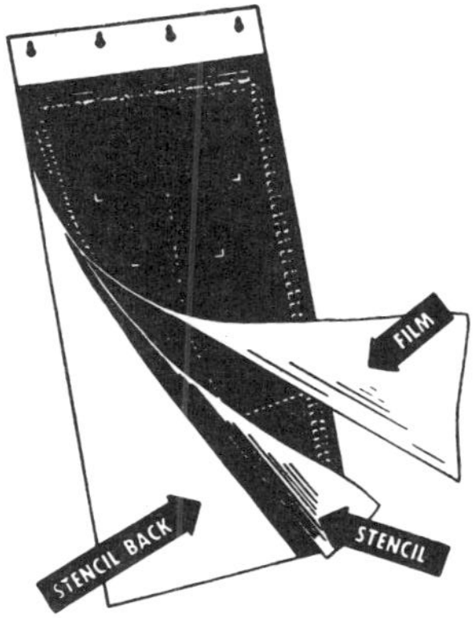

DO NOT REMOVE FILM
FROM STENCIL UNTIL
TYPING IS COMPLETED

After stencil is cut, tear off along perforation line—the remaining film covers the glue line. This completely eliminates any possibility of glue on operator's hands, glue on mimeograph machine, and sticking together of stencils when filed away.

SPECIAL STENCILS

These three special stencil sheets have special guide marks to show you exactly where to type when you use the 4 page folder stencil, the newspaper stencil, or the addressing stencil. Ask for these stencils by name. We will be glad to send you samples of some with complete instructions.

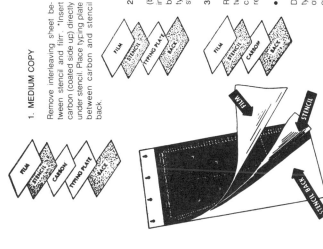

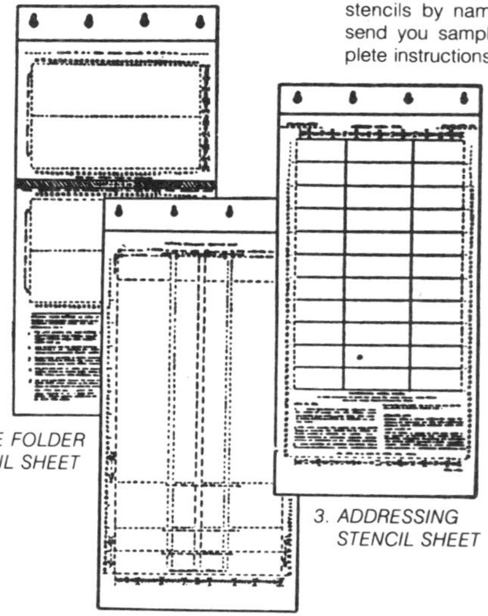

1. 4 PAGE FOLDER STENCIL SHEET

2. SCHOOL NEWSPAPER STENCIL SHEET

3. ADDRESSING STENCIL SHEET

STENCILS FOR ALL MAKES
OF DUPLICATORS

In addition to making stencils for all American model machines, we also manufacture stencils for all foreign make machines such as Gestetner, Roneo, and Rex Rotary duplicators.

Courtesy of Frankel Manufacturing Company,
285 Rio Grande Blvd., Denver, Colorado 80201.

Figure 12-13

MONEY SAVING IDEAS FOR MAILERS

- Be thoroughly familiar with postal rates. The post office will supply current rate cards.
- Take advantage of postal clinics to keep up-to-date with new rules and techniques.
- Check scales regularly. Nine pennies equal one ounce.
- Consider alternate payment modes for postage: precanceled stamps, postage meters, permit indicia.
- Take advantage of meter setting in your office. Slight charge.
- Consider possible use of first-class permit imprint when pieces are identical in weight and size. Envelopes can be printed months in advance.
- Use "Address Correction Requested" and "Return Postage Guaranteed" on various kinds of third- and fourth-class mail, and random use on all or selected first-class mailings.
- Fold mail to letter size.
- Use business reply instead of prestamped envelopes when minimal return is expected.
- Be sure post cards are proper size.
- Use a single cover for collective mailing pieces going to the same person or same address.
- Use certified rather than registered mail when contents have no monetary value.
- Use prominently identified, large first-class envelopes. If plain envelopes are used, mark both sides to ensure the desired result. (Large envelopes are sometimes handled as third-class matter if not identified.)
- Program mailing releases. This provides a more even workload.
- Stay in close contact with local post office customer service representative for advice on postal products, services, and current procedures.

TIPS FOR CREATING A MAILING LIST

Sources

- Your own customers
- Your own suppliers
- People who have called on ads
- Newspaper announcements of births, engagements, marriages, wedding anniversaries, deaths (also available from public records at courthouse)
- Assessor's rolls
- Voter registration rolls
- Building and remodeling permits
- Telephone directories
- Reverse directories
- City directories
- Business and industrial directories
- Chamber of Commerce directories
- Dunn and Bradstreet's Million Dollar Directory and Middle Market Directory
- Credit rating books
- Thomas's Register
- MacRae's Blue Books
- The Standard Directory of Advertisers
- Poor's Register
- The Who's Who
- The social registers
- Association membership rosters
- Labor organizations
- Religious organizations
- Convention lists
- Subscription lists
- Business services lists
- Construction lists

If mailing lists are to be purchased (usual price *approximately* $50 per thousand) check the library for the catalogs of lists available by different business list brokers.

If you rent a list, regardless of the source, it is delivered to you on labels or in envelopes supplied by you.

BIBLIOGRAPHY

Be certain to use the latest editions of these books.

Postal Sources

Your local Postmaster has these and other helpful free booklets readily available to help your mailing operation and to make sure you're as up-to-date as possible.

1. *A Consumer's Guide to Postal Services and Products*—Publication #201.
2. *Guidelines for Designing and Printing Envelopes for Machine Processing*—Notice 23E.
3. *Zip Code Directory.*
4. *What Mailers Should Do to Get the Best Service*—Publication #153.
5. *Express Mail Service*—Publication #163.
   Express Mail Here Today ... There Tomorrow. We Guarantee It!—Notice 43.
6. *Addressing for OCR—Optical Character Reading*—Publication # 114.
7. *Presorting—The Way to Fast, Dependable Mail Service*—Publication #54.

Books

Hodgson, Richard S., *Direct Mail and Mail Order Handbook*, Chicago: The Dartnell Corporation.

Advertising and Mail Order Directories

Direct Mail Lists, Rates & Data, Standard Rate & Data Service, semi-annual with bi-weekly supplements.

Directory of Mailing List Houses, New York: B. Klein.

Gebbie House Magazine Directory, House Magazine Publishing Company.

Guide to American Directories for Compiling Mailing Lists, New York: B. Klein.

Standard Directory of Advertisers, National Register Publishing Company, annual with nine supplements.

Standard Directory of Advertising Agencies, National Register Publishing Company, three times a year with monthly supplements.

Periodicals

Direct Marketing, published monthly by The Reporter of Direct Mail Advertising, Inc., 244 Seventh Street, Garden City, Long Island, New York 11530.

Advertising Age, published weekly by Crain Publications, Inc., 740 Rush Street, Chicago, Illinois 60611.

13

Examples of Clever Brochures and Mailers

A checklist of general criteria to be answered before embarking on a project is presented here as a guide for applying the techniques described in the last chapter. Add the particular questions you will need for a thorough picture of your project before you begin.

Three totally different advertising brochures will also be discussed and illustrated to show what others have done. Given the same situations, you might have thought up something entirely different.

CRITERIA FOR DESIGNING FORMS AND MAILERS

1. What is the total budget?
2. How much is allocated for design, printing, paper, envelopes, mailing?
3. When is the deadline?
4. Is it a mailer? What about reply?
5. If it is a handout, can it be used later as a mailer?

6. Two-sided printing?
7. What kind of folding, if any?
8. What kind of illustrations?
9. Must a cut be made?
10. Is a professional photographer or artist required?
11. What printing process will be used? Colored inks? Colored paper?
12. Is an advertising agency involved?
13. Can the copy be assembled so that key portions can be changed for future use (dates, floor plans)?
14. What is mailing list status?
15. Will a letter accompany the mailing? Individual inside address? Typed? Printed? Signed—each? Letterhead? Letterhead envelopes?
16. Enclose business card?
17. How will the mailer be addressed and who will do it?
18. Have bulk mailing rates and permits been considered?

Nordic-Schultz, Inc., of Colorado Springs, Colorado, builder of new residential homes, thinks it is important for each prospective client to have one of their brochures *in hand* for comparison when visiting other models.

These brochures were made up by a rearrangement of letterhead and envelope, type-set copy, a reduced 3″ × 5″ black and white photo of actual houses, and a reduced 18″ × 24″ floor plan. All of this was combined on a negative and transferred to a printing plate, which was then used to print the brochures. The finished product is black and white with shades of gray, on approximately 40-pound bond, size 8½″ × 11″. The brochures are given out at the model homes themselves, and at the office of the real estate builder. They also can be used as mailers to new prospects. See Figure 13-1.

Notice that each page is balanced. Each presented a different design problem because of the different shapes involved. Look at the subtleties of placement, darks and lights, the use of white space, and the use of light and dark lines in floor plans. The finished products clearly and pleasingly describe the necessities.

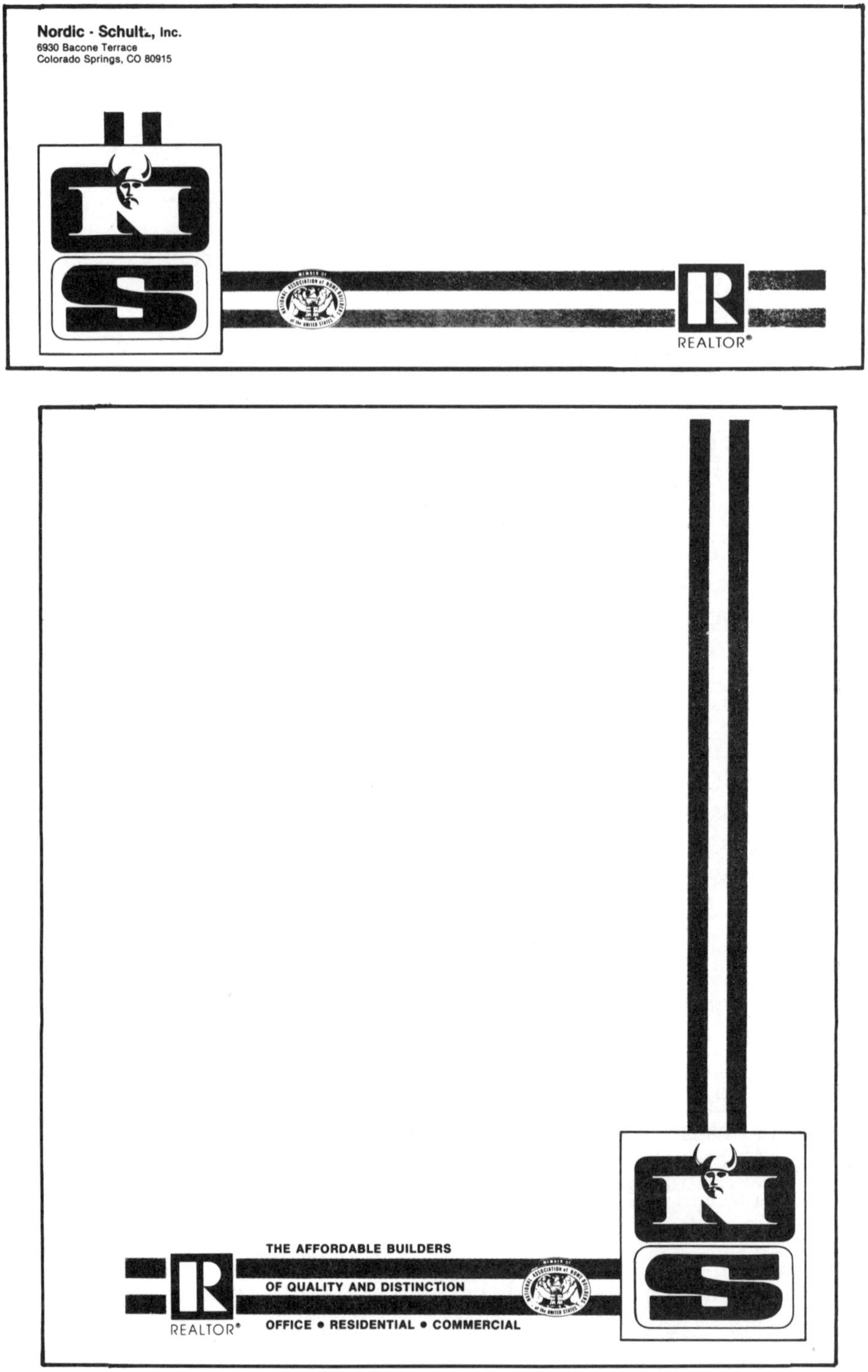

Figure 13-1

From the component parts of this letterhead and envelope come the following pages.

NORDIC-SCHULTZ, INC.
Phone 596-1100
6930 Bacone Terrace
Colorado Springs, Colo. 80915

REALTOR®

"THE INDEPENDENCE"

(Bi-Level)

THE INDEPENDENCE is a convertible, Bi-Level, consisting of a large living rm., dining area, kitchen with illuminated ceiling lights & standard Hotpoint appliances, 2 bedrooms, full bath, 2 car garage, utility room in the bsmt., rear wood deck & 2500 sq. ft. of sod.

OPTIONS available: fireplace, sliding glass door, rough-in plumbing lower level, full bath l.l., brick wainscot-front only, full finished lower level including bedrooms, family or recreation room with carpet. (All options vary in individual homes and vary in additional cost.)

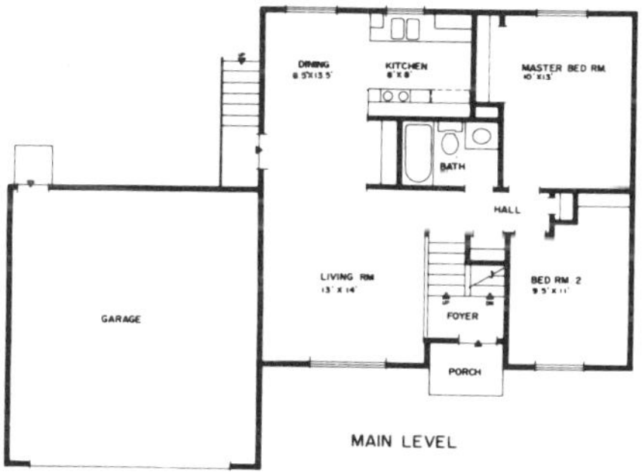

MAIN LEVEL

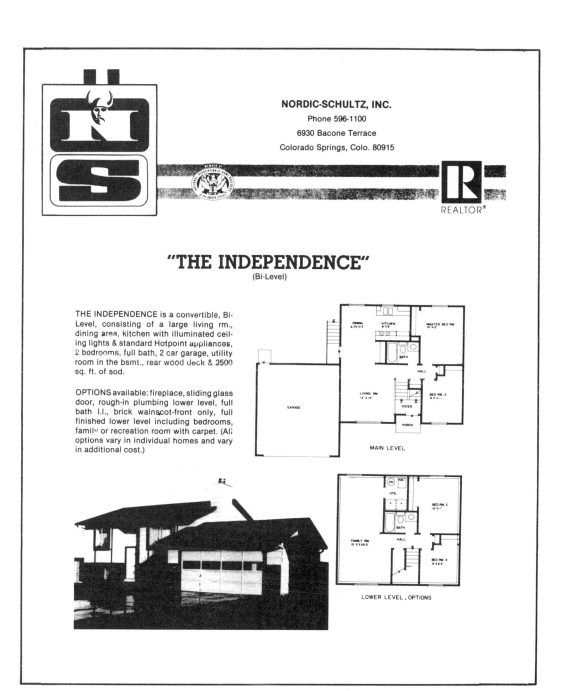

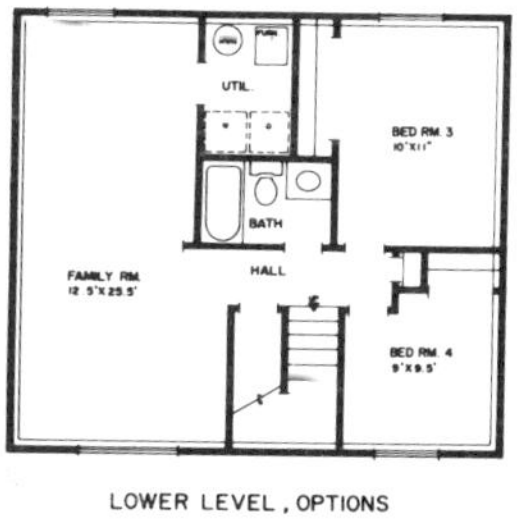

LOWER LEVEL, OPTIONS

Figure 13-1 (cont'd)

The use of only verticals and horizontals makes this very neat and orderly. The parts make up the whole—if you squint, it is almost a framed picture. You are comfortable reading it.

NORDIC-SCHULTZ, INC.

Phone 596-1100

6930 Bacone Terrace

Colorado Springs, Colo. 80915

REALTOR®

LITTLE HOUSE — BIG HOUSE

ALL WITH TODAY'S LIVING IN MIND

Nordic-Schultz takes the same special care to include quality and craftsmanship; that is why we can say, "The Affordable Builders of Quality and Distinction."

We build 3 basic Homes: THE LIBERTY (rancher); THE INDEPENDENCE (bi-level); and THE CONSTITUTION (tri-level) with a number of options available.

"We don't just TALK Energy Savings, we actually build it into our homes." ½" Double Foil Faced Thermax wall insulation, 3½" fiberglass bat insulation, Visqueen vapor barrier on outside walls, 10" ceiling insulation, insulated front metal door, Thermo glazed windows.

Our outside walls carry an engineered weather protection rating factor in excess of 50% greater than a typical outside wall.

STANDARD FEATURES: appliances include self-clean range, hood and fan, dishwasher and disposal. Kitchen includes quality cabinets, baths include marble or formica top vanities and ceramic showers. Living areas are full carpeted over ½" pad, or hard surfaced in many available patterns. We also include thermo glazed windows, smoke detector, washer-dryer outlets, and the energy package previously mentioned. All interior walls are Hand Textured, and 2500 sq. ft. of sod is installed at time of closing. Most plans include as standard, two car garage.

NORDIC-SCHULTZ, INC.

Members of National Association of Home Builders, Colorado Springs Chapter
National, State and Local Board of Realtors — Colorado Springs Chamber of Commerce

596-1100

HOME OWNERS WARRANTY

EQUAL HOUSING OPPORTUNITY

Figure 13-1 (cont'd)

The logo on top is heavy and dark. To offset what could easily be imbalance, the heaviness is spread across the bottom line. Everything coordinates. Only verticals and horizontals are used. except for the logo, which fades.

Realty USA, in St. Louis, Missouri, mails out the brochure shown in Figure 13-3 in response to ads in *Business Week, Fortune, Forbes, Money, The Wall Street Journal* (illustrated), *The Christian Science Monitor*, and the *Army, Navy and Air Force Times*. The ad is illustrated in Figure 13-2.

REAL ESTATE SERVICE
Realty USA
HOUSE HUNTING?
. . . or selling
Find out how fast and easy it really can be! Write for our FREE booklet - "TAKING THE HASSLE OUT OF HOUSE HUNTING ... and how to sell your home for the right price fast."
No obligation!
M
name
address
city state zip
RELOCATING?
CALL TOLL FREE FOR RELOCATION ASSISTANCE ANYWHERE!
800-325-3777
Realty USA®
P.O. Box 5780 W
St. Louis, MO 63121

Figure 13-2

The booklet is intended to introduce the *service* of the company, in answer to a blind inquiry. To hold the reader's interest the booklet speaks directly, pointing out the specific values and benefits that Realty USA will offer the buyer. The back cover is the reply, so all that has to be done is to tear off the postage paid card and mail. The booklet has the company motif in red, white, and blue, which keeps the theme and completes the message.

Figure 13-4 is another example of an effective and well-designed booklet, also in business reply format. This booklet is distributed by Jackson-Cross Company, of Philadelphia, Pennsylvania.

NEW INSIGHTS
Taking the Hassle out of House Hunting
. . . and how to sell your home for the right price fast!
TOLL FREE 1-800-325-3777 . . . IN MISSOURI 314/389-1111
CUT HERE

The size of this is 4½″ × 7″; the front and back covers are done in shiny white card stock. The background strip upper left is red, the rest of the lettering is white. The illustration is royal blue and light blue.

Notice:
1. Red, white and blue color scheme to coordinate with name (Realty USA).
2. The positive approach—the text tells what and how, and the illustration shows it happening with smiling faces.

Figure 13-3

"And each heart
is whispering,
Home,
Home at last!"
– HOOD

Realty USA
3855 Lucas and Hunt Rd.
St. Louis, MO 63121
TOLL FREE: 1-800-325-3777
In Missouri 314/389-1111

Serving You a Better Way

© 1978 REALTY USA ★ ST. LOUIS, MO 63121

This is the face page of the inside front cover; black on white.
Notice: One whole page is devoted to the concept of "home" rather than house.

Figure 13-3 (cont'd)

TAKING THE HASSLE OUT OF HOUSE HUNTING . . . and how to sell your home for the right price fast!

Have you ever been loaded into a real estate salesperson's car, driven for what seemed to be endless miles and hours and shown "everything available"? In real estate jargon this is referred to as "converting a suspect to a prospect." It's the old fashioned "hunt and peck" way to determine a buyer's desires. It's also one of the surest ways to turn a lot of people off - *and never see them again!*

WE WANT TO SERVE YOU THE NEXT TIME TOO!

At Realty USA we want your house hunting experience to be as pleasant, professional and expedient as possible. We want you to feel you are being assisted . . . *rather than pressured.* We understand this will probably not be the last home you will purchase and we want to give you reason to *want* to do business with us again! We're also working for your recommendation of friends, relatives, business associates, and neighbors.

1

This begins the inside and it is as shown—black and gray on white. The concept of personal service is continued and the reader is beginning to be instilled with confidence ... for this and future sales.

Figure 13-3 (cont'd)

Quality Product

PROFESSIONAL PAMPERING

Salespeople of Realty USA franchised firms are trained to provide an excellence of service. We urge the owners and operators of these firms to select *only* salespeople with the desire to put into practice the Realty USA SIMPLE SIX $_{tm}$ PHILOSOPHY. (You can use it to evaluate the service you are receiving.)

THE REALTY USA SIMPLE SIX $_{tm}$ PHILOSOPHY

- **KNOW YOUR PRODUCT**

(Is the salesperson familiar with what he or she is selling - or are they meeting a home for the first time when they thumb through their listing book with you?)

- **KNOW YOUR PROSPECTS**

(Does the salesperson take the time to learn details of your family's living patterns - or are you subjected to long dissertations on why "this is such a great buy"?)

- **KNOW YOUR MARKET**

(Can the salesperson give you an accurate detailing of business conditions and trends in the area - or does he or she have difficulty answering even your most basic questions?)

2

Figure 13-3 (cont'd)

- **WHERE'S THE MONEY?**

(Like most people, you'll probably be looking for mortgage money. Can the salesperson intelligently counsel you on your mortgage requirements?)

Quality Product

- **BE A SUCCESS**

(Real estate salespeople don't have to be driving a current model Cadillac or Lincoln, but if they aren't successful themselves, how do you know they won't try to talk you into buying *anything,* just so they can "earn" a commission?)

- **BE OF SERVICE**

(If you indicate you may not be able to buy right away, are you treated as though you might have the plague? Realty USA salespeople are expected to live up to the company motto - WHAT ARE YOU DOING TO HELP SOMEONE ELSE. Many times a sale doesn't come as easily or quickly as a salesperson would like. This is what separates the pros from the dropouts.)

REALTY USA FIRMS WERE SELECTED FOR EXCLUSIVE AREA REPRESENTATION FOR A <u>REASON</u>

Just as physicians, attorneys, and engineers work hard, long, and continuously to

Quality Product Because

3

Figure 13-3 (cont'd)

learn their professions, so must real estate salespeople. It is important for the salesperson, who is helping you with one of the most important decisions of your life, to be thoroughly trained in all phases of service to the public. Selecting a dedicated professional is your best assurance of taking the hassle out of house hunting. We hope your selection of a real estate firm agrees with ours!

Serving You a Better Way

Relocation Assistance Anywhere!

4

Because (continued)

Figure 13-3 (cont'd)

TAKING THE HASSLE OUT OF HOUSE HUNTING . . . **and how to sell your home for the right price fast!**

Sometimes people think of trying to sell their home themselves. The reason is usually to "save the commission." But a lot of people who shop for-sale-by-owners are bargain hunters who are also trying to "save the commission." *How can both parties save the same commission?*

WHO CAN SELL YOUR HOME?

Selecting a real estate firm to sell your home can be a hit and miss proposition since there are no established methods of rating a firm's performance. However, you can gauge the percentage possibility of a firm selling your home by asking the salesperson or broker - "What percentage of your firm's listings are sold, either by your firm or a cooperating firm, during the initial listing period?" Be prepared for some blank stares or some very interesting and amusing answers. If they tell you about 50%, they'll be around the national average - as closely as we've been able to determine. Stop and think for a minute. *Would you let a doctor who lost about 50% of his or her patients on the operating table operate on you?*

5

Quality Product Because of Good Reason

Figure 13-3 (cont'd)

More Good Reasons

PICK A PRO!

Realty USA franchised firms are provided the tools and technology to score much higher than 50%! *In fact we urge them to strive for the 90+% plateau of success.*

EXPOSURE - EXPOSURE - EXPOSURE

Our national advertising regularly in publications such as Business Week, Fortune, Forbes, Money, The Wall Street Journal, The Christian Science Monitor, Army, Navy, and Air Force Times, is run to attract buyers nationally as well as from all parts of the world.

ADVERTISING SHOULD BE REPETITIVE

Participating Realty USA firms running the following ad format are advertising your home 24 hours a day - seven days a week!

We'll advertise your home every day until it's SOLD! tm

While your home is listed with us, it will be advertised *every day* locally and nationally in our Handy HOUSE HUNTER'S Helper booklets, beginning with the next issue. No extra charge. Call us today!

© 1978 Realty USA ★ St. Louis, MO 63121

6

Figure 13-3 (cont'd)

ACE-IN-THE-HOLE

Participating Realty USA firms utilize their Handy HOUSE HUNTER'S Helper$_{tm}$ booklets to super marketing advantage both locally and nationally. A copy of this pictorial booklet of homes is distributed to other Realty USA firms from coast to coast. These booklets are sent to people moving to the Realty USA member firm's area so that they can preview homes and prices before making their initial trip. Handy HOUSE HUNTER'S Helper$_{tm}$ booklets are also:

- ☐ Displayed at motels, hotels, offices, restaurants and retail stores
- ☐ Distributed at new and used home open houses
- ☐ Direct mailed
- ☐ Delivered to their established clients

Truly the Ace

SELLING A HOME TAKES MUCH MORE THAN A SIGN IN FRONT AND AN AD IN THE CLASSIFIED SECTION OF A NEWPAPER

Realty USA member firm salespeople are trained to use every one of their professional and personal contacts to uncover buying

Competent Salespeople

7

Figure 13-3 (cont'd)

prospects. They are taught to utilize Marketing, Advertising, and Professionalism to produce results. We encourage them to start cultivating early - *by giving talks at kindergartens and giving each child a Handy HOUSE HUNTER'S Helper*$_{tm}$ *to take home!*

May We Offer You Our Sales Ability?

MAY WE BE OF SERVICE TO YOU . . .

We would like the opportunity to prove that our network of Realty USA firms is anxious to serve you . . . whether you're buying or selling . . . moving across town or across the nation. Please call toll free or return the postage paid card - then get ready to START SMILING!

Thank you.

And a Gracious Close

Serving You a Better Way

Relocation Assistance Anywhere!

8

Figure 13-3 (cont'd)

TOLL FREE 1-800-325-3777 . . . IN MISSOURI 314/389-1111

CUT HERE

To: Realty USA ®

We're interested in:

BUYING A HOME IN ______ city ______ state

SELLING A HOME IN ______ city ______ state

PLEASE PRINT CLEARLY

M ______ name

______ address

______ city ______ state ______ zip

______ area code ______ telephone

Best time to call is between ______ AM PM and ______ AM PM

Inside Back Cover

Clear Instructions, Enough Line Length

Figure 13-3 (cont'd)

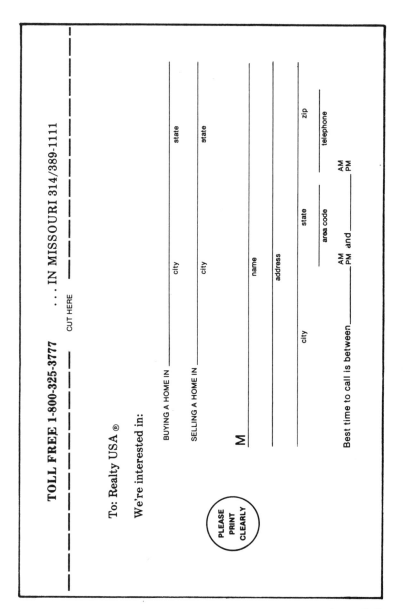

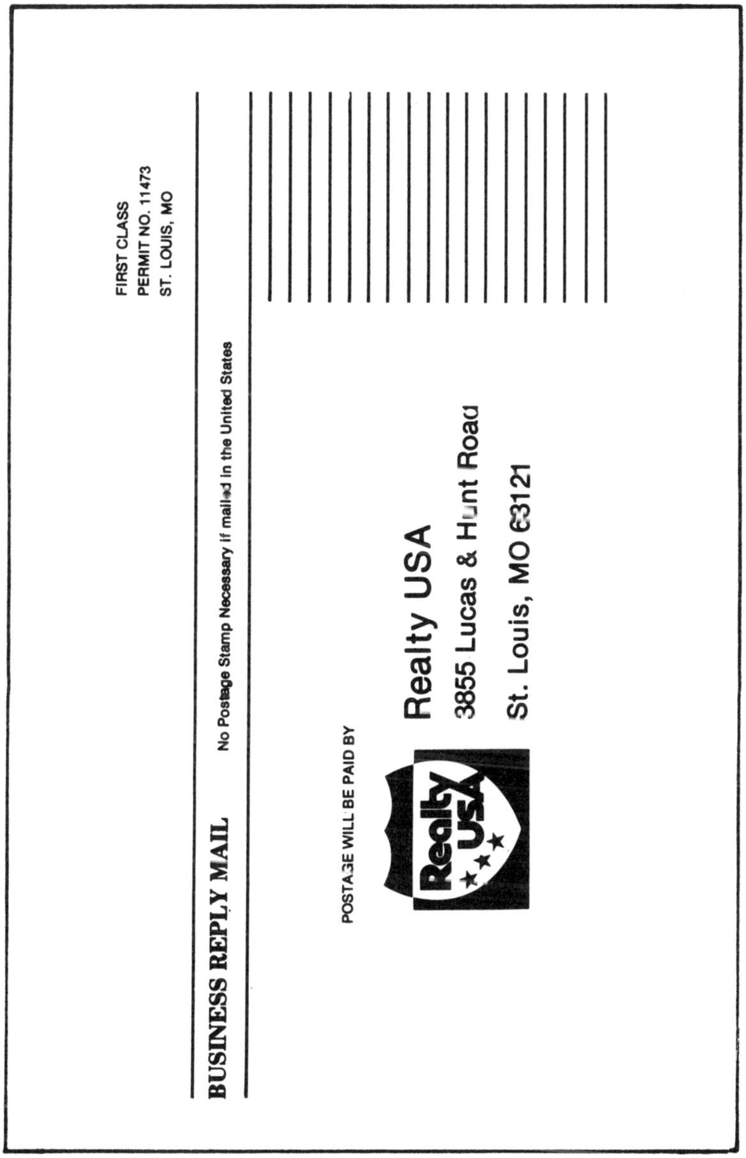
BUSINESS REPLY MAIL

FIRST CLASS
PERMIT NO. 11473
ST. LOUIS, MO

No Postage Stamp Necessary if mailed in the United States

POSTAGE WILL BE PAID BY

Realty USA
3855 Lucas & Hunt Road
St. Louis, MO 63121

Outside Back Cover

All There Is to Do Is Cut

Figure 13-3 (cont'd)

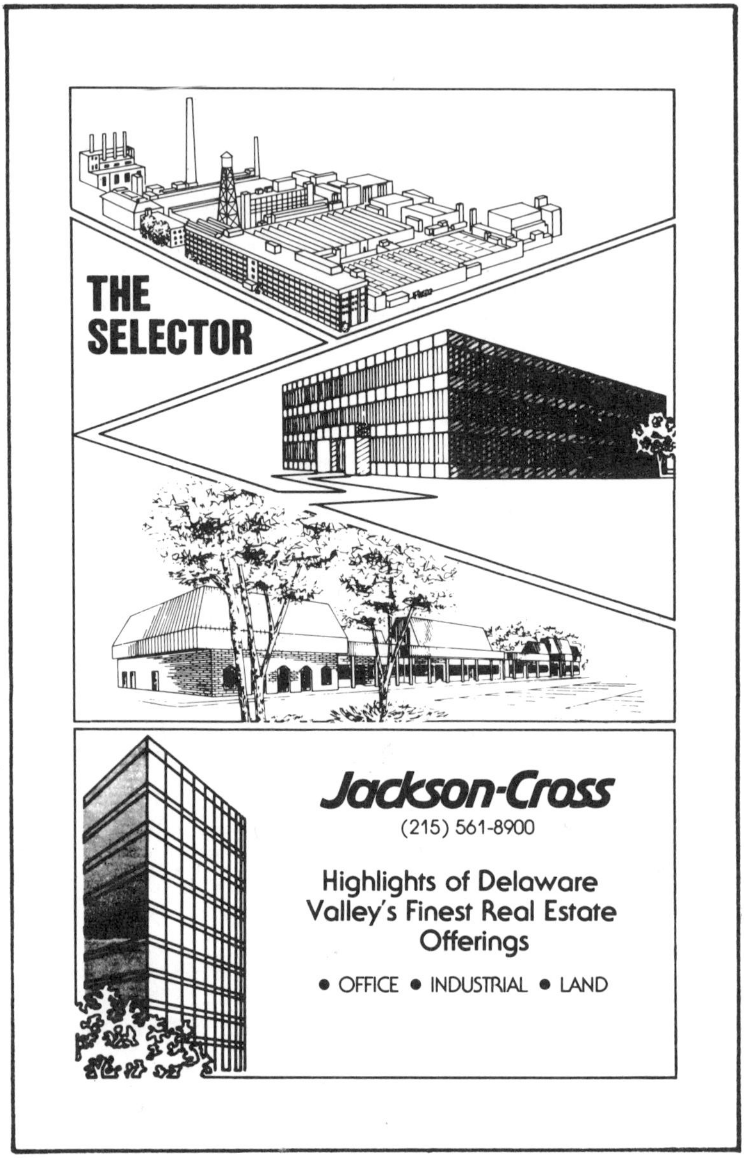

Buff-colored card stock is used for this handsome cover.
The drawings and dark lettering are black; the gray lettering and dots are brick red.

Courtesy
Jackson-Cross
JACKSON-CROSS COMPANY • **REALTORS®**
2000 Market Street, Philadelphia, PA 19103

Figure 13-4

Jackson-Cross

Jackson-Cross is a dynamic real estate organization providing solution-oriented service to all our clients regardless of their size or the complexity of the assignment.

A team of experienced, knowledgeable professionals, the firm enjoys a national reputation for excellence.

Jackson-Cross. . .Real Estate Results.

Sales & Leasing

We offer clients full services in industrial, commercial, office, residential and investment properties. Services include the total marketing of real estate including sales and leasing, as well as the acquisition of sites, buildings, and investment real estate in the Delaware Valley and on a national basis.

Appraisal & Counseling

Our capabilities include the valuation of real estate, feasibility and market analyses, property damage evaluation, tax appeals, fire insurance reports, cost analysis breakdowns, going concern and liquidation values, the appraisal of equipment and machinery, and real estate counseling.

Property Management

We offer owners professional management and innovative methods to maximize income from real estate investments. We currently manage diverse industrial and commercial facilities and over 2 million square feet of first-class office buildings.

Property Maintenance

Our specialists offer comprehensive maintenance and cleaning services for office buildings, industrial plants, commercial facilities and multi-tenant residential properties. Property maintenance is a vital part of real estate management and can be efficiently and effectively handled only by experts.

THE OFFICE NETWORK, INC.

INDIVIDUAL MEMBER
SOCIETY OF
INDUSTRIAL REALTORS

Information concerning this offering is from sources deemed reliable but no warranty as to the accuracy thereof and it is submitted subject to errors, omissions, change of price or other conditions, prior sale or lease or withdrawal without notice.

This inside front cover is, of course, buff; the dark lettering and illustrations are black and the gray is brick red.
Note that balance is achieved by use of type face as well as good design.

Courtesy
Jackson-Cross
JACKSON-CROSS COMPANY • **REALTORS®**
2000 Market Street, Philadelphia, PA 19103

Figure 13-4 (cont'd)

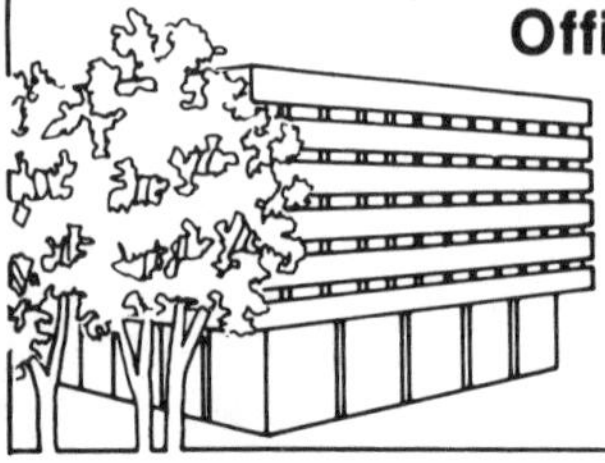

Office Buildings

—Looking for efficient office space in prime locations?
—Has your growth caused you to expand your needs, or has change necessitated a reduction of your space?
Return the enclosed post card, or call:
ROBERT F. BOWMAN Senior Vice President
215/561-8930

1/LEASE

2000 Market St., 20th & Market Sts. Philadelphia, Pa.

- 25,000 Sq. Ft. per floor
- 29 story office tower
- Flexible interior design
- Convenient to public transportation, major arteries
- Concourse-level courtyard, covered street level service area
- 3,100 Sq. Ft. retail area available

2/LEASE

Chestnut East Building
9th & Chestnut Sts., Phila., Pa.

- 250,000 Sq. Ft., divisible
- Air-conditioned
- 25′6″ column spacing
- Convenient to public transportation, shopping, hotels and restaurants
- Full floor 50,490 Sq. Ft.

3/LEASE

Rohm and Haas Bldg., Independence Mall West, Philadelphia, Pa.

- 12,000 Sq. Ft.
- Maximum flexibility
- 5′ module design
- Climate control air-conditioning
- Transportation to all sections of Delaware Valley
- Restaurant and bank on premises

This is the face page to the inside cover. It is glossy white, black and white photos; headings, lead-in lines, and Jackson-Cross logo in chocolate brown.

Courtesy
Jackson-Cross
JACKSON-CROSS COMPANY • **REALTORS®**
2000 Market Street, Philadelphia, PA 19103

Figure 13-4 (cont'd)

SHOPPING CENTERS

For additional information on these or other Centers, call with your requirements:

PG

JOHN W. LAMBERT, Director of Leasing
The Phoenix Group, Inc.
(609) 234-4521 and (215) 925-5393
AND
JOSEPH E. DISBOT, Vice President
Jackson-Cross
(215) 561-8987

CASTLE MALL
G L.A. 220,000
**4/ Chestnut Hill Rd. & S. Chapel St.
Newark, Delaware**

- A & P, K Mart, Thrift Drug
- Open seven days a week
- Enclosed air-conditioned community center of 32 sotres
- Parking for 1,136 cars
- Fully sprinklered
- Greater Newark has population of 130,000, including 5,000 University of Delaware students

VILLAGE MALL
G L.A. 221,000
**5/ Blair Mill Rd. at Moreland Rd.
Horsham, Pa.**

- Only one remaining pad site of 3,000 SF
- Woolco, Acme/Super Saver, Thrift Drug, Singer
- Enclosed air conditioned mall of 45 stores
- Strong walk-in traffic
- High density population
- Fully sprinklered
- Accesible by public bus

NORCO MALL G.L.A. 423,633
**6/ Route 724 & Route 100 Bypass
North Coventry Township (Pottstown), Pa.**

- Sears, Roebuck & Co., Hess's Department
- Store, J.M. Fields
- Enclosed air-conditioned regional mall of 50 stores
- Situated on 50 acres
- Parking for 2,800 cars
- Fully sprinklered
- Accessible by public bus
- Expansion plan to include space for 90,000
- SF two-story department store
- Greater Pottstown average household income (1976) $20,839

This is an inside page; same color scheme, but shown here to depict design and balance.

Courtesy
Jackson-Cross
JACKSON-CROSS COMPANY • **REALTORS®**
2000 Market Street, Philadelphia, PA 19103

Figure 13-4 (cont'd)

33/SALE

Skyron Industrial Park, Cold Spring Creamery Rd., Doylestown, Pa.

- 45 acres
- 10 lots—from 3 to 6 acres available
- Adjacent to general aviation airport
- Improved, subdivided and ready to build
- Pleasant rural location in Buckingham Twp.
- Only industrially zoned land

34/SALE/LEASE

County Line Industrial Park
Bucks County, Upper Southampton, Pa.

- Located on a 100 acre site
- Excellent commercial location
- Pa. Turnpike frontage
- Municipal water & sewer
- Tax-free county financial available
- Sites from 2 acres are available

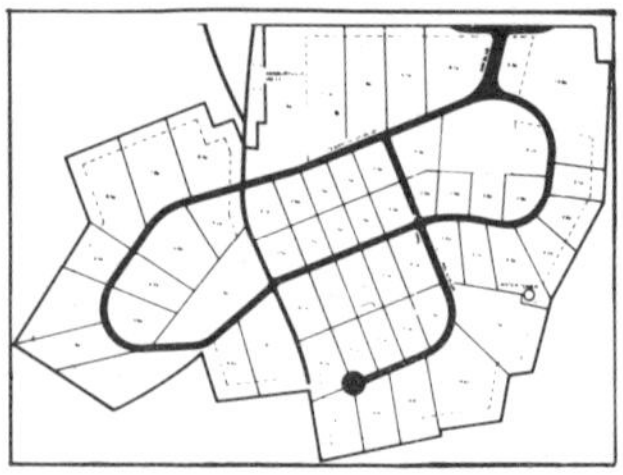

35/SALE

Airport Industrial Mall
Chester County, Pa.

- Central to Eastern Pennsylvania, New York, New Jersey, and Maryland markets
- Neighboring county airport accommodates small jets.
- Most attractive setting in rural Chester County
- Utilities and subdivision approvals in place

Industrial Leasing Strong

The semi-annual survey of industrial and distribution space in the eight-county Delaware Valley area showed a very high rate of demand, with over 5,725,000 square feet absorbed. A total of 388 buildings in the eight-county area were included in the survey.

Total inventory at the end of June was 15 million square feet—part of this by virtue of completion of 33 new buildings, which created 1.3 million square feet.

Industrial Space		
Bucks County	1,762,000	699,000
Montgomery County	368,000	1,166,000
Chester County	342,000	687,000
Delaware County	147,000	3,100,248
Philadelphia	2,364,120	7,056,048
So. New Jersey	742,000	2,310,000

Another inside page; same color scheme but entirely different design and balance.

Courtesy
Jackson-Cross
JACKSON-CROSS COMPANY • **REALTORS®**
2000 Market Street, Philadelphia, PA 19103

Figure 13-4 (cont'd)

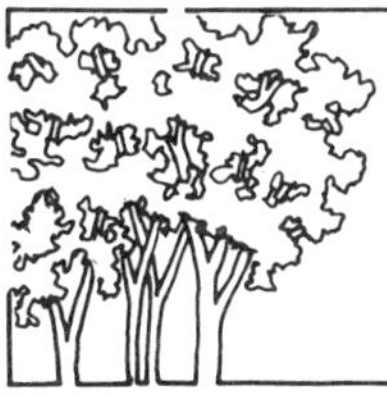

Selected Land Listings

—Contemplating a new development?
—Need riparian rights?
—Is rail a problem?
For further information on these or other land listings, return the enclosed post card, or call:
DAVID H. GLOVACH Vice President
215/561-8935

47 Chesapeake Turkey Point Rd., Cecil Co., Md.
352 acres • On Chesapeake Bay • Zoned recreational, residential.

48 RTE. 22 & 100, Upper Macungie, Lehigh Co., Pa.
3-70 acres • Industrial, rail • Will divide.

49 Pa. Turnpike off Davisville Rd., Upper Moreland, Pa.
33 acres • Limited industrial • Water, sewer, rail.

50 Expressway 283, Old Harrisburg Pike & State Rd. Lancaster, Pa. area.
160 acres • Industrial potential • Water • Sewer • Rail possible • Will divide

51 Sproul Rd (#320) North of Baltimore Pike, Springfield, Del. Co., Pa.
63 acres • Water-sewer • Zoned special use, possible townhouses, apartments, condominiums.

52 Aberdeen, Hartford County, Maryland
50 acres • Heavy industrial—approved for chemical operations or storage • Water • Sewer • Rail • Division possible.

53 Central City Philadelphia, 23rd & Cherry Streets
36,600 Sq. Ft. • Zoned RC4—High rise, residential-commercial • full city services • more ground available adjacent.

54 Rte. 44 & Delaware River, West Deptford, N.J.
243 acres, more available • On 40′ channel in Delaware River • Heavy industrial • Water, sewer, rail.

55 Crownpoint Rd. & Rte. 44, West Deptford, N.J.
214 acres—more available • Public water-sewer • Rail, zoned heavy industrial • Subdivision possible.

56 Fellowship Rd. North of Rte. 73, Mt. Laurel, N.J.
8 acres • Water-sewer • Zoned industrial • Office possibility • Adjacent Holiday Inn.

57 Beverly-Mt. Holly Rd. & JFK Blvd., Willingboro, N.J.
2 parcels • 7.8 acres • 1.125 acres • Municipal water-sewer • Zoned administration and professional.

58 Dulty's Lane & Penn-Central RR, Burlington, N.J.
26.284 acres • Penn Central siding • Water-sewer • Zoned industrial.

59 I-95 Delaware Industrial Park, New Castle County, Delaware
95 acres • water • sewer • rail

This is the face page to the inside back cover. Same color scheme but the design gives the feeling of ending and closing.

Courtesy
Jackson-Cross
JACKSON-CROSS COMPANY • **REALTORS®**
2000 Market Street, Philadelphia, PA 19103

Figure 13-4 (cont'd)

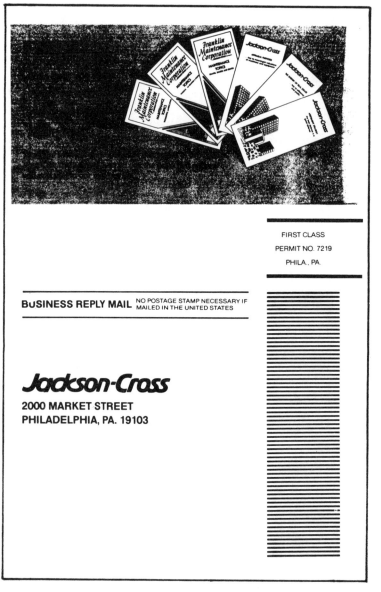

FIRST CLASS
PERMIT NO. 7219
PHILA., PA.

BUSINESS REPLY MAIL NO POSTAGE STAMP NECESSARY IF MAILED IN THE UNITED STATES

Jackson-Cross
2000 MARKET STREET
PHILADELPHIA, PA. 19103

Inside back cover; buff card stock; gray is brick red and black is black. Perforated for mailing under top illustration and along seam.

Courtesy
Jackson-Cross
JACKSON-CROSS COMPANY • **REALTORS®**
2000 Market Street, Philadelphia, PA 19103

Figure 13-4 (cont'd)

Jackson-Cross
JACKSON-CROSS COMPANY • REALTORS®
2000 Market Street, Philadelphia, PA 19103

Bulk Rate
U.S. Postage Paid
#270
Phila., Pa.

Jackson-Cross
JACKSON-CROSS COMPANY • REALTORS®
2000 Market Street, Philadelphia, PA 19103

☐ YES . . . I'm interested! Please send me additional information on Item Number__________
☐ Also, please forward to me, absolutely free, the Topic of Interest booklets.

FIRM__________

NAME AND TITLE__________

ADDRESS__________

CITY__________ ZIP__________

STATE__________

TELEPHONE (AREA CODE PLEASE)__________

Outside back cover; buff card stock (of course), gray is brick red, black is black. Note: word "yes" is in red so it jumps out; lines are long enough for information.

Courtesy
Jackson-Cross
JACKSON-CROSS COMPANY • REALTORS®
2000 Market Street, Philadelphia, PA 19103

Figure 13-4 (cont'd)

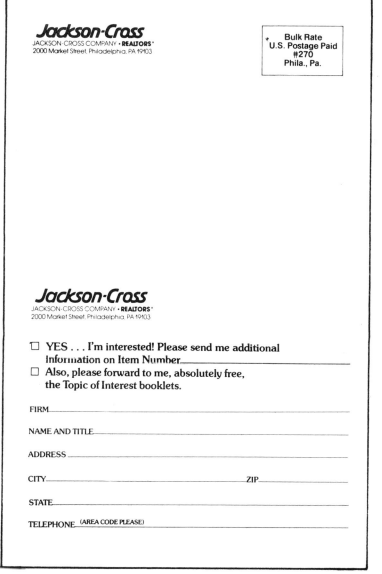

14

Charts of Handy Information

No matter what position you hold in the real estate office, it is sometimes necessary to be an encyclopedia of bits of knowledge for the general public. In order for you to perform this function capably, here are ready-reference charts and tables for that unusual answer you need immediately.

- *Text description of 13 different architectural styles* (Figure 14-1).
- *Drawings of 8 different roof types* (Figure 14-2).
- *Illustration showing 113 different details of a building's construction and a list of definitions of each part* (Figure 14-3).

All of this will help you write ads, answer phones and mail, make presentations, create window displays and slide shows, deal with other real estate people, contractors, buyers, sellers, and architects, and much more.

- *A temperature conversion chart,* because climate and seasons are a vital part of real estate, especially to someone from another state who may be inquiring about purchasing property many miles away, or to a business opportunity franchise which is seasonal (Figure 14-4).

- *Tables of weights and measures* and conversions to metric units are a must for measuring lots, rooms, yards, blocks, and property descriptions (Figure 14-5).
- *Think Conservation!* Energy-Saving Tips (Figure 14-6).
- *A checklist for homebuyers* (Figure 14-7).
- *Chart of moving reminders* (Figure 14-8).

ARCHITECTURAL STYLES

California bungalow or ranch house. One story; stucco with wood trim; often on concrete slab; shingle or shake roof; low and rambling; generally attached garage; indoor-outdoor living.

Colonial. Cape Cod and Cape Ann styles are generally quite small in size—minimum with good taste; symmetrical—windows balanced on both sides of front door; either one or one and one-half stories with little head room upstairs; fairly steep gable or gambrel roof covered with wood shingles; exterior of wood siding.

Georgian and Southern colonial. These styles have elaborate front entrances with plain or fluted columns; are generally of brick or wood; have prominent gable roofs, often hipped; are very symmetrical; require large plots of land; large scale—not suitable for a minimum-sized house; either two, two and one-half, or three stories.

New England colonial. A square or rectangular box-like structure having maximum of usable space; symmetrical—windows balanced on both sides of front door; either two or two and one-half stories; gable roof covered with wood shingles; exterior of wood generally painted white; impressive front entrance usually with transom fan of glass above the door.

Contemporary and modern. Generally one story; usually flat or low-pitched roof; often on concrete slab; large amount of glass; indoor-outdoor living.

Figure 14-1

English Elizabethan. This style has Gothic refined lines with moulded stone around windows and doors; generally of brick, stucco, or stone; steep pitched roof, covered with slate or shingle; usually leaded metal casement windows; requires a large building site.

English half-timber. This style has protruding timber faces with stucco between the faces; lower story of heavy masonry; steep pitched roof; generally two stories; requires a large lot area.

French Normandy. Generally has turrets at entry; walls of brick or stone; symmetrical; steep pitched shingle roof.

French provincial. Usually a large house on a sizable plot; masonry exterior walls with very high roofs; large high windows with long shutters; one and one-half or two and one-half stories.

Regency. A generally symmetrical style with front entrance in center; exterior of brick or stone; shutters on each side of windows; low-hipped roof; two stories in height; octagonal window on second floor over front door.

Small California Spanish. Stucco exterior; flat composition roof with mission tile trim in the front; suitable for small lots; no patio; one story only.

Monterey Spanish. Two stories; stucco (generally white); red mission tiled roof; second story balconies; decorative iron railings.

True Spanish. Enclosed patios, red mission tiled roof; wrought iron decorations; stucco walls (usually white).

Figure 14-1 (cont'd)

ROOF TYPES

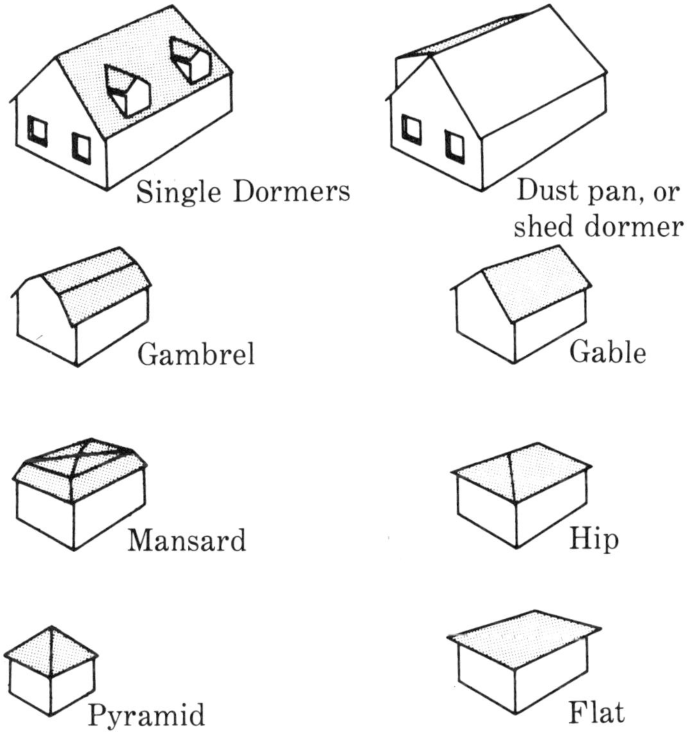

Figure 14-2

KEY TO DETAILS OF STANDARD CONSTRUCTION

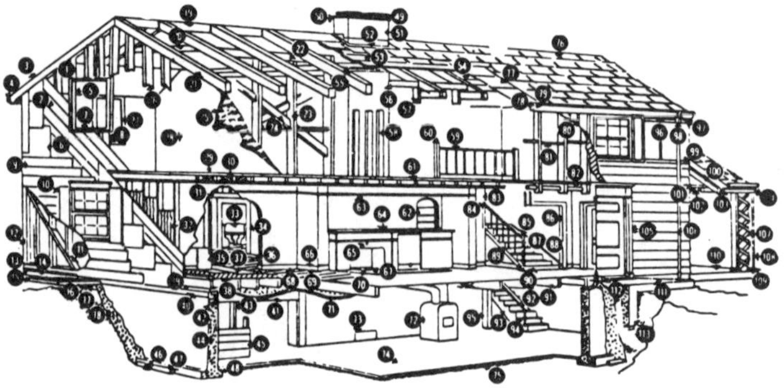

KEY TO DETAILS OF STANDARD CONSTRUCTION

1. Window Head Frame
2. Wall Sheating, Diagonal
3. Verge Board
4. Gutter
5. Window Jamb Trimmer
6. Wall Building Paper
7. Window Sill Frame
8. Cripple Stud
9. Wall Siding
10. Window Shutters
11. Corner Bracing 45
12. Corner Studs, Double
13. Sole Plate
14. Box Sill
15. Basement Areaway
16. Basement Sash
17. Grade Line
18. Gravel Fill
19. Ridge Board
20. Collar Beam
21. Roof Rafters
22. Interior Partition Plates
23. Interior Studs
24. Cross Bracing
25. Plaster Base, Lath
26. Gable Studs
27. Interior Window Trim
28. Plaster Walls
29. Cross Bridging
30. Second Floor Joists
31. Arch Framing
32. Insulation, Batts
33. Dining Nook
34. Interior Door Trim
35. Plaster Base, Rock Lath
36. Finish Floor
37. Floor Lining Felt
38. Sub-Flooring, Diagonally
39. Sill Plate
40. Termite Shield
41. Girder
42. Plate Anchor Bolt
43. Post
44. Foundation Wall
45. Frame Partition
46. Tarred Felt Joint Cover
47. Drain Tile
48. Footing
49. Flue Liner Tops
50. Chimney Cap
51. Brick Chimney
52. Flashing & Counter Flashing
53. Spaced 1" x 4" Sheathing (Wood Shingles)
54. Tight Roof Sheathing (All Other Coverings)
55. Ceiling Joists
56. Exterior Wall Plates
57. Lookouts
58. Furring Strips
59. Stair Rail & Balusters
60. Stair Landing Newel
61. Finish Floor Over Felt Over Sub-flooring on Wood Joists
62. Book Shelves
63. Picture Mould
64. Mantel and Trim
65. Damper Control
66. Base Top Mould
67. Ash Dump
68. Baseboards
69. Shoe Mould
70. Hearth
71. Plaster Ceiling
72. Boiler or Furnace
73. Cleanout Door
74. Basement Concrete Floor
75. Cinder Fill
76. Roof Cover (Shingles)
77. Roofing Felts
78. Soffit or Cornice
79. Facia of Cornice
80. Vert Board & Batten Siding
81. Fire Stops
82. Ribbon Plate
83. Stair Wall Partition
84. Stair Rail or Easing
85. Starting Newel
86. Cased Opening Trim
87. Main Stair Treads & Risers
88. Wall Stair Stringer
89. Face Stringer & Moulds
90. Starting Riser & Tread
91. First Floor Joists
92. Basement Stair Rail & Post
93. Basement Stair Horses
94. Basement Stair Treads & Risers
95. Basement Post
96. Facia board
97. Cornice Bed Mould
98. Leader Head or Conductor Head
99. Belt Course
100. Porch Rafter
101. Porch Ceiling Joists
102. Porch Ceiling Soffit
103. Porch Roof Beam
104. Porch Beam Facia
105. Entrance Door Trim
106. Leader, Downspout or Conductor
107. Porch Trellis
108. Porch Column
109. Porch Column Base
110. Concrete Porch Floor
111. Concrete Stoop
112. Entrance Door Sill
113. Stoop Foundation

Figure 14-3

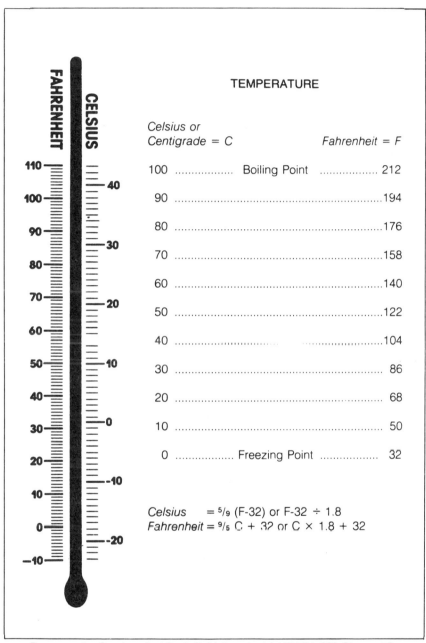

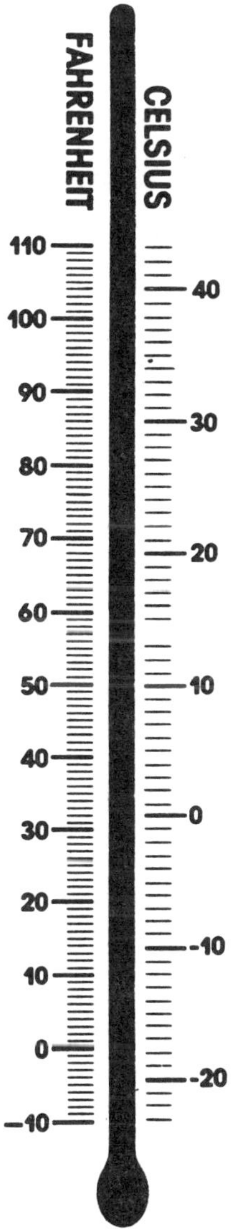

TEMPERATURE

Celsius or Centigrade = *C*		*Fahrenheit* = *F*
100	Boiling Point	212
90		194
80		176
70		158
60		140
50		122
40		104
30		86
20		68
10		50
0	Freezing Point	32

Celsius = $^{5}/_{9}$ (F-32) or F-32 ÷ 1.8
Fahrenheit = $^{9}/_{5}$ C + 32 or C × 1.8 + 32

Thermometer Courtesy Joel Bartlett, Meteorologist, KPIX TV, CBS Channel 5, San Francisco, California.

Figure 14-4

TABLES OF WEIGHTS AND MEASURES

Linear Measure

1 mil	= 0.001 inch	=	0.0254 millimeter
1 inch	= 1,000 mils	=	2.54 centimeters
12 inches	= 1 foot	=	0.3048 meter
3 feet	= 1 yard	=	0.9144 meter
5½ yards or 16½ feet	= 1 rod (or pole or perch)	=	5.029 meters
40 rods	= 1 furlong	=	201.168 meters
8 furlongs or 1,760 yards or 5,280 feet	= 1 (statute) mile	=	1.6093 kilometers
3 miles	= 1 (land) league	=	4.83 kilometers

Square Measure

	1 square inch	=	6.452 square centimeters
144 square inches	= 1 square foot	=	929.03 square centimeters
9 square feet	= 1 square yard	=	0.8361 square meter
30¼ square yards	= 1 square rod (or square pole or square perch)	=	25.292 square meters
160 square rods or 4,840 square yards or 43,560 square feet	= 1 acre	=	0.4047 hectare
640 acres	= 1 square mile	=	259.00 hectares or 2.590 square kilometers

Cubic Measure

	1 cubic inch	=	16.387 cubic centimeters
1,728 cubic inches	= 1 cubic foot	=	0.0283 cubic meter
27 cubic feet	= 1 cubic yard	=	0.7646 cubic meter

(in units for cordwood, etc.)

16 cubic feet	= 1 cord foot	=	0.453 cubic meter
128 cubic feet or 8 cord feet	= 1 cord	=	3.625 cubic meters

Chain Measure

(for Gunter's, or surveyor's, chain)

7.92 inches	= 1 link	=	20.12 centimeters
100 links or 66 feet	= 1 chain	=	20.12 meters
10 chains or 220 yards	= 1 furlong	=	201.17 meters
80 chains	= 1 mile	=	1.6093 kilometers

(for engineer's chain)

1 foot	= 1 link	=	0.3048 meter
100 feet	= 1 chain	=	30.48 meters
52.8 chains	= 1 mile	=	1,609.3 meters

Surveyor's (Square) Measure

625 square links	= 1 square pole	=	25.29 square meters
16 square poles	= 1 square chain	=	404.7 square meters
10 square chains	= 1 acre	=	0.4047 hectare
640 acres	= 1 square mile or 1 section	=	259.00 hectares or 2.59 square kilometers
36 square miles	= 1 township	=	9,324.0 hectares or 93.24 square kilometers

Nautical Measure

6 feet	= 1 fathom	=	1.829 meters
100 fathoms	= 1 cable's length (ordinary) (In the U.S. Navy 120 fathoms or 720 feet, or 219.456 meters, = 1 cable's length; in the British Navy, 608 feet, or 185.319 meters, = 1 cable's length.)		
10 cables' length	= 1 international nautical mile (6,076.11549 feet, by international agreement)	=	1.852 kilometers (exactly)
1 international nautical mile	= 1.150779 statute miles (the length of a minute of longitude at the equator)		
3 nautical miles	= 1 marine league (3.45 statute miles)	=	5.56 kilometers
60 nautical miles	= 1 degree of a great circle of the earth = 69.047 statute miles		

Dry Measure

	1 pint	= 33.60 cubic inches	=	0.5506 liter
2 pints	= 1 quart	= 67.20 cubic inches	=	1.1012 liters
8 quarts	= 1 peck	= 537.61 cubic inches	=	8.8098 liters
4 pecks	= 1 bushel	= 2,150.42 cubic inches	=	35.2390 liters

According to United States government standards, the following are the weights avoirdupois for single bushels of the specified grains: for wheat, 60 pounds; for barley, 48 pounds; for oats, 32 pounds; for rye, 56 pounds; for shelled corn, 56 pounds. Some States have specifications varying from these.

The British dry quart = 1.032 U.S. dry quarts

Liquid Measure

1 gill	= 4 fluid ounces (see next table)	= 7.219 cubic inches	=	0.1183 liter
4 gills	= 1 pint	= 28.875 cubic inches	=	0.4732 liter
2 pints	= 1 quart	= 57.75 cubic inches	=	0.9464 liter
4 quarts	= 1 gallon	= 231 cubic inches	=	3.7854 liters

The British imperial gallon (4 imperial quarts) = 277.42 cubic inches = 4.546 liters. The barrel in Great Britain equals 36 imperial gallons, in the United States, usually 31½ gallons.

Figure 14-5

TABLES OF WEIGHTS AND MEASURES

Apothecaries' Fluid Measure

	1 minim	= 0.0038 cubic inch	=	0.0616 milliliter
60 minims	= 1 fluid dram	= 0.2256 cubic inch	=	3.6966 milliliters
8 fluid drams	= 1 fluid ounce	= 1.8047 cubic inches	=	0.0296 liter
16 fluid ounces	= 1 pint	= 28.875 cubic inches	=	0.4732 liter

See table immediately preceding for quart and gallon equivalents.
The British pint = 20 fluid ounces.

Circular (or Angular) Measure

60 seconds (″)	= 1 minute (′)
60 minutes	= 1 degree (°)
90 degrees	= 1 quadrant or 1 right angle
180 degrees	= 2 quadrants or 1 straight angle
4 quadrants or 360 degrees	= 1 circle

Avoirdupois Weight

(The grain, equal to 0.0648 gram, is the same in all three tables of weight.)

1 dram or 27.34 grains		= 1.772 grams
16 drams or 437.5 grains	= 1 ounce	= 28.3495 grams
16 ounces or 7,000 grains	= 1 pound	= 453.59 grams
100 pounds	= 1 hundredweight	= 45.36 kilograms
2,000 pounds	= 1 ton	= 907.18 kilograms

In Great Britain, 14 pounds (6.35 kilograms) = 1 stone, 112 pounds (50.80 kilograms) = 1 hundredweight, and 2,240 pounds (1,016.05 kilograms) = 1 long ton.

Troy Weight

(The grain, equal to 0.0648 gram, is the same in all three tables of weight.)

3.086 grains	= 1 carat	= 200.00 milligrams
24 grains	= 1 pennyweight	= 1.5552 grams
20 pennyweights or 480 grains	= 1 ounce	= 31.1035 grams
12 ounces or 5,760 grains	= 1 pound	= 373.24 grams

Apothecaries' Weight

(The grain, equal to 0.0648 gram, is the same in all three tables of weight.)

20 grains	= 1 scruple	= 1.296 grams
3 scruples	= 1 dram	= 3.888 grams
8 drams or 480 grains	= 1 ounce	= 31.1035 grams
12 ounces or 5,760 grains	= 1 pound	= 373.24 grams

THE METRIC SYSTEM

Linear Measure

	1 millimeter	= 0.03937 inch
10 millimeters	= 1 centimeter	= 0.3937 inch
10 centimeters	= 1 decimeter	= 3.937 inches
10 decimeters	= 1 meter	= 39.37 inches or 3.2808 feet
10 meters	= 1 decameter	= 393.7 inches
10 decameters	= 1 hectometer	= 328.08 feet
10 hectometers	= 1 kilometer	= 0.621 mile or 3,280.8 feet
10 kilometers	= 1 myriameter	= 6.21 miles

Square Measure

	1 square millimeter	= 0.00155 square inch
100 square millimeters	= 1 square centimeter	= 0.15499 square inch
100 square centimeters	= 1 square decimeter	= 15.499 square inches
100 square decimeters	= 1 square meter	= 1,549.9 square inches or 1.196 square yards
100 square meters	= 1 square decameter	= 119.6 square yards
100 square decameters	= 1 square hectometer	= 2.471 acres
100 square hectometers	= 1 square kilometer	= 0.386 square mile or 247.1 acres

Land Measure

1 square meter	= 1 centiare	= 1,549.9 square inches
100 centiares	= 1 are	= 119.6 square yards
100 ares	= 1 hectare	= 2.471 acres
100 hectares	= 1 square kilometer	= 0.386 square mile or 247.1 acres

Volume Measure

1,000 cubic millimeters	= 1 cubic centimeter	= 0.06102 cubic inch
1,000 cubic centimeters	= 1 cubic decimeter	= 61.023 cubic inches or 0.0353 cubic foot
1,000 cubic decimeters	= 1 cubic meter (the unit is called a *stere* in measuring firewood)	= 35.314 cubic feet or 1.308 cubic yards

Capacity Measure

10 milliliters	= 1 centiliter	= 0.338 fluid ounce
10 centiliters	= 1 deciliter	= 3.38 fluid ounces or 0.1057 liquid quart
10 deciliters	= 1 liter	= 1.0567 liquid quarts or 0.9081 dry quart
10 liters	= 1 decaliter	= 2.64 gallons or 0.284 bushel
10 decaliters	= 1 hectoliter	= 26.418 gallons or 2.838 bushels
10 hectoliters	= 1 kiloliter	= 264.18 gallons or 35.315 cubic feet

Weights

10 milligrams	= 1 centigram	= 0.1543 grain or 0.000353 ounce (avdp.)
10 centigrams	= 1 decigram	= 1.5432 grains
10 decigrams	= 1 gram	= 15.432 grains or 0.035274 ounce (avdp.)
10 grams	= 1 decagram	= 0.3527 ounce
10 decagrams	= 1 hectogram	= 3.5274 ounces
10 hectograms	= 1 kilogram	= 2.2046 pounds
10 kilograms	= 1 myriagram	= 22.046 pounds
10 myriagrams	= 1 quintal	= 220.46 pounds
10 quintals	= 1 metric ton	= 2,204.6 pounds

Figure 14-5 (cont'd)

THINK CONSERVATION!
ENERGY SAVING TIPS

Thoughtful Landscaping

...A beautiful way to save energy

Energy conservation has become a full-time consideration for all of us in both our private lives and in our business careers. It is particularly important to those entrusted to manage and maintain commercial and office structures where large losses are the penalty for inattention to energy-saving details.

A building's energy configuration is established when it is built, but many changes can be made to alter energy usage—often overlooked is landscaping.

Esthetics and energy

Many people think of landscaping as only of cosmetic value to a structure, rarely considered is the impact it can have on energy usage. The esthetic and energy considerations on a low-rise suburban building can be considerable.

Among other things, trees can block or reduce radiation from the sun, ground covers can control reflection radiation and lower air temperatures on hot summer days, and properly located wind breaks can significantly reduce winter winds.

Windbreaks work

A windbreak can be instrumental in reducing heat loss from inside the building by cutting down on the winds that reach, and flow over the windows. A layer of relatively still air at windows retards heat transmission through the glass.

Interestingly, a windbreak should not present a solid front; it works more efficiently if some wind is allowed to penetrate. Wind blowing against and over a solid barrier produces turbulence and eddy currents behind the windbreak, and greatly increases wind flow over the leeward side of the building. Allowing some of the wind to pass through the break tends to minimize the eddy currents.

Results of a Princeton University study showed that a single row of evergreens, as high as the building, would reduce air infiltration 40%, and when used in combination with a five-foot

Courtesy
Jackson-Cross
JACKSON-CROSS COMPANY • REALTORS®
2000 Market Street, Philadelphia, PA 19103

Figure 14-6

fence, would cut air infiltration by 60%.

This research also indicated that the best location for the windbreak was upwind from the building at a distance 1½ to 2½ times the height of the building. For example, if the building is 20 feet high, the windbreak should be located from 30 to 50 feet from the building.

Prevailing winds in the Philadelphia area are out of the northwest at 8 to 10 mph. Prevailing summer winds are out of the southwest at 7 to 9 mph.

Because of this direction change between winter and summer winds, a windbreak can be placed to divert winter wind away from a building without interfering with the breezes of summer.

Shade trees

Planting shade trees of the deciduous variety can provide summer shade and desired window cooling, and still admit sunlight during winter months. And, oddly enough, a tree-shaded window on the south side of a building receives less solar heat than an un-shaded, north facing window; diffused radiation comes from clouds through that north window.

Shading not only cuts window heat, it also reduces ground surface temperature, which then produces cooler air temperatures in the window area, and reduces window heat gain.

Is the effect of shade trees significant? A test conducted at Indiana University, in an air temperature of 84 F, showed that concrete exposed to direct sunlight heated up to 108 F; concrete shaded by a maple tree was only 88 F.

Ground cover

A couple of other interesting points: light-colored ground surfaces reflect sunlight into windows potentially reducing the need for lighting; dark surfaces absorb sunlight, raise outside temperatures and may require additional interior lighting.

Planted surfaces will absorb sunlight and lower outside temperatures, at the expense of reflected light. Careful study of a building, its site location, window configuration and the wind direction will allow landscaping to be designed to take energy as well as esthetic factors into account.

Landscaping can truly be a beautiful way to save energy.

Courtesy
Jackson-Cross
JACKSON-CROSS COMPANY • **REALTORS®**
2000 Market Street, Philadelphia, PA 19103

Figure 14-6 (cont'd)

Windows . . . for Comfort and Profit!

What's a window?

Well, it provides a view of the outside world. But those interested only in the view are missing the boat.

A window can be:

- a solar collector to reduce heating bills;
- a transmitter of natural light to cut use of electricity;
- a ventilator to reduce air conditioning requirements.

As an energy tool a window relies on the building's interior design: colors of room surfaces, placement of large components, floors and walls that act as heat absorbers/radiators, and lighting circuits.

Lighting configuration

Two rows of lights for instance—one near the window, one deeper in the room—would mean that an outer row could stay off during daylight hours. Electricity savings and the reduced air conditioning load are instant benefits.

Photocells or timers can even further cut power usage.

Colors

Light-colored surfaces reflect more light inside a building, thereby increasing the light levels. White gives the highest reflection factor—80 to 90 percent—followed by pastels, all in the 70 to 80 percent range.

Carrying this a step further, ceilings should have an 80 percent reflection factor, and walls (in poorly lighted rooms) 70 percent, (25 percent in well-lighted rooms), 80 percent for walls containing windows, and 25 percent from floors.

Another factor to be considered is that large window areas, particularly in small rooms, can transmit so much solar energy that overheating can occur.

Solar Energy

A partial solution is to place heavy, massive materials in the path of the sunlight to absorb the energy. When room temperature later drops, the stored heat is released into the room.

Consider also the fact that dark colors—blue and black—absorb 80 to 90 percent of the energy. And, the denser a material and the greater its conductivity, the better it is as a storage medium.

According to the Standard Handbook for Mechanical En-

Courtesy
Jackson-Cross
JACKSON-CROSS COMPANY • REALTORS®
2000 Market Street, Philadelphia, PA 19103

Figure 14-6 (cont'd)

gineers by Baumeister, water has the relatively high capacity to hold heat of 62.0, but its conductivity is 0.35 (BTU/hr ft° F). Red-enameled steel, on the other hand has a lower thermal capacity of 58.8, but a conductivity rating of 26.2, making it the better heat storage material.

To better increase the efficiency of something like a heavy slab wall, and to augment a heating/cooling system, air ducts or copper tubing can be embedded in the material to force the heat from the material.

So what's a window? It's a vital, important part of building design in so many ways: it can help to control or regulate light, heat, and cooling, while increasing overall employee comfort.

Drapes, Shades and Blinds

. . . Energy saving tools

We know for a fact that opening or closing windows affects the heating or cooling of a room—so let's look at interior accessories as a way of managing and conserving energy.

Draperies, shades and venetian blinds, properly used, can accomplish this.

Venetian Blinds

Because they can be raised, lowered and tilted to different angles venetian blinds can both vary and diffuse sunlight entering a room, as well as reflect direct rays back through the window.

Venetian blinds do not offer a good insulation barrier to keep out winter's cold.

Drapes

Drapes can reduce winter heat loss and summer heat buildup. Tight-weave fabrics are best to cut heat loss.

Drapes should hang against walls or windows, and be in contact with either floor or window sill for best insulating value.

Drapery tracks should extend well beyond the sides of the window, to allow full clearance of the glass area. This allows the

Courtesy
Jackson-Cross
JACKSON-CROSS COMPANY • REALTORS®
2000 Market Street, Philadelphia, PA 19103

Figure 14-6 (cont'd)

maximum amount of direct sunlight to heat and illuminate the room.

Summer heat can be reduced by draperies, with three factors determining efficiency:

- Amount of sunlight reflected back
- Amount of solar energy absorbed by fabric
- Amount of solar energy transmitted through the fabric

And then the key to the drape's effectiveness in energy conservation, beyond material and installation configuration, rests with the people in the office—to open and close them as conditions warrant.

Film shades

Clear or coated-transparent roll shades can be used singly, or in multiple, separated layers—reducing solar heat gain in summer and cutting winter heat losses.

A low emissivity film shade can reduce a single glazed window's absorption of heat from interior surfaces by as much as 64 percent.

Three types of film—reflecting, clear, and heat absorbing—can be used singly or together, and because the shades are magnetically sealed against the frame and sill there's the additional advantage of reduced infiltration of incoming air.

Opaque roll shades

Opaque shades in white, dark, or light colored translucent, have certin advantages.

- Reduced solar heat gain in summer
- Reduced conducted heat loss on winter nights
- Glare control
- Privacy

An opaque white shade can reflect up to 80 percent of incoming solar energy back through the glass, while absorbing only about 20 percent, substantially reducing summer heat gain in a room.

A dark opaque shade will reflect only about 12 percent but will absorb up to 88 percent solar energy—a useful factor during winter months.

The light colored translucent shade both reflects, absorbs, and allows a certain amount of light into the room, reflection rate is about 60 percent, absorption rate 15 percent.

Some shades are white on one side, and dark on the other. By simply reversing the shade as seasons change, it can be both a solar collector and a shading device.

Courtesy
Jackson-Cross
JACKSON-CROSS COMPANY • REALTORS®
2000 Market Street, Philadelphia, PA 19103

Figure 14-6 (cont'd)

A Checklist for Homebuyers

Comparison shopping is a must when you're looking for a new home. Yet, after inspecting a number of possibilites, the features offered in individual houses are apt to become blurred.

Was the house with good financing available the one that had small bedrooms? Was public transportation accessible to the well-landscaped one? And that scribbled note reading "insulation"—which house was that and what does it mean?

Here's a chart that is designed to help straighten out the confusion. Carry it with you as you house hunt. You'll not only have a permanent record of every house you've looked at, but also a basis for making sound, comparative judgments.

	HOUSE #1 Address:	HOUSE #2 Address:	HOUSE #3 Address:	HOUSE #4 Address:	HOUSE #5 Address:	HOUSE #6 Address:	HOUSE #7 Address:	HOUSE #8 Address:
Location								
Price								
Number of rooms								
Size of lot								
Financing available								
Taxes/ Assessments								
Neighborhood								
Shopping								
Schools								
Landscaping								
Transportation								
Floor plan								
Appliances								
Resale value								
Special features (Fireplace, pool, etc.)								
General impression								

San Francisco Newspaper Agency

Figure 14-7

MOVING REMINDERS— BEFORE YOU LEAVE YOUR PRESENT ADDRESS

1. Order a final reading of:
   Gas meter
   Electric meter
   Water meter
2. Request termination of services:
   Milk delivery
   Newspaper delivery
   Cleaning service
   Diaper service
   Telephone service
3. Have your refrigerator and other appliances serviced for the trip.
4. Write the utility companies in the city to which you are moving and inquire about the necessary fees or deposits required for installation of services. Remit the utility deposits requested with information as to when and where you will want the following services:

Electricity	Water
Gas	Telephone

5. Send your forwarding address to the local post office and send change of address cards to:

Insurance companies	Friends
Magazine companies	Merchants with whom you conduct business
Book and record clubs	Secretaries of clubs and organizations to which you belong

6. Transfer your insurance:

Life	Household goods and personal possessions (check to see that they will be properly covered enroute and at your new home)
Hospitalization	
Auto	

Figure 14-8*

*Suggested by Mrs. Dian L. Coleman, Secretary in the offices of Members Realty Corporation, 6061 N.W. Expressway, San Antonio, Texas 78201.

7. Notify the principal of your children's school about your intended move. Request a letter from him covering the status of your children in school.
8. Notify your church pastor that you are leaving.
9. Obtain birth and baptism records of your children.
10. Obtain all medical records of shots, dental records, and eyeglass prescriptions.
11. If your car or other possessions are not paid for, obtain permission to move them.
12. Transfer your bank accounts.
13. Have your present bank arrange references for establishing new accounts in the city to which you are moving.
14. Arrange sufficient cash or travelers checks to cover the cost of moving services and expenses until you make banking connections in the city to which you are moving. Cash or certified check is generally required by the transfer company.
15. Personal items. Pick up:

Furs	Shoes being repaired
Dry cleaning	Laundry

16. Leave the keys for your old property with the real estate agent or a neighbor.

MOVING REMINDERS—AT YOUR NEW ADDRESS

1. Check on service of:
   Telephone
   Electricity
   Water
   Gas
2. Check pilot light on the hot water heater, heating, and air-conditioning units.
3. Obtain emergency numbers for ambulance, police, and fire departments and post them near telephone.

Figure 14-8 (cont'd)*

*Suggested by Mrs. Dian L. Coleman, Secretary in the offices of Members Realty Corporation, 6061 N.W. Expressway, San Antonio, Texas 78201.

4. Have the refrigerator, stove, automatic washer, dryer, and television checked.
5. Have hot water heater serviced and check the pilot light.
6. Ask the mailman for mail which he may be holding for your arrival.
7. Have new address recorded on your driver's license or apply for issuance of new license, whichever is required in state to which you move.
8. Register your car within a reasonable time after arrival in a new state or a penalty may be imposed when acquiring license plates.
9. Visit the city office and register to vote.
10. Register your family in your new place of worship.
11. Register your children in school.
12. Notify all credit card companies for which you have credit cards of your change of address.
13. Notify auto club or other travel or road service organization of your change of address.
14. Obtain names of doctors, dentists, and veterinarians.
15. Obtain a map of the new city to help you find your way around better.
16. Call transportation company and get map of bus routes.
17. Check with friends and neighbors on best places to do shopping.
18. Check on requirements for licensing of pets.
19. Call Chamber of Commerce and request brochures on points of interest and things to do and see in the city and surrounding area.

Figure 14-8 (cont'd)*

*Suggested by Mrs. Dian L. Coleman, Secretary in the offices of Members Realty Corporation, 6061 N.W. Expressway, San Antonio, Texas 78201.

15

Real Estate Reference Sources

You are expected to think on your feet and to know and understand the world in which you work. Economic conditions, laws, and even the value of money change frequently, making every day different and keeping you alert. You can never know everything, but you can know where to go for an answer.

City, county, state, and federal agencies will give telephone information, and public records are open for inspection.

Public, private, and university librarians will give telephone information and will guide you to all sources and cross-references for a topic if you visit.

The Department of Real Estate of each state publishes brochures and booklets (some free and some for sale). Call or write for information. The public library can give you out-of-state addresses.

The United States Government bookstore, if you live in a city which has one, sells many fine publications including, but not limited to, environmental studies, geography, home improvement, history, and energy conservation. If you don't have such a bookstore in your city, check the library. Catalogs available free with lists of pamphlets are:

Selected U.S. Government Publications. Covering topics such as agriculture, business, commerce, energy, environmental protection, Federal Home Loan Bank Board,

Housing and Urban Development, Interior, Securities and Exchange, and more.

Prentice-Hall, Inc., through Executive Reports Corporation, Englewood Cliffs, New Jersey, 07632, publishes two biweekly secretarial newsletters that are available by subscription.

The Creative Secretary. Ideas from and for secretaries all over the country for efficiency, diplomacy, ingenuity, and more.

The Creative Real Estate Secretary. Ideas for forms, sales promotions, money savers, profit makers, and more from and for real estate secretaries all over the country.

Parker Publishing Company, West Nyack, New York, publishes the book *The Successful Creative Secretary*, which gives all the necessary and practical information to make the secretary's job easier and more rewarding.

Your local Board of Realtors has many fine programs and publications and you can obtain information by telephone or letter.

The California Association of Realtors and the National Association of Realtors have an educational program with an excellent selection of books, cassettes, slides, and movies for sale, which can be used in any state.

Magazines are important informational material to be read by clients, and by a well-versed sales and office staff. Information begets ideas and it is the application of knowledge that creates and sells. Publications on real estate and related topics, such as architecture, decorating, economics, and more, are in this chapter for easy reference.

Real estate law varies from state to state so check for those texts pertaining to your specific state in the library or bookstore. Excellent books with general real estate knowledge are available and some are listed here.

You may be asked to research public records and you will be shown here the procedure when you know the person's name, address, telephone number, or business name, address, and telephone number. The contents of basic directories, such as the *Realty Index*, *Polk's City Directory*, *Telephone Company Cross Directory*, and *Haine's Criss Cross Directory* are reviewed here so you will know where to find the information you need.

This chapter also includes definitions of the function of and the documents found in the Assessor's Office, Tax Collector's Office, Recorder's Office, County Clerk and Superior Court

(Civil), Municipal and Small Claims Court, Registrar of Voters, Board of Equalization, Secretary of State, Department of Motor Vehicles, Zoning and City Planning, Purchasing and Engineering.

The following is a partial list of available material from the California Association of Realtors, 505 Shatto Place, Los Angeles, California 90020. Price catalog on request.

BOOKS

Closing Guidelines—closing costs, salary requirements, qualifications guide, loan amortization payments, subescrow fees, estimated and allowable closing costs, and many charts and tables.

How to Sell Mobile Homes—provides information on mobile home valuation and regulations, and gives background required to properly list and sell used mobile homes.

Industrial and Commercial Real Estate—detailed procedures are outlined for evaluating and analyzing commercial and industrial property, followed by step-by-step procedures for listing, selling, and leasing. Included is a formal example of an appraisal of a commercial building by an MAI.

**Listing Real Estate*—covers all aspects of listing and reflects the hard-earned experience of some of the most successful Realtors and salesmen in the United States.

Real Estate Counseling—topics covered vary from basic concepts of real estate counseling through more advanced theories and complex case studies.

Real Estate Economics—among the subject matter contained in this book are discussions of private enterprise and "free" market systems, money, credit, and real estate marketing behavior, business and real estate cycles, analyzing a property's economic potentials, economic foundations of appraising, and more.

Selling Real Estate—Consistent work habits, close attention to details, full disclosure and negotiations, methodic accumulation of factual data, thorough follow-through, and empathy for the buyer and seller are listed as the most important keys to successful selling.

---

*Coordinating motion picture available.

BOOKS AND CASSETTES

Apartment Houses ... How to Invest, How to Sell—covers investment and operational aspects; financing, taxation, legal aspects, management, advertising, exchanges, analyses, estimates, cash flow, and calculation techniques.

Closing the Sale—closing for the appointment, closing the listing, closing the buyer, closing the seller.

How to Convert Apartments to Condominiums—condominium updating and briefing, selections of the property, feasibility study and analysis, acquisition and financing, processing and documentation, preparing for marketing, marketing and management.

How to List and Sell Condominium Homes—guidelines and techniques for listing and selling condominiums, including emphasis on financing, marketing, and closing the sale.

How to Manage an Apartment House—maintenance, management policy and procedures, and credit and collection.

How to Manage Condominium Developments—topics include importance of advance planning for condominium management, condominium insurance, and condominium law.

How to Negotiate in Listing and Selling Homes—six experts discuss how to negotiate in such areas as financing, qualifying, showing the home, obtaining and presenting the offer, closing, and follow-up. Various forms and examples are presented.

**In Search of Agreement*—negotiating is brought into focus by eight experts. Selling the owner, qualifying the buyer, obtaining and presenting the offer and the counteroffer are only a few topics covered.

**I Would If I Only Had The Time*—topics covered include listing, selling, negotiating, financing, goal setting, and memory training.

---

*Coordinating motion picture available.

Selling Income Property Successfully—filled with "how to" techniques to make money in listing and selling income property. The situations are real and the lessons have been extracted from countless closed transactions.

**You Gotta Work the Territory*—contains, in detail, eight prospecting techniques that work. Among approaches discussed are prospecting by telephone, door-to-door, open houses, use of newspapers, community service work, the positive attitude in prospecting, time management, and communicating.

CASSETTES

Condominiums—six one-hour cassettes covering the condominium concept, the market for condominiums, financing condominiums, marketing condominiums, step-by-step processing in development of condominiums, condominium success story, low, medium and high price units, apartment house conversion to condominiums.

For Sale By Owner—shows why owners feel this way and how to successfully deal with them.

SLIDE CASSETTE SALES TRAINING PROGRAMS

What the Seller Doesn't Know Can Hurt You—carousel tray, 80 color slides, audio cassette, illustrated text, leader's guide, 6 trainee workbooks. Instructional program designed to help salespeople improve their listing techniques.

How to List Real Estate—carousel tray, 80 color slides, a cassette tape, workbooks for class members, an illustrated text and leader's guide. Subjects: listing objectives, selling the owner, competitive market analysis, the financing analysis, the listing agreement, servicing the listing.

How to Sell Real Estate—carousel tray, 80 color slides, a cassette tape, workbooks for class members, an illustrated text and leader's guide. Subjects: answering ad calls, qualifying the buyer, showing property, obtaining the

---

*Coordinating motion picture available.

offer, presenting the offer, presenting the counteroffer and follow-through.

EDUCATIONAL MOTION PICTURES

Don't Take Their Word for It—20 minutes running time, 16 mm, in color. Depicts the importance of knowing what your clients really want so that misunderstandings are avoided.

Prospecting Listings ... The Professional Approach—31 minutes running time, 16 mm. Follow along with a successful salesperson as she demonstrates how success can be achieved by simple and thorough preparation and good communication.

What The Seller Doesn't Know Can Hurt You—20 minutes running time, 16 mm, in color. Explains what to tell sellers about financing at the time the listing is taken in order to get the property exposed to 100 percent of the market.

A New Way of Living—30 minutes running time, 16 mm, in color. Dramatically portrays the different closing techniques in a story that follows the closing of a sale on a home and a follow-through with the sellers in closing the sale on a condominium.

**You Gotta Work the Territory*—30 minutes running time, 16 mm, in color. The value of the farm system to salespersons, the creative market analysis, and need for specialization are presented.

**In Search of Agreement*—30 minutes running time, 16 mm, in color. In this film two salesmen learn the art of negotiating the hard way.

**I Would ... If I Only Had the Time*—30 minutes running time, 16 mm, in color. In this film salesmen present the wrong way and the right way to approach goal setting and time management.

**The Sale of Investment Property ... Apartment Houses*—32 minutes running time, 16 mm, in color. Traces the sale of an apartment house from listing to closing.

---

*Coordinating book and cassette available.

Selling Is Communicating—32 minutes running time, 16 mm, in color. How often have you made a simple statement of fact or opinion to someone and then discovered they have interpreted your remarks entirely differently from what you had intended?

Presenting the Offer—20 minutes running time, 16 mm, in color. Illustrates a methodical approach to preparing for and completing the presentation of an offer. Emphasis is on the development of factual data, anticipating the seller's objections, and techniques for bringing the negotiation to a successful close.

How to List Real Estate in a Competitive Market—20 minutes running time, 16 mm, in color. Features a professional procedure for Realtors and salesmen to follow in obtaining listings at current market prices. Emphasis is given to research and preparation performed before talking to the seller.

Qualifying the Buyer—21 minutes running time, 16 mm, in color. Presents correct techniques for converting ad calls into appointments with buyers, illustrates ways to recognize buyer's motivations and find home buyer's real desires.

Showing the Property and Obtaining the Offer—20 minutes running time, 16 mm, in color. Dramatically presents the correct techniques for showing a property in such a way that buyers "discover" it for themselves. Shows how to recognize and solve problem of buyers. Covers referrals.

The following is a partial listing of materials available from the National Association of Realtors®, 430 N. Michigan, Chicago, Illinois 60611. Price catalog on request.

BOOKS

Marketing Investment Real Estate—this provides a comprehensive, uniform, analytical approach to investment real estate and introduces new techniques of discounting cash flows.

Real Estate Office Management—complete guide for the person who manages the office.

Real Estate Advertising Ideas—30 Realtors from every part of the country have written case studies on their utilization of advertising to the best advantage. Hundreds of illustrations.

Houses: Illustrated Guide to Construction, Design and Systems—basic information about houses from the significance of land use, planning, and site improvement, to architectural styles.

COLOR SOUND/SLIDE PRESENTATIONS

America's Real Estate ... The Soil of America's Economy—comprised of 75 slides, a cassette, and script, this demonstrates the real estate industry as the vital foundation of the American economic system and its practitioners as models of free enterprise in action.

For Sale By Owner?—comprised of 68 slides, a cassette, and script, this illustrates the pitfalls of a buyer selling his or her own home.

CATALOGS, BOOKLETS, CARDS

Audio-Visuals for Real Estate Instruction—this catalog provides brief descriptions of audio/visual aids which may be used for instructional purposes and includes listings from private and association sources, cost, availability, and how-to-order information.

Community Projects Workbook—this booklet provides general how-to information and brief descriptions of more than 100 community projects successfully implemented by Realtors.

America's Real Estate ... The Soil of America's Economy—this booklet is designed for the general consumer and describes the impact that real estate and its uses have had on the American economy.

Buying/Selling a Home? Here's What a Realtor Does for You!—A card for the consumer that highlights the advantages of using Realtor services when buying or selling a home.

EDUCATIONAL MATERIAL

A Basic Course in Real Estate—a comprehensive instructor's guide that provides detailed lecture outlines, suggestions to instructors, instructions to students, reading assignments, principal textbooks of listings, questions and problems, and listings of terms to be defined for a seven-session, 36-classroom-hour course.

Conference Package—a comprehensive guide for staging educational and sales conferences. Included are: lecture outlines on 23 topics; suggestions for conference organization, promotion, and presentation; printed promotion materials; sources of conference speakers; procedures for conference chairman; copy for news releases, and more.

Real Estate Fundamentals—a set of 15 lecture outlines and a bibliography for the instructor. Sample topics: economic and social significance of real estate, vocational opportunities in the real estate business, local ordinances and regulations.

Real Estate Practice—a set of 15 lecture outlines and a bibliography for the instructor. Sample lecture topics: establishing the real estate office, real estate management as a business, selling income property, appraising (parts 1 and 2), and insurance.

Realtors® Institute Reference and Practice Book, Vol. 1—includes chapters on organized real estate industries, urban development, legal environment, construction, prospecting for listings, real estate contracts, market analysis for listing price, financing, qualifying the buyer, showing the property, obtaining and presenting the offer, and career management.

Realtors® Institute Reference and Practice Book, Vol. 2—(builds upon information included in Vol. 1). Included are chapters on communication, real estate market analysis, real property and capital gains taxation, subdivision, condominiums, creative finance, advertising, and residential trade-ins and guaranteed sales.

Realtors® Institute Reference and Practice Book, Vol. 3—includes information on investment real estate, investment financing, taxation, residential and special purpose cost estimating, industrial real estate, managing investment property, managing brokerage operations, and exchanges.

LISTS

List of Real Estate Commissioners—a listing of persons in each of the 50 states who may be contacted for detailed information on licensure as a real estate broker and/or salesperson.

National Directory of Speakers—a compilation of more than 185 speakers throughout the country and their 57 topics listed alphabetically by both speakers' names and topics. Also included are: subject material covered by each speaker, presentation type and length, travel limitations, fee structures, speaker references and experience, and contact information.

LIBRARY

Bibliography Series—revised as needed, the series lists materials in specific subject areas available on loan from the National Association's library.

COURSES AND SEMINARS AVAILABLE THROUGH AFFILIATES OF THE NATIONAL ASSOCIATION OF REALTORS®

This information has been compiled by the Department of Education of the National Association of Realtors. Unless otherwise indicated, address all written inquiries to the appropriate Affiliate at 430 N. Michigan, Chicago, Illinois 60611, or call the phone number shown.

AMERICAN INSTITUTE OF REAL ESTATE APPRAISERS (312) 440-8135

Course I-A	... Basic Appraisal Principles, Methods, and Techniques
Course I-B	... Capitalization Theory and Techniques
Course II	... Urban Properties—Real Estate Appraisal
Course III	... Agricultural Properties

Course IV	... Condemnation—Real Estate Appraisal
Course VI	... Real Estate Investment Analysis
*Course VII	... Industrial Properties
Course VIII	... Single Family Residential Appraisal
Course IX	... Appraisal Administration and Review
**EDUCARE	... Computer Applications

AMERICAN SOCIETY OF REAL ESTATE COUNSELORS (312) 440-8092

Workshop	... Analysis for Real Estate Market Decisions
Workshop	... Case Studies in Real Estate Counseling

FARM AND LAND INSTITUTE (312) 440-8043

Course	... Exchanging Farms, Ranches, and Rural Properties
Course	... Federal Taxes and Real Estate
Course	... How to Establish the Market Value of Agricultural Land
Course	... How to Market Commercial Sites to Retail Chains and Franchises
Course	... Land Brokerage, Introduction to
Course	... Land Return Analysis
Course	... Listing, Packaging, and Presenting Effectively
Course	... Planning of Your Personal Estate, The
Seminar	... One-day Tax Seminar

INSTITUTE OF REAL ESTATE MANAGEMENT (312) 440-8069

REM 101	... Successful On-Site Management
REM 102	... Successful Management of Public Housing
REM 301	... Market and Management of Residential Property
REM 302	... Leasing and Management of Office Buildings
REM 303	... Leasing and Management of Commercial Buildings and Shopping Centers

---

*Jointly sponsored by the American Institute of Real Estate Appraisers and the Society of Industrial Realtors®.

**Jointly sponsored by the American Institute of Real Estate Appraisers, American Society of Real Estate Counselors, Society of Real Estate Appraisers, and SREA Market Data Center, Inc.

REM 401	...	Managing Real Estate as an Investment
REM 501	...	Long-Range Management Plan for Residential Properties
REM 502	...	Long-Range Management Plan for Office Buildings
REM 503	...	Long-Range Management Plan for Commercial Stores and Shopping Centers
REM 601	...	Condominiums, The Management of
REM 602	...	Workout of Troubled Properties, The
REM 603	...	Managing the Development Process
REM 701	...	Managing the Management Office
Seminar	...	How to Make Money Leasing Office and Commercial Space
Seminar	...	Investment Opportunities in Upgrading Older Properties
Seminar	...	Merchandising Apartments for Maximum Rents
Seminar	...	Real Estate Finance—What You Always Wanted to Know but Were Afraid to Ask
Seminar	...	Real Estate Investment Analysis

NATIONAL ASSOCIATION OF REALTORS®
(312) 440-8081

RS 101	...	Advanced Listing Practices
RS 102	...	Advanced Selling Practices
RS 103	...	Successful Career Planning Through Organization and Time Management Practices

REAL ESTATE SECURITIES AND SYNDICATION INSTITUTE (312) 440-8507

Course I	...	A Workshop in Syndication
Course II	...	Advanced Techniques in Real Estate Syndication

REALTORS® NATIONAL MARKETING INSTITUTE
(312) 440-8507

CI INTRO	... Commercial and Investment Real Estate, Introduction
CI 101	... Fundamentals of Real Estate Investment and Taxation
CI 102	... Fundamentals of Creating a Real Estate Investment
CI 103	... Advanced Real Estate Taxation and Marketing Tools for Investment Real Estate
CI 104	... Case Studies in Commercial Investment Real Estate Brokerage
CI 105	... Skills and Techniques of Effective Communication for Commercial-Investment Selling
GSP	... Guaranteed Sales Plan Clinic
MM 201	... Introduction to Real Estate Office Management
MM 202	... Communications and Leadership
MM 203	... Principles of Real Estate Marketing Management
MM 204	... Recruiting, Selecting, Training and Retaining Sales Associates
MM 205	... "Broker": A Computer Simulation of Marketing Management Techniques

SOCIETY OF INDUSTRIAL REALTORS® 925 15th St. NW, Washington, DC 20005, (202) 637-6884

Course I	... Industrial Real Estate, Principles and Practices
Course II	... Industrial Real Estate, Advanced Principles and Practices

WOMEN'S COUNCIL OF REALTORS® (312) 440-8085

Course	... Basics of Residential Real Estate

MAGAZINES

Architecture

AIA Journal, Washington, DC
American Builder, New York, NY
American Home, Philadelphia, PA
Architectural Index, Norman, OK
Architecture Metals, Oak Park, IL
Architectural Record, New York, NY
Better Homes and Gardens, Home Building Ideas, Des Moines, IA
Better Homes and Gardens, Home Improvement Ideas, Des Moines, IA

Building and Buildings

Construction Reports, Washington, DC
Construction, Washington, DC
Contractor Leader, Los Angeles, CA
Daily Pacific Builder, San Francisco, CA
Flooring, New York, NY
Home Center, Chicago, IL
House and Home, New York, NY
House Beautiful's Houses and Plans, New York, NY
Hudson Home Guide, Los Altos, CA
Marshall Valuation Service, Los Angeles, CA
Modern Concrete, Chicago, IL
Modern Steel Construction, New York; NY

Business

Capital Goods Review, Washington, DC
Chartbook on Prices, Wages, and Productivity, Washington, DC
Columbia Journal of World Business, New York, NY
Commerce America, Washington, DC
Commerce Business Daily, Washington, DC
Commodities, Columbia, MD
Consumer Price Index, Washington, DC

Cities and Towns

American City and County, Pittsfield, MA

American Institute of Planners Journal, Washington, DC
American Municipal News, Chicago, IL
HUD Newsletter, Washington, DC
Landscape Architecture, Louisville, KY
Public Works, Ridgewood, NJ
Water and Sewage Works, Chicago, IL

City Planning

Downtown Idea Exchange, New York, NY
Nation's Cities, Washington, DC

Housing

Communities, Sacramento, CA

Real Estate Business

California Real Estate, Los Angeles, CA
Farm Real Estate Market Developments, Washington, DC
Housing and Urban Development Trends, Washington, DC
Journal of Property Management, Chicago, IL
National Real Estate Investor, New York, NY
Real Estate Appraiser, Chicago, IL
Real Estate News, San Francisco, CA

United States Commerce

Duns Review, New York, NY
Nation's Business, Washington, DC

United States Economic Conditions

Across the Board, New York, NY
American Affairs, The Economic Record, NY
American Economic Review, Evanston, IL
American Federation of Labor, *Survey of Current Business*, Washington, DC
Economic Indicators, Washington, DC
Manufacturer's Hanover Trust Company, *Economic Forecast*, New York, NY
Survey of Current Business, Washington, DC
Wholesale Prices and Price Indexes, Washington, DC

HOW TO RESEARCH PUBLIC RECORDS FOR INFORMATION*

If You Know the Person's Name

Go to *D* to find index of transactions involving this person and property deals.
Go to *C* to find a list of all property now owned by this person.
Go to *A* & *H* to find the person's address, occupation, telephone number, height, social security number, and birth date.
Go to *E, F, G, P,* and *Q* to find any court cases against the individual or by him.

If You Know the Person's Address

Go to *A* to find the tenant and phone number at the address.
Go to *B* to find the name of the owner at that address.
Go to *M* to find zoning information.
Go to *I* if any business is at that address, to find the business name and owner.
Go to *C* if any business is at that address, to find the business name.

If You Know a Telephone Number

Go to *A* to find the name of the owner of that number and the address at which it is located.

If You Know a Business Name

Go to *A* to find manager, address, phone number.
Go to *C* to find owner.
Go to *D* to locate property transactions by business.
Go to *E* to find officers or owners.
Go to *E, F,* and *G* to find court cases by or against the business.
Go to *J* to find officers and tax standing.

A. Directories

Realty Index— listed alphabetically by the street names and each street name has the street address listed numerically. Given with owner's name is block and lot number.

---

*This section, to page 256, from *A Guide to Public Records,* © 1973, by San Francisco Consumer Action & People's Law School.

Polk's City Directory

1. "Yellow pages"— advertising like yellow pages of phone book.
2. "White pages"—alphabetical listing of people and companies, giving occupations, home addresses, managers, and spouse information.
3. "Green pages"—addresses as in the Realty Index, except this shows tenant's name and phone number.
4. "Blue pages"—numerical list by telephone number, showing holder's name.

Telephone Company Cross Directory—listed by street address. Shows name and telephone number there.

Haine's Criss Cross Directory—like the "blue pages" of Polk's Directory.

B. Assessor's Office

This office is responsible for appraising land and buildings and keeping track of the owners.

Duplicate Assessor's Roll—indexed by block and lot number, shows:

1. Property address
2. Assessed and cash value of land
3. Assessed and cash value of building
4. Miscellaneous improvements (rooms added on, etc.)
5. Mailing address where tax statement is sent (of owner, complete with zip code)
6. Annual tax amount paid
7. Owner's name
8. Exemptions
9. Personal property (such as furnishings)

Sales Ledger—contains the sales description and ownership activity for each lot on each block.

1. Grantor (seller's name)
2. Grantee (buyer's name)
3. Transaction and date

C. Tax Collector

Has the duty of collecting the tax owed.

Secured Assessment Roll—same as Duplicate Assessor's Roll.

Property Index contains alphabetical list of owners of land and property.

Unsecured Assessment Roll contains alphabetical listing of both owners of business and businesses themselves.

1. Tax account number
2. Owner or business name
3. Address of business
4. Business name or owner

Assessment Statements are computer produced descriptions of inventory and office supplies, along with improvements and deductions for each business listed in the Unsecured Assessment Roll.

Personal Property Declaration by Location—same as Unsecured Assessment Roll, except listed alphabetically by address.

D. Recorder's Office

Holds records of all transactions involving every piece of property in the city: deeds, mortgages, second mortgages, liens, etc. Also recorded are agreements, judgments, notices, etc.

E. County Clerk and Superior Court (Civil)

The County Clerk is the hand of the Superior Court. In this office are all matters pertaining to the Court, plus miscellaneous registration papers. This court deals with matters for more than $5000, divorces, writs of mandate, etc.

Superior Court Indexes

These indexes are organized in two sets—PLAINTIFF and DEFENDANT, and contain:

1. Defendant
2. Plaintiff
3. Case number
4. Date case was filed

Look under both indexes, since one party may have simply "beat the other to the punch."

Case Files can be found once you find the case number.

Fictitious Names Index

Contains the names of businesses and the owners of those businesses. If you want to sue, you must use the name of the owner of the business. The fictitious name of the business is not sufficient. Sole proprietorships are required to register in the county in which they are doing business and corporations need only register in the county in which they are doing business and in the capital of the state. If you cannot locate a business, write the District Attorney. The entries yield:

1. Fictitious name
2. Owner's name
3. Date of filing
4. Filing number of file, which will give you copy of publication of notice of business and home address of owner of business

Corporation Index

Shows:

1. Articles of incorporation
2. Home addresses of initial members of the board of directors

Probate Index and Register of Actions—Probate

Listed by name of deceased and indicates where to find what has happened in the probate of the Will and the Will itself.

Register of Actions—Civil

A summary of what happened in the civil cases and is arranged numerically by case number.

F. Municipal Court

Handles matters between $500 and $5000 (civil).

Index—Plaintiff and Defendant

Lists the defendant's name, the plaintiff's name, the case number, and the date of filing. Files are available.

G. Small Claims Court

Handles matters for less than $500, and is part of the Municipal Court.

Index—Defendant and Plaintiff

Lists defendant's name, plaintiff's name, case number, and date of filing. Files are available.

H. Registrar of Voters

Gives:

1. If someone is a registered voter
2. When registered
3. Place of residence at the time of registering
4. Occupation listed
5. Petitions signed, if any
6. Height
7. Social Security number
8. Appearance of signature
9. Charts of city showing voting precincts, polling places, precinct workers
10. Registration affidavit number
11. Party affiliation
12. Congressional district
13. Assembly district
14. Voting history showing which election or primaries the person voted in

I. Board of Equalization

The state agency responsible for collection of state sales tax. If you give them the address of the business, they will give you:

1. The exact business name
2. The name of the person or business paying the tax (usually the owner)
3. The state tax account number
4. The date the account was opened

J. Secretary of State

At the State Capitol of each state, will give:

1. The date the corporation was started (if not, the fact that the corporation doesn't exist)
2. If the corproation is paying state income tax, and if not, the date they last paid
3. The county in which the principal office is located
4. The person to send the summons to (agent designated to accept service of process)
5. In some states there is a fee for the names of the officers and their home addresses obtained from the Secretary of State.

K. Department of Motor Vehicles

Will give the name of the registered owner and legal owner if you have license plate number, for a fee. Also gives driver license information and driving record if you know the driver license number.

L. Zoning and City Planning

Maintains all records pertaining to the unusual use of land, such as opening a business in a residential area, or converting a single-family dwelling, in a residential area, into an apartment house. Each new use must be applied to the city for permission. Go to the Assessor's Office, Tax Collector's Office, or Recorder's Office with street address to obtain the block number from the Realty Index.

Zoning Block Book

Shows you a picture of the block and a lot-by-lot breakdown, is similar to block and lot charts usually found in City Hall offices, shows nonconforming uses on the block and what date these are legally required to stop being nonconforming, specifies current size of lots on the block, the lot's zoning, and any setback requirements.

Zoning Commission Files

Available if you want to look up a particular case that was heard by the Zoning Commission. Thc street address is all that's needed. Some of the cases are about zone changes, but most will concern an application for variance. In the file will be found:

1. The application for variance submitted by the property owner
2. Copies of the notices of the hearing which must be mailed to all neighbors within 300 feet of the applicant
3. The minutes of the hearing
4. The results of the hearing

M. Purchasing Department

Usually in City Hall, has available to the public copies of maps of the city showing block numbers, individual block charts, and aerial photo survey maps for sections of the city.

N. Bureau of Engineering

Gives you information on:

1. Streets and sidewalks
2. Permits
3. Inspections

GLOSSARY

Abstract of title—A summary of the recorded documents affecting the title to a specific piece of real property.

Amortize—To pay the principal payments of a loan in installments.

Assign—Transfer in writing of claim, right, or title to property from one to another.

Bank—An establishment which receives, keeps, lends, and sometimes issues money.

Beneficiary—A person named in a will to receive income or inheritance.

Bond—An interest bearing certificate which promises to pay the holder a certain sum on a certain date.

Capital—Money or property (wealth) used in business.

Chattel—Movable personal property such as furniture, livestock, automobiles.

Contiguous—That which adjoins or touches, like land parcels next to each other.

Conveyance—A written document transferring title.

Corporation—A group of people legally authorized to act as a single individual.

Credit—An asset.

Debt—An obligation to pay money.

Deed—A written document which transfers title.

Draft—A document which transfers money.

Depreciation—Loss in value.

Duress—Illegal force which compels a person to do something against his will.

Easement—A privilege to use another's land.

Escrow—The delivery, by one person to a third, of title evidence, which the third person holds until certain conditions are met.

Estate—A person's ownership in real property.

Estoppel—Preventing a person from making an affirmation or a denial because it is contrary to a previous affirmation or denial.

Executed—A fully performed contract.

Fee simple absolute—Unconditional marketable title to property.

Fictitious name—An alias used for business purposes.

Foreclose—To sell property pledged as security for a debt to pay the debt when default occurs.

Grant—To transfer property.

Injunction—A court order stopping or requiring an act.

Interest rate—The percentage charged for the use of money.

Intestate—To die without leaving a will.

Irrevocable—Unchangeable.

Joint tenancy—Two or more people own property with the right of survivorship.

Liability—Money owed.

Liens—The charges against a property to pay debts.

Loan—To use temporarily.

Mortgage—The document which makes property security for the payment of a loan.

Net—That remaining after deductions.

Note—A document promising payment of a debt.

Notary public—A person authorized to certify and/or attest documents and to take depositions.

Option—The right to buy, sell, or lease property within a stated period of time and under particular conditions.

Ordinance—A regulation of the government.

Ownership—Legal right or possession.

Parcel—A specific piece of land.

Principal—The investment amount, less interest, or the amount on which interest is figured.

Property—That which is owned. *Real property* is affixed to the land; *Personal property* is movable.

Quit-claim—To release a claim.

Reconveyance—The return of ownership of real property to a prior owner.

Redemption—The re-acquiring of property lost through foreclosure within the specified time limit.

Restriction—A limit on the use of property.

Rider—An addition or an amendment to a document.

Riparian rights—Rights of a landowner for the use of water on, under, or next to his land.

Sandwich lease—A sublease which is sublet but is subject to an original lease—an "in-between" lease.

Severalty—Solely owned.

Setback ordinance—A law which prohibits building to a certain distance from lot boundaries.

Solvent—The ability to pay all debts.

Specific performance—A court order requiring a person to do what he has agreed to do.

Statute of Limitations—A state law which limits the time in which certain court actions can be brought.

Straight note—Payable in one lump sum—not installments.

Sublet—To rent property which one is renting to another.

Surety—A guarantee.

Syndicate—An association of individuals formed to transact financial business.

Title—Evidence of ownership and the lawful possession thereof.

Trustor—The borrower on a trust deed note.

Use tax—Sales tax on goods purchased out of state.

Vendee—The buyer.

Vendor—The seller.

Void—Having no legal effect.

Waive—To surrender.

Writ—A court document commanding or prohibiting a person from doing specific acts.

Zone—The limiting of property to a specific use.

Index

A

N

O

P